Pentecostals and Charismatics in Britain

Pentecostals and Charismatics in Britain

An Anthology

Edited by

Joe Aldred

scm press

© Churches Together in England 2019

Published in 2019 by SCM Press
Editorial office
3rd Floor, Invicta House,
108–114 Golden Lane,
London EC1Y 0TG, UK
www.scmpress.co.uk

SCM Press is an imprint of Hymns Ancient & Modern Ltd
(a registered charity)

Hymns Ancient & Modern® is a registered trademark of
Hymns Ancient & Modern Ltd
13A Hellesdon Park Road, Norwich,
Norfolk NR6 5DR, UK

British Library Cataloguing in Publication data

A catalogue record for this book is available
from the British Library

978 0 334 05711 6

Typeset by Regent Typesetting
Printed and bound by
CPI Group (UK) Ltd, Croydon

Contents

Part Four Pentecostal and Charismatic and Socio-Political Issues

Foreword

by the Most Reverend Justin Welby

Throughout Christian history disciples of Jesus Christ have sought to live holy lives and have striven to find a foretaste of heaven on earth. From time to time a significant movement arises, prompted by the Holy Spirit, that stands the test of time and has a lasting effect on the Church for years or centuries to come. One can point to historical examples such as the rapid spread of the medieval friars and the increase in piety, preaching and the call to repentance that stemmed from the ministry of St Francis and St Dominic. In England and beyond in the eighteenth century the Evangelical Revival, and in particular the ministry of John Wesley, brought people to faith, called them to holiness of life and enabled them to be open to experiencing God's perfect love in worship and fellowship. In the nineteenth and early twentieth centuries the Anglo-Catholic revival in the Church of England and Anglican Communion sought to bring people to an experience of the transcendent presence of God in the here and now through 'the beauty of holiness' in worship.

The Charismatic revivals that brought about what we now know as Pentecostalism stand in this tradition. Conceived both in traditional denominations and in the ministry of individuals and small groups, the Pentecostal and Charismatic movements have grown into significant, Spirit-filled churches. What is more, the influence of Charismatic Christianity is now felt in virtually every church and denomination. This volume is both an introduction to and an analysis of the growth and significance of Pentecostal and Charismatic Christianity in Britain.

My own faith was, to a large extent, formed and nurtured in the Charismatic tradition within the Church of England. Charismatic worship and preaching are able to transcend denominational divides. Today, Pentecostal and Charismatic churches, both networked and independent, have taken their proper place as significant partners with other churches and denominations in ecumenical bodies, particularly in bringing the good news of Jesus Christ, in word and deed, to the people of this land.

The Most Reverend Justin Welby
Archbishop of Canterbury

Contributors

Babatunde Aderemi Adedibu holds a PhD in Missiology from North-West University, South Africa. He was the Mission and Ecumenical Manager at the Redeemed Christian Church of God, Central Office, UK until April 2015 before his appointment as Provost of the Redeemed Christian Bible College, Nigeria. He is a Research Fellow in the Department of Practical Theology and Missiology, University of Stellenbosch, South Africa. Babatunde is also a Research Associate in the Research Project on Biblical Theology and Hermeneutics in the Department of New Testament, University of Pretoria, South Africa. He is the author of *Coat of Many Colours: Origin, Growth Distinctives and Contributions of Black Majority Churches to British Christianity* (2012).

Daniel Akhazemea is the Rector of Christ the Redeemer College, London. He holds a Post-Graduate Certificate in Higher Education (PGCHE); Master of Divinity; Master of Art in Missional Leadership; and a PhD in Biblical Counselling. He is a Provincial Pastor of the Redeemed Christian Church of God (RCCG). He is a member of the Theology Advisory Group of the Evangelical Alliance. A regular speaker in seminars and conferences, his articles have been published in academic journals, and he is the author of three books. His published articles include 'The RCCG, A Missionary Global Player: What Is Her Message Regarding Human Development?' A recent article is 'Building a Stable College in a Dynamic Global Education Culture'. His research interests are in cross-cultural missions and theological development in black majority churches.

Joe Aldred is responsible for Pentecostal and Multicultural Relations at Churches Together in England and is a bishop in the Church of God of Prophecy. He has a PhD in Theology from Sheffield University, is editor of *Preaching with Power* (2000), *Sisters with Power* (2000) and *Praying with Power* (2000) and author of *Respect: Understanding Caribbean British Christianity* (2005), *The Black Church in the Twenty-first Century* (2010), *Thinking Outside the Box: On Race, Faith and Life*

(2013) and *From Top Mountain: An Autobiography* (2015). He is a regular contributor to periodicals including the College of Preachers' *The Preacher*. Joe is Honorary Research Fellow at Roehampton University and has experience as bishop and pastor, chair and member of strategic councils, boards and committees mainly in the areas of religion, education, health and community relations.

Allan H. Anderson has been at the University of Birmingham since 1995, where he is Professor of Mission and Pentecostal Studies. Before that he was a Pentecostal minister in Southern Africa for 23 years and published his master's and doctoral theses on African Pentecostalism in the early 1990s. He has written many articles and books since, the latest being *To the Ends of the Earth* (2013), *An Introduction to Pentecostalism* (2nd edition, 2014), and *Spirit-Filled World* (2018).

Andrew Davies is a Reader in the Public Understanding of Religion at the University of Birmingham, where he works on the reception history of the Bible, particularly its handling by Pentecostals and Evangelicals, and its interpretation in music and the other arts. Both these concerns have encouraged his broader fascination with how the Bible and religion in general impact public life, particularly in the social and political spheres. He joined the University of Birmingham in January 2010, after ten years at Mattersey Hall Bible College, the last five of them as Vice Principal. He now serves as Head of the Department of Theology and Religion and Director of the Edward Cadbury Centre at the University of Birmingham. Recent research projects include the AHRC-funded Megachurches and Social Engagement in London project, while still sharing leadership of an inner-city Pentecostal Church in Sheffield with his wife Lesley.

Anne E. Dyer, initially an archaeology graduate (1977), worked with her husband and two children in Thailand with OMF (1980–93). She gained her PhD from Bangor University, Wales (2008). Since 2000 she has worked for Mattersey Hall college as librarian and also became secretary (2004–17) and is co-editor for the *Journal of the European Pentecostal Theological Association*. After a one-year cover as PhD Missiology programme leader at Cliff College, she returned to Mattersey Hall as Research Centre and Archives manager and supervises students in all levels of research. Beyond college, she is a Methodist local preacher, tutor and District Mission representative.

Roger Forster attended St John's College, Cambridge, where he graduated in mathematics and theology. After a period in the Royal Air Force, he worked as an itinerant evangelist until 1974 when he established the Ichthus Christian Fellowship. Among his many responsibilities over the years, he has chaired the Evangelical Alliance's council, served on a number of EA committees and was an honorary vice president of Tearfund. Roger was one of the founders and leaders of March for Jesus, and was on the board of the international AD2000 Movement. He is the author or co-author of more than 20 books, including *God's Strategy in Human History* (1989), *Suffering and the Love of God* (2006), *Trinity: Song and Dance God* (2015), *Prayer* (2007), *The Kingdom of Jesus* (2014), *Women and the Kingdom* (2010), *Reason, Science and Faith* (1999), *Finding the Path* (1991), *Explaining Fasting* (1994) and *Christianity: the Evidence* (2015).

David Hilborn is Principal of Moorlands College, Dorset. Previously he was Principal of St John's College, Nottingham, Assistant Dean of St Mellitus College and Head of Theology at the Evangelical Alliance UK. He has written and edited several books, including *One Body in Christ* (with Ian Randall), *'Toronto' in Perspective* and *God and the Generations* (with Matt Bird). He served for ten years on the Church of England's Faith and Order Commission, where he helped pioneer dialogue between Anglicans and Pentecostals. He is a member of the Society for Pentecostal Studies and chairs the Evangelical Alliance's Theological Advisory Group. He is married to Mia, a hospital chaplain, and they have two grown-up children.

Emmanuel Kapofu is senior pastor at the International Life Centre, a multicultural church that he and his wife Ivy founded in 2001 in the city of Wolverhampton. The ILC has several daughter churches in the United Kingdom. He runs a School of Ministry in Wolverhampton and in Zimbabwe, raising tomorrow's leaders today. He holds a BA in Religious Studies and Sociology from the University of Wolverhampton, an MA in Evangelical and Charismatic Studies from the University of Birmingham and is currently a PhD research student at the University of Wolverhampton exploring multiculturalism among African Pentecostals in the West Midlands.

William Kay studied at the Universities of Oxford, London, Nottingham and Reading and is now Emeritus Professor of Theology at Wrexham Glyndŵr University and Honorary Professor of Pentecostal Studies at the University of Chester. He is a former Senior Lecturer in the

Department of Education and Professional Studies at King's College London. He has published widely on religious education, often using empirical methods to verify or challenge contemporary orthodoxies. Similarly, he has used empirical methods in conjunction with the study of Pentecostalism. He edits *The Journal of the European Pentecostal Theological Association*. He has published widely on Pentecostalism including *Pentecostals in Britain* (Paternoster, 2000) and *Apostolic Networks in Britain* (Paternoster, 2007). His most recent books are *Pentecostalism: A very short introduction* (Oxford University Press, 2012) and *George Jeffreys: Pentecostal Apostle and Revivalist* (CPT Press, 2017). He is co-editor of Brill's Global and Pentecostal Studies series.

Dionne Lamont is the Lead Pastor and Founder of Bethesda Ministries, UK which offers empowerment to people from all walks of life. She holds an LLB in Law, a BA in Theology and a Diploma in Christian Counselling. As well as being the CEO of Phareznow Limited, a company which seeks to enhance the life chances of women, she is a fashion designer who specializes in bespoke designs for leading women in ministry. Dionne has now authored her first book *Public Success, Private Struggle* and travels extensively as an international speaker to countries including Bulgaria, Cyprus and Canada, in the West Indies and Africa and over 35 States of America.

R. David Muir BA (Hons), Dip. Th., PGCE, MA, PhD is Senior Lecturer in Ministerial Theology and Public Theology at Roehampton University. His research interests include the intersection between religion and social justice and the role of African and Caribbean churches in society. Before joining Roehampton University, he was executive director of Public Policy and Public Theology at the Evangelical Alliance. He was an independent adviser to the Home Secretary and Police Minister from 2003 to 2008, as well as a member of the Advisory Board for Naturalisation and Integration. Recent publications include *Theology and the Black Church* (2010) and a chapter entitled *London's Burning: Riots, Gangs, and Moral Formation of Young People* (2014). David is a member of the Kirby Laing Institute for Christian Ethics (Cambridge University) and a UK board member of the Transatlantic Roundtable on Religion and Race. He is also Co-Chair of the National Church Leaders Forum – A Black Christian Voice.

Mark Sturge is Head of the London Region at Christian Aid and has over 22 years senior management experience in the charity sector and 30 years in Christian leadership. For eight years he was the General Director of the African and Caribbean Evangelical Alliance (ACEA). He then became the Assistant Director (Services) for Lewisham's Council for Voluntary Services and the Chief Operating Officer of the Lokahi Foundation. In 2006, Mark received a full scholarship from Cranfield University to study for an Executive MBA. He also has a BEng (Hons) degree in Electrical and Electronic Engineering and a BA (Hons) in Theology. Mark is the author of *Look What the Lord Has Done: An Exploration of Black Christian Faith in Britain*. In July 2018, he received the London School of Theology's Alumnus of the Year Award.

Introduction

JOE ALDRED

The origins of this collection lie in the providential emergence of a Pentecostal Leaders Forum within Churches Together in England (CTE), made up of representatives from over 20 Pentecostal and Charismatic national churches and agencies, all members of CTE. Since 2014 the Forum has met twice yearly, chaired by the CTE Pentecostal President, to consider relational and missional matters that flow from Christian life and witness together in Britain. Pentecostals and Charismatics put a lot of store by the 'moving of the Spirit'; that a space has been created for prayerful reflection by a wide range of Pentecostals and Charismatics of British African, British Caribbean and European descent, and continues to meet, is best ascribed to a move of the Holy Spirit.

The CTE Pentecostal Leaders Forum is now established as a meeting point for Pentecostal and Charismatic leaders in Britain and is keen to support its presence by conferences and publications emanating from within the constituency. Although some of its intellectual agency is in developmental transition, the Forum is supported by some key established Pentecostal and Charismatic academic practitioners and centres, evidenced in this publication. In an age of sound bites and scepticism toward faith the Forum hopes to develop a literary corpus that speaks with integrity for and about itself.

In the autumn of 2016 the Forum organized its first Theological Symposium in London, followed by another in Birmingham in spring 2018. It became apparent from these discourses that an opportunity had presented itself to make a significant contribution to public awareness of Pentecostal and Charismatic religious traditions in Britain. While there are some British luminaries in the field of Pentecostal and Charismatic study, this is a first attempt to pull together in one publication such a wide range of contributions on a subject that still has something of the esoteric about it for the general public, including theological and sociological practitioners.

This anthology provides insightful perspectives on key areas of Pentecostal and Charismatic expression of Christian faith in Britain. As a reader, expect to deepen your understanding of British Pentecostals and Charismatics which we hope will engender better engagement with this religious phenomenon, practically and intellectually. The work seeks to debunk the folklore of Pentecostals and Charismatics in Britain as primarily an African and Caribbean religious expression that was brought to Britain by *Windrush* migration. What will emerge instead is that Pentecostals and Charismatics in Britain are an ethnically and denominationally diverse faith expression that dates back to the early twentieth century and is now nationally and internationally among the fastest growing religious groupings. By delineating the contours of key areas of Pentecostal and Charismatic life and belief in an academic yet accessible way, this anthology aims to help to demythologize this religious expression and to challenge its anti-intellectual label. Further, this anthology puts into the public domain theological and sociological literature that posits contemporary thinking in key areas of British Pentecostal and Charismatic thought. A key authoritative trait of this book is that these are voices from within telling their story.

Inevitably, some topics relevant to Pentecostals and Charismatics in Britain are not covered by this short volume, such as Oneness Pentecostals who have a significant presence particularly as an expression of Britain's black church movement, and the area of human sexuality and its implications for a largely conservative expression of Christian faith. It is hoped that these and other issues will be explored by future writing initiatives.

The work is broken into four main sections that deal with the history, diversity, relationship with mainstream Christianity, and social and political considerations of Pentecostal and Charismatic faith in Britain. This project is indebted to all contributors, CTE staff, and the Commissioning Editor and staff at SCM Press.

Joe Aldred
Editor

Part One

Pentecostal and Charismatic History

I

Heritage and Hope:
A Story of British Pentecostalism

ANDREW DAVIES

There comes a moment on any long journey when it is helpful to pull over and pause for a while, for us to catch our breath, check our progress and review our journey so far. This volume provides a useful opportunity for such reflection at the heart of Pentecostalism. And, just as any resting traveller would seize the opportunity to check the map or the sat-nav to look for upcoming challenges, delays or obstacles and make sure they are on track for the next phase, so too it seems to me that re-evaluating the story of over 100 years of British Pentecostalism can leave us with significant insight into its possible futures. The potential of Pentecostalism to reshape and remodel the role of Christianity in British society is immense, and its increase already impressive. In the face of a general decline in Christian observance, its future looks rather more secure than that of some other groupings and denominations. However, if its significant growth is to be sustained and the nation transformed, then the great heritage of Pentecostalism in this country must, I think, become a hopeful spur to continuing positive change within the movement.

First, let me explain precisely what I mean by Pentecostalism, since defining this movement is perhaps not quite as simple as we might have thought. In a nutshell, I think of classical Pentecostals as the self-contained, stand-alone denominations which, in terms of the white-majority traditions – such as Elim (www.elim.org) (Kay 2009; Frestadius 2016), Assemblies of God (www.aog.org.uk) (Kay 1990), and the Apostolic Church (www.apostolic-church.org) (Worsfold 1991) – mainly have their origins in the revival meetings of the early twentieth century and, in terms of the black majority traditions, first began to emerge in Britain in the 1940s to 1960s with the advent of large-scale immigration from the Empire and Commonwealth (Edwards 1997; Cartwright 2007). These Pentecostal migrants came first principally from the Caribbean, leading to the establishment of the Church of

God in Christ (www.cogic.org.uk), the New Testament Church of God (www.ntcg.org.uk) and the Church of God of Prophecy (www.cogop.org.uk). As more recent Christian migration into the UK has come from Africa, the Nigerian-led Redeemed Christian Church of God (www.rccg.org), the Ghanaian-focused Church of Pentecost (www.copuk.org) and other transnational denominations have grown in number and influence since the 1980s and have expressed repeatedly their passionate commitment to work for the re-evangelization of the UK, a phenomenon which has become known as 'reverse mission' (Catto 2008, 2012; Freston 2010). Both black-led and white-led movements have their own denominational structures and are very often part of bigger global networks. While they do collaborate to a measure at national level, there remains something of a structural and cultural division between the black-led and the white-led churches, and it seems to me important for the future of British Pentecostalism that we move to address this practically and forthrightly, as I will discuss further below.

Alongside the denominations, London in particular has seen the rise of freestanding transnational megachurches, with membership of over 2,000, over the last two decades or so (http://hirr.hartsem.edu/mega church/megachurches.html, Cartledge and Davies 2014; Thumma and Bird 2015). Many of these are classically Pentecostal in orientation and structure, including both Hillsong Church (www.hillsong.com/uk) and Kingsway International Christian Centre (www.kicc.org), which are the country's two biggest churches. In the UK, these traditional Pentecostal denominations account for around 250,000 people, with perhaps another 30–40,000 or so in the independent Pentecostal megachurches.

Then we have the Charismatics, and I see this group as falling into two halves. Both have their origins in a renewal movement among the established churches in the 1960s and 1970s. On one side the denominational Charismatic movement comprises those who share a broadly Pentecostal experience and theology of the Spirit's work but have remained in the traditional denominations, such as Anglican and Catholic Charismatics. The New Wine network (www.new-wine.org/network) falls into this category, as does Holy Trinity Brompton, also known as HTB Church (www.htb.org), the megachurch home of the Alpha Course which in recent times has begun to evolve into a church planting movement in its own right, although in conjunction with Anglican dioceses. The striking tale of Charismatic Anglicanism is that through the influence of John Wimber, New Wine and HTB Church it now has rather more in common with the theology and culture of Wimber's Vineyard movement than with the ideas of more conservative evangelicals such as John Stott, who led another great Anglican megachurch just up the road from HTB at All Souls Langham Place.

But, on the other side of the equation, not all the Charismatics stayed within the traditional denominations. Some left for the 'new wineskins' of apostolic networks centred around the ministry of an individual or group of prominent leaders (Kay 2007). Some structural change has taken place in these networks over the last few years as those original apostolic leaders have begun to step back from active leadership, but many of those networks continue to prosper even if in altered form – take for example New Frontiers (www.newfrontierstogether.org), which has now become something of an apostolic network of apostolic networks. 'Pentecostalism' is appropriately often used as a catch-all to cover all these variant traditions, which account together for around a million people in the UK and quite probably around two thirds of a billion worldwide (Weigel 2015); though the 'Pentecostal/Charismatic movement' is perhaps more precise a title, since it does a little more justice to the cultural differences which do exist between Pentecostals and Charismatics.

Pentecostal spirituality has been responsive to the denominational traditions it works within, as well as transformative for them so, while they share a common core culture, there is much, obviously, that distinguishes high church Catholic Charismatics from urban classic Pentecostals. Indeed, I have characterized Pentecostalism elsewhere as 'a metadenomination – a metatradition, even … offering an over-arching cultural and theological mindset which works within, as it binds itself into, the classical denominations, traditions and streams of Christianity, and in the process changes them, as much as it itself is changed by them' (Davies 2009). That we can even talk about so many variant denominational perspectives as being a part of one move-ment shows how much this tradition has learned to be flexible and responsive to changing contexts. Its success has come from its creativity and innovation. It has flourished and prospered by being so responsive to external cultural changes in at least as many aspects. In some areas – particularly around social ethics, for example – it has been incredibly conservative, and that will confront it with challenges in years to come. But in general, the entrepreneurial spirit of Pentecostalism has encour-aged it to engage proactively with other Christian traditions and the outside world and influence both positively.

Indeed, it is often forgotten that the advent of Pentecostalism in the UK was in the Church of England – the first significant 'outpouring of the Spirit' in this country in the twentieth century was in a series of revival meetings led by an Anglican priest, Revd Alexander Boddy, at All Souls Parish Church, Monkwearmouth, Sunderland. Boddy continued to have a significant influence upon the culture and style of Pentecostalism in its earliest days in the UK, and it was really first the issue of how Christians should respond to the onset of the Great War which began to move the nonconformist away from his orbit and eventually provoked the establishment of the British Pentecostal denominations (Wakefield 2007).

Taking account of the distinctions I have highlighted as well as the commonalities, I write here principally with the classical Pentecostal denominations in mind, and readily acknowledge that my experience is fundamentally among the white-led Pentecostal churches. The huge diversity of this movement here and abroad means that it is always difficult to generalize, but there are clear familial connections and shared priorities, ideas and cultures which unite the global Pentecostal communion (Kay 2009). Pentecostals now understand their shared history better than ever before and have a deeper understanding of what they can distinctively contribute to the wider body of Christ. So let me begin by outlining what I think are some of the more important aspects of Pentecostal heritage in terms of their potential contribution to global Christianity.

Pentecostal Heritage

The theological cohesiveness of Pentecostalism, of course, depends upon adherence to a variety of theological distinctives: belief in divine healing, in a second and subsequent reception of the Holy Spirit after conversion (the baptism in the Spirit) resulting in empowerment for service, in the gifts of the Spirit – including speaking in tongues, and (historically at least) a distinctive premillennial eschatology. Pentecostals have always claimed to be a people of the Spirit, and even where these ideas have influenced other Christian traditions they should still be seen as distinctively Pentecostal perspectives. My interest here is much more in the non-theological Pentecostal distinctives, especially the cultural features which combine to shape the environment and atmosphere of the Pentecostal movement.

So, what lessons can we learn from the earliest days of the Pentecostal movement?

Many narratives point to what has become known as the Azusa Street revival of 1906 as the real origin of Pentecostalism as a movement and the locus of the eschatological restoration of the gifts of the Spirit to the Church (Roebeck 2006; Alexander 2011; Synan and Fox 2012). The

Azusa Street story tells how a young black pastor William Seymour, the son of freed slaves and blind in one eye, who had suffered as a student the indignity and humiliation of being kept out in the hallway and forced to listen to his Bible school lectures through the half-open door, began to believe in what he saw as the biblical experience of speaking in tongues and to preach about this in a small Holiness church in Los Angeles. When he was locked out of the church because its elders could not accept his ideas, he was welcomed into the home of one of the congregation members and conducted services there with a small group of supporters. There, in a private home on Bonnie Brae Street, after five weeks of prayer, fasting and Bible study, on 9 April 1906, God's Spirit fell upon the people present and a number of them began to speak in tongues (Synan 2001). Seymour received his own baptism in the Holy Spirit just a few nights later. As the congregation outgrew the house and moved to new premises on Azusa Street (a former African Methodist Episcopal church in one of the poorest areas of the city), the curious events there began to attract the attention of the wider population and the local press. Within months, people were flocking from all over the world to see what was happening, and some nights well over 1,000 people squeezed into the building.

The *Los Angeles Times* was not impressed with this new Pentecostal spirituality, accusing worshippers of 'breathing strange utterances and mouthing a creed which it would seem no sane mortal could understand'. They continued:

> Devotees of the weird doctrine practice the most fanatical rites, preach the wildest theories, and work themselves into a state of mad excitement ... night is made hideous in the neighborhood by the howlings of the worshippers who spend hours swaying forth and back in a nerve-racking attitude of prayer and supplication. (Bartleman, p. xviii)

Despite some hostility from the wider community, however, for the spiritually hungry who came from far and wide to receive their Pentcostal experience, 'the very atmosphere of heaven' had descended, according to one attender. A Baptist pastor visiting the meetings described his experience this way: 'The Holy Spirit fell upon me and filled me literally, as it seemed to lift me up, for indeed, I was in the air in an instant, shouting, "Praise God", and instantly I began to speak in another language. I could not have been more surprised if at the same moment someone had handed me a million dollars' (Bartleman, p. 61; McGee 1999; http://enrichmentjournal.ag.org/199904/026_azusa.cfm). It would have been

7

a remarkable experience to have attended those meetings, for sure, and over the next six years or so, many thousands did, and many of them took its message away back home with them. The Azusa Street experience has been hugely significant in terms of its continuing influence on Pentecostal self-understanding (Synan 2006; Anderson 2006; http://enrichmentjournal.ag.org/200602/200602_142_Legacies.cfm; http://enrichmentjournal.ag.org/200602/200602_164_AllPoints.cfm).

However, in the last 20 years or so, scholars have developed a new and broader understanding of the earliest history of Pentecostalism. We have come to appreciate that Azusa Street was only one part of a wider move of God across the nations of the earth in that era. Just a little earlier in Wales, revival had swept the land and over 100,000 people were converted to Christianity in just one year, 1904 (Evans, pp. 190–6; Bundy). Numerous local clusters of revival were reported in Pyongyang, now capital of North Korea (Blair and Hunt 1977; Lee, pp. 80–90). By 1905, in India, Pandita Ramabai was leading 500 young women every day in prayer and sending them out as 'praying bands' and 'Holy Ghost missionaries' who spread revival wherever they went, resulting in thousands across the subcontinent coming to Christ (Anderson 2007, pp. 75–89).

What happened in Los Angeles was significant, therefore, but it was not unique. It was part of a broader reawakening of the church to the gifts and power of the Spirit in response to a cry for a Christian experience more in line with that described in the New Testament. Pentecostalism was a global Spirit-led response to a global spiritual hunger. In other words, Pentecostalism is a faith for the whole world, which arose from the four corners of the world and, as a missionary faith, it went out to the four corners of the world too. Allan Anderson is surely right to suggest that 'Pentecostalism is above all else a missionary movement' and to highlight this as 'the primary motivation for its global expansion throughout the twentieth century' (Anderson 2013, p. 2).

Many of the earliest Pentecostals believed that speaking in tongues specifically, as well as the baptism in the Holy Spirit more generally, was intended to equip them for missionary service. More than one alumnus or alumna of Azusa Street headed out to China, Africa or India with no experience of missionary ministry, just a sense of calling and a conviction that their glossolalic expression would suffice as they stood in the village market places and proclaimed the gospel. Many tried and failed. Some died in the attempt. But still within its first decade it is estimated that Pentecostalism had reached some 50 countries (Anderson 2013, p. 2). By the end of the last century, the missionary instinct of

Pentecostalism had transformed the global shape of Christianity and moved its power base away from Europe to sub-Saharan Africa and Latin America. These transitions are thoughtfully explored in detail in the series of essays collated by Stephen Hunt (Hunt 2015). Some of the earliest British Pentecostal denominations had their origins in missionary support networks, most prominently the Pentecostal Missionary Union which later became a part of Assemblies of God (Andrews, pp. 18–20).

Pentecostal evangelistic activity was not only limited to foreign climes, either. Pentecostalism had been birthed in revivalism in the UK, and it grew to maturity as a church planting movement. Between the two world wars, thousands flocked to hear the preaching of the great Pentecostal evangelists like George Jeffreys, and hundreds of them made the decision to follow Christ (Kay 1990, pp. 155–67, 209–14). And when they did, among the first things they would have been told was the need to testify to the world of what God had done in their life and to bring others to know him too.

Any assessment of the story of Pentecostalism, therefore, must engage with its global origins, its missionary history and its evangelistic culture, and these are to this day some of the most significant Pentecostal contributions to the global Church. Yet it is also important to note that throughout much of its history, Pentecostalism has been notable for its inclusive culture. 'Whosoever will may come' was one of the rallying cries of the early Pentecostal preachers, based on Philip P. Bliss' hymn 'Whosoever Will' that featured in the three most prominent British classical Pentecostal hymnbooks Redemption Songs (1937, no. 93), Redemption Hymnal (1951, no. 274) and Making Melody (1983, no. 300). Race, gender and social status were not obstacles to coming to faith.

Perhaps one of the most interesting sociocultural distinctions between the Charismatics and the Pentecostals in the UK is that while the Charismatic movement is in general a little more middle class, the most rapid growth of Pentecostalism has been among the working classes. Until around the 1980s and increasing national prosperity, it was often joked that the Pentecostal Church in any town could be found inhabiting a tin hut behind the gas works! Indeed, my childhood home church was first based in a former jam factory in the 1920s, and my wife's was initially located in an old dairy! To this day established classical Pentecostal congregations can most frequently be found in the UK's industrial heartlands – the north-east, Yorkshire, South Wales and the Midlands in particular – and in the inner cities. It has to be acknowledged that these are difficult communities to work in, with low rates of church attendance, and many of the long-established Pentecostal congregations in the towns are small and have remained so for many years, though happily city-based Pentecostalism has tended to prosper a little more.

The movement's working-class origins made for something of a double-edged sword; they gave Pentecostalism a certain pragmatic earthiness which rooted the movement in the realities of daily life, for one thing. But the northern industrial towns and mining villages were often very deeply conservative communities which were hostile to change, and particularly in the latter half of the twentieth century, many small Pentecostal congregations found themselves bound up by leadership structures which were no longer fit for purpose, but rather embodied adversarial workplace mentalities and a hostility to any external authority. Pentecostalism's preference for 'flat' organizational structures has not always worked in its favour and, within the UK and internationally, regional cultures among other factors have often shaped and nuanced the governmental model of individual congregations. Indeed, not least but by no means only for reasons of ecclesiology, it is critically important that any analysis of Pentecostal belief and practice attends not only to the formal, official teaching and culture of the established denominations but the actual, everyday, belief and practice of 'ordinary' Christians (Astley 2002; Cartledge 2010). Lived practices are, on a number of levels, sometimes rather different from espoused beliefs, and it is all too easy for those outside the Pentecostal movement to overlook its lack of homogeneity and see only the distinctive commonalities.

However, Pentecostalism's more egalitarian approach to church life did have plenty of advantages. One of the most important aspects of the Azusa Street revival, as I noted, was its recognition of the role of women and people of colour, both of whom had roles of significant influence and worked together effectively across sharp cultural divides – at least at first. Many of the greatest early Pentecostal missionaries were women, as were some of the prominent early evangelists, such as Amy Semple McPherson, Carrie Judd Montgomery, Florence Crawford and, rather later, Katherine Kuhlman. Many of the earliest Pentecostal denominations ordained women from the outset; it is to my mind a great travesty that the movement has to some extent rowed back from that initial commitment. Ugly sexism and racism have raised their heads in some quarters at various times in Pentecostal history, rather too frequently for us to be comfortable, but at its heart, I believe Pentecostalism remains a faith which empowers the disempowered and reasserts the rights of the disenfranchised. And that is just one aspect of its transformational power. Pentecostalism makes a difference wherever it goes. It does not believe in just improving the world, but in transforming it.

Fundamentally, this commitment boils down to issues of soteriology. Historically for Pentecostals, salvation has been viewed as a total and immediate transformation. They do not conceive so much of a 'journey to faith', but simply to a before and an after. The classic Pentecostal testimony amounts to 'Once I was lost – now I am found'. Just as Pentecostals believe they will be 'changed in the twinkling of an eye' at the return of Christ, so too they believe they instantly gain a new hope, a new life, a new destiny and a new Lord at the moment of conversion. Pentecostals seek to believe the Bible over their experience at every stage and to trust in the word of the Lord over their feelings, and even the evidence of their sight, because they understand the overwhelming capacity of God to reverse any negative situation for his glory in just a moment.

It is worth noting though that historically, this expectation of transformation has been very much focused on the individual rather than the transformation of society. Even though many Pentecostals work, believe and pray for a great end time revival that will usher millions into the kingdom of God, they believe that winning the world begins with one, that the gospel changes lives one person at a time. Pentecostals share the evangelical belief that every individual needs to make their own choice to follow Christ. However, for much of Pentecostal history, this came along with the assumption that it was not the Church's role to seek to address social challenges. The 'social gospel' was seen as purely a liberal agenda emerging from an apostate mainstream church. When Peter once acknowledged the disciples' economic poverty to a lame man at the temple gate (Acts 3.1–10), it was principally so he and John could offer the man healing instead of alms. Many Pentecostals saw a paucity of spiritual riches in the established denominations which, Pentecostals thought, left-wing clergy were attempting to replace with political campaigning. There was also an ecclesiological element to their thinking; whereas the Anglican parish system entrusts the care of a whole community to its priest, Pentecostal churches believed it was their responsibility to attend to the spiritual and physical well-being of their membership, not of the wider population.

This failure to engage socially and politically for much of Pentecostal history is, with the benefit of hindsight, one of the movement's greatest missed opportunities. Even the black majority churches, whose congregations arguably had most to gain from addressing issues of systemic injustice, tended to take a back seat on such issues. Yet the Pentecostal messages of hope, aspiration, self-betterment and of the transformative power of salvation were powerful motivations for pursuing social change. Sadly, however, it is only really after the rise of the Charismatic movement and with their increasing influence over classical Pentecostals that we see the rise of what Donald Miller and Tetsuano Yamamori have labelled 'progressive Pentecostalism' (Miller and Yamamori, pp. 15–38). The transformation over the last 30 years has been comprehensive, however, and today you would be hard pressed to find a Pentecostal church that does not offer a variety of services to the community beyond its own congregation. Furthermore, Pentecostal social and political engagement is increasingly a topic of scholarly reflection, with some exciting work emerging in this field including a 2018 special edition of the *Journal of the European Pentecostal Theological Association* (see particularly Homfray Cooper; Stone; Nyandoro; cf. also Muir 2018).

One further, final aspect of Pentecostal heritage deserves acknowledgement, however, and that is Pentecostalism's expert use of the popular media. Pentecostalism was always reliant upon the printed word, from its earliest days. Perhaps this ultimately goes back to their committed dependence upon the written word of scripture. There is something of a contradiction, actually, in that Pentecostal leaders sometimes told their congregations 'the only book you need to read is the Bible', but that the explosive early growth of Pentecostalism was promoted and propelled by a wealth of early publications – most prominently *The Apostolic Faith* from Azusa Street, which had a circulation of some 50,000 by 1909, *Confidence* from Sunderland and later denominational journals such as *Redemption Tidings* and *Church of God Evangel*. The apparent anomaly can be resolved, however, if we consider what it was that those early periodicals sought to do, which was to propagate revival news; provide Bible studies supporting Pentecostal readings of scripture and offering sound teaching; and promote testimonies of people's experience of salvation, of healing and of baptism in the Spirit. These magazines sought to comment on the Bible and demonstrate that its truths were still in action in the here-and-now. The significance and influence of such publications cannot be overestimated; it is perhaps noteworthy that one of the earliest major disagreements in Pentecostalism was at least partially over who owned and controlled the *Apostolic Faith* mailing list from the Azusa Street church. Clara Lum and Florence Crawford took the list to Portland with them when they left Azusa Street after a dispute apparently concerning William Seymour's marriage (Martin, pp. 279–80).

Yet despite that somewhat bitter experience, Pentecostal publishing continued to grow and flourish and as new technologies came along they were grasped enthusiastically. The BBC first put a Pentecostal worship service out on radio in July 1952 and within four years British Assemblies of God had established a radio council to take forward opportunities for broadcasting the gospel. Soon after that their American colleagues were taking regular TV slots and we see the origins of televangelism. Though restrictions on channel ownership in the UK meant that it was a while before the phenomenon reached here, Christian broadcasting is now well and truly established as a result of multichannel TV. And as 'on demand' delivery has begun to replace even multichannel TV and the prominence of the internet has risen, even more churches have taken the opportunity to go online, whether just posting sermons or live videocasting their services. Others just Instagram them!

Religious broadcasting is not without its challenges and downsides. It can be hugely expensive, and we all know that some of its proponents have not been the greatest examples morally. There is arguably a risk that Christian TV simply brings Christians out of the 'secular' media world where they would have better opportunities to be salt and light. But certainly, British networks such as United Christian Broadcasters, Premier Christian Radio and God Channel are well supported and having significant impact, and are quite heavily used by Pentecostals. Many of the African-led churches rely on specific black networks to take their material, too. Perhaps broadcasting attracts a particular non-representative subset of Pentecostalism which is less accessible and comprehensible outside the Christian world, but it is nevertheless undeniable that Pentecostals have seized wholeheartedly the opportunities that come their way.

Pentecostal Hope

The story of British Pentecostalism so far, then, is broadly if not unremittingly one of success and growth. But going forward, the continuing influence and growth of the movement in the UK depends upon it tackling a number of significant challenges.

The first of these is race and the integration of the black- and white-led congregations. It is to the UK's great and continuing shame that those citizens of its former empire and colonies who answered the call to come and rebuild Britain after World War Two were not welcomed and appreciated as they should have been, and this inhospitality was not uncommon in the churches either. The Windrush Generation did not find the warm welcome they expected from their brothers and sisters in the white churches, and Pentecostals were at fault here as much as any other tradition. Much of this rejection was out-and-out racism. Some of it arose from uncertainty on the white churches' part as to how to engage and build community with new people whose culture, priorities and experiences were so very different from their own. Some of it was concern about the new, more enthusiastic style of worship these people brought with them – post-war Britain was a cautious, risk-averse and introverted nation – but either way, my estimate is that at least 90 per cent of the cause of the racial divide at the heart of British Pentecostalism belongs at the feet of the white churches who, albeit through omission as much as commission, failed to rise to the challenge in the 1950s.

The resulting racial divide at the heart of Pentecostalism has, arguably, harmed wider race relations and integration, hindered the growth of the Church, and hampered the development of positive development opportunities for immigrant communities by excluding them from access to networks and from integration into church life. While massive progress in healing that rift has been made, the hurt still needs to be healed and stronger bridges between the two communities still need to be built. If the British Pentecostal Church is ever to fully reflect the beautiful image presented in Revelation 5 of a church of all generations, races and cultures gathering together in worship around the throne of God, then more needs to be done here urgently.

Second, Pentecostals need to deal with their hostility to education, and theological education in particular. This is a long-standing challenge which depends upon outdated, historic assumptions. Many early Pentecostals expressed considerable resistance to any formal theological education, because they saw universities as hotbeds of liberalism that had no place for anyone outside the liberal intelligentsia. They were not thought of as places for the working classes to aspire to attend, and few Pentecostal leaders felt that anyone outside the movement itself had anything to teach them about theology. Indeed they were even sceptical about educational opportunities offered by good Pentecostal women and men. Bible college training was not required for anyone seeking recognition as a minister in my former denomination, and when I was invited in the 2000s to oversee its ministerial training programme, it had at that time the lowest expectation for clergy training of any group in the UK.

The narrative was that academic study drained the spiritual life from a leader and distracted them from the more important and visionary tasks. 'We don't need training, we just need the Spirit' was a common assertion. Considerable progress on this issue was made in the 1990s when the established Pentecostal Bible colleges first achieved validation from the universities and approval to offer their own degree programmes. The more progressive church leaders saw this for the important recognition of the movement's influence that it was, and welcomed it with open arms, but for sceptics, secular recognition of the colleges' academic virtues was merely further acknowledgement that they had become too intellectual and were failing to develop the pastors the movement needed. Pentecostalism has therefore had to endure something of an uneasy truce with scholarship for the last generation. It is interesting to note, however, a very distinct cultural difference among the British African churches, which have been very quick to encourage their pastors to pursue academic training including up to doctoral level.

The long and short of this matter is, however, we are living in a much more professionalized world where the aspiration is that half our teenagers will attend university, where continuing professional development is part of the lifeblood of any large organization, and where the experience, training and capability of our leaders is under more scrutiny than ever before. In such a context, the traditional Pentecostal hostility to education has to be revisited and their models of leadership re-evaluated. Critical academic reflection could and should feed into Pentecostal appreciation and understanding of what leadership looks like and how it might be sustained in a changing world, balance apostolic vision with accountability, participation and engagement. These were issues that the new church apostolic networks had to engage with from their inception, though the retirements of some of their most senior leaders in recent years have provoked some re-evaluation.

Classical Pentecostals have, I think, so far largely failed to appreciate how cultural change demands organizational change and are still too frequently reliant on dated models of leadership which fail to recognize altered social perceptions and expectations. In this regard, it seems to me that Pentecostalism has been trying to march forward with its legs tied together by an outdated and ill-informed perspective on the significance of ministerial training and theological education. Until the spiritual aspiration of Pentecostal excellence is mirrored by a commitment to intellectual excellence, the movement will continue to restrict its opportunities for growth and alienate potential adherents.

Finally, there is I believe one additional challenge that the Pentecostal movement in the UK still needs to address, and that is the question of its distinctiveness. When Charismatic-style worship music is the norm – when all flavours of the church are becoming more global – why do we still need the Pentecostals? Have they become so successful that they have now 'Pentecostalized' UK Christianity more widely and their mission is now complete? Do they – and here I do very much mean the classical Pentecostal denominations – still have something to offer the British church? You will not be surprised, perhaps, to hear that I think they do.

Classical Pentecostals share an inherent and intrinsic hope and optimism, a positivity, that is not quite mirrored in any other grouping. It comes from the committed belief that no matter what circumstances life throws up, the believer is seated in heavenly places in Christ Jesus and is more than a conqueror in every situation. This is not just something Pentecostals confess, it is the core assumption at the very heart of their spirituality, and everything else arises from and depends upon this claim. Because Jesus is King over all, then all that matters in life is living for him and serving him. This remarkable self-sacrificial dedication means that Pentecostal believers can live by faith in every circumstance and find something to rejoice in even in their bleakest hours. To lose that hope from British Christianity would be a tragedy.

References

Alexander, Estrelda Y., 2011, *Black Fire: One Hundred Years of African American Pentecostalism*. Downers Grove, IL: IVP Academic.

Anderson, Allan H., 2006, 'To All Points of the Compass: the Azusa Street Revival and Global Pentecostalism', *Enrichment: A Journal for Pentecostal Ministry*, Vol. 11 No. 2 (Spring), pp. 164–72.

Anderson, Allan H., 2007, *Spreading Fires: The Missionary Nature of Early Pentecostalism*, London: SCM Press.

Anderson, Allan H., 2013, *To the Ends of the Earth: Pentecostalism and the Transformation of World Christianity*. 2nd edn. Cambridge: Cambridge University Press.

Andrews, John, 2004–05, 'The Pentecostal Missionary Union: a brief history', *Assemblies of God Heritage*, Vol. 24 No. 4.

Astley, Jeff, 2002, *Ordinary Theology: Looking, Listening and Learning in Theology*. Explorations in Practical, Pastoral and Empirical Theology. London: Routledge.

Bartleman, Frank, 1980, *Azusa Street*. South Plainfield, NJ: Bridge Publishing.

Blair, William N. and Bruce Hunt, 1977, *The Korean Pentecost and the Sufferings which Followed*. Edinburgh: Banner of Truth.

Bundy, D. D., 2002, 'Welsh Revival' in S. M. Burgess and E. M. van der Maas (eds), *New International Dictionary of Pentecostal and Charismatic Movements*, pp. 1187–8. Grand Rapids, MI: Zondervan.

Cartledge, Mark J., 2010, *Testimony in the Spirit: Rescripting Ordinary Pentecostal Theology*. Explorations in Practical, Pastoral and Empirical Theology. Aldershot: Ashgate.

Cartledge, Mark J. and Andrew Davies, 2014, 'A Megachurch in a Megacity: A Study of Cyberspace Representation', *PentecoStudies*, Vol. 13 No. 1.

Cartwright, Desmond, 2007, 'Black Pentecostal Churches in Britain', *Journal of the European Pentecostal Theological Association*, Vol. 27 No. 2, pp. 128–37.

Catto, Rebecca, 2008, 'Non-Western Christian Missionaries in England: Has Mission been Reversed?', in S. Spencer (ed.), *Migration and Mission: Papers Read at the Biennial Conference of the British and Irish Association for Mission Studies at Westminster College, Cambridge 2–5 July 2007*. Sheffield: Cliff College Publishing.

Catto, Rebecca, 2012, 'Reverse mission: From the Global South to Mainline Churches', in David Goodhew (ed.), *Church Growth in Britain: 1980 to the Present*. Farnham: Ashgate.

Davies, Andrew, 2009, 'Reading in the Spirit: Some Brief Observations on Pentecostal Interpretation and the Ethical Difficulties of the Old Testament', *Journal of Beliefs and Values*, Vol. 30 No. 3, pp. 303–11.

Davies, Andrew, 2019 (forthcoming), '"The Evangelisation of the Nation, the Revitalisation of the Church and the Transformation of Society": Megachurches and Socio-Political Engagement', in S. Hunt (ed.), *The Brill Handbook of Megachurches*. Leiden: Brill.

Edwards, Joel, 1997, 'Afro-Caribbean Pentecostalism in Britain', *Journal of the European Pentecostal Theological Association*, Vol. 17, pp. 37–48.

Evans, Eifon, 1969, *The Welsh Revival of 1904*. Bridgend: Evangelical Press of Wales.

Frestadius, Simo, 2016, 'The Elim Tradition: "An Argument Extended through Time" (Alasdair MacIntyre)', *Journal of the European Pentecostal Theological Association*, Vol. 36 No. 1, pp. 57–68.

Freston, Paul, 2010, 'Reverse Mission: a Discourse in Search of Reality?', *PentecoStudies* Vol. 9 No. 2.

Hillborn, David, n.d., 'Charismatic Renewal in Britain', www.eauk.org/church/resources/theological-articles/charismatic-renewal-in-britain.cfm

Homfray Cooper, Trevor, 2018, 'Is a Theology for the Poor Relevant in a British Society Supported by Benefits and a Free NHS?', *Journal of the European Pentecostal Theological Association*, Vol. 38 No. 1, pp. 3–23.

Hunt, Stephen (ed.), 2015, *Handbook of Global Contemporary Christianity: Themes and Developments in Culture, Politics, and Society*. Leiden: Brill.

Kay, William K., 1990, *Inside Story: a History of British Assemblies of God*. Mattersey: Mattersey Hall Publishing.

Kay, William K., 2007, *Apostolic Networks in Britain: New Ways of Being Church*. London: Paternoster.

Kay, William K., 2009, *Pentecostalism*. SCM Core Texts. London: SCM Press.

Kay, William K., 2017, *George Jeffreys: Pentecostal Apostle and Revivalist*. Cleveland, TN: CPT Press.

Kay, William K. and Anne E. Dyer (eds), 2011, *European Pentecostalism*. Leiden: Brill.

Lee, Young Hoon, 1996, 'The Holy Spirit Movement in Korea: Its Historical and Doctrinal Development'. PhD thesis, Temple University.

McGee, Gary, 'William J Seymour and the Azusa Street revival', *Enrichment*, Fall 1999. http://enrichmentjournal.ag.org/199904/026_azusa.cfm

Martin, Larry, 1999, *The Life and Ministry of William J. Seymour.* Joplin, MO: Christian Life Books.

Miller, Donald and Tetsuano Yamamori, 2007, *Global Pentecostalism: the New Face of Christian Social Engagement.* Oakland, CA: University of California Press.

Muir, R. David, 2018, 'Pentecostalism & Socio-political Engagement: A Prolegomenon for the Common Good', *Journal of the European Pentecostal Theological Association*, Vol. 38 Issue 2.

Nyandoro, Pious H., 2018, 'Beyond Charity: Towards a Classic Pentecostal Vision for Promoting an Enterprising Spirit in Britain's Deprived Communities', *Journal of the European Pentecostal Theological Association*, Vol. 38 No.1, pp. 39–49.

Robeck, Cecil M., 2006, *The Azusa Street Mission and Revival: the Birth of the Global Pentecostal Movement.* Nashville, TN: Thomas Nelson.

Robeck, Cecil M. and Amos Yong (eds), 2014, *The Cambridge Companion to Pentecostalism.* Cambridge: Cambridge University Press.

Stone, Selina, 2018, 'Pentecostal Power: Discipleship as Political Engagement', *Journal of the European Pentecostal Theological Association*, Vol. 38 No. 1, pp. 24–38.

Synan, Vinson, 2001, *The Century of the Holy Spirit: 100 Years of Pentecostal and Charismatic Renewal, 1901–2001.* Nashville, TN: Thomas Nelson.

Synan, Vinson, 2006, 'The Lasting Legacies of the Azusa Street Revival', *Enrichment Journal.* http://enrichmentjournal.ag.org/200602/200602_142_Legacies.cfm.

Synan, Vinson and Charles R. Fox, Jr, 2012, *William J. Seymour: Pioneer of the Azusa Street Revival.* Alachua, FL: Bridge-Logos.

Thumma, Scott and Warren Bird, 2015, 'Megafaith for the Megacity: The Global Megachurch Phenomenon', in S. Brunn (ed.), *The Changing World Religion Map.* Dordrecht: Springer.

Wakefield, Gavin, 2007, *Alexander Boddy: Pentecostal Anglican Pioneer.* Milton Keynes: Paternoster.

Weigel, Charles, 2015, 'World Christianity by the Numbers', *First Things*, Issue 25, www.firstthings.com/web-exclusives/2015/02/world-christianity-by-the-numbers accessed 21 May 2018.

Worsfold, James, 1991, *The Origins of the Apostolic Church in Great Britain.* Wellington, NZ: Julian Literature Trust.

2

African and Caribbean Pentecostalism
in Britain

BABATUNDE ADEREMI ADEDIBU

The twenty-first century has heralded a new phase in the history of Christianity with the emergence and proliferation of Pentecostalism across various cultural frontiers. The growth and impact of Pentecostalism is not restricted to the global South, which incidentally is now the centre of gravity of Christianity, but resonates in the global North as Pentecostalism, particularly African and Caribbean Pentecostalism is now everywhere including Britain. The rise of Pentecostalism has undermined the claims of secularization, and some advocates of secularization acknowledge that 'today it is secularity, not spirituality, which may be heading for extinction' (Cox, p. xv). The emerging currents within the British Christian landscape reflect cultural and religious changes due to migration, globalization and technological advances. The changes result not only from secularization or the dwindling influence of Christianity in the public life, but also from the proliferation of African and Caribbean Pentecostal churches. Such a development coincides with the change in missionary direction: the erstwhile hub of the European missionary enterprise to Africa and the rest of the world has become the recipient of missionaries from Africa and the Caribbean intent on re-evangelizing Britain, a Protestant nation by law. This supports the opinion of some Western missionaries to Africa in the 1800s that a time would come when Africans would strengthen the Western churches, referred to as 'blessed reflex' (Kwiyani, pp. 70–1). This change coincided with the various social, economic and political challenges that accelerated migration from many countries of the Commonwealth to Britain, many bringing to the motherland their sociocultural as well as religious affiliations.

Britain's African and Caribbean Pentecostal churches are diverse but intertwine historically, theologically and practically. The title of this chapter refers to a broad, largely heterogeneous class of churches differing in their theological affiliations and exegetical traditions, their cultural nuances reflecting the lived experiences of Africans and Caribbeans in Britain (Adedibu 2012, p. 79). The mapping of African and Caribbean Pentecostalism below gives an overview of the antecedents of the movement in the British religious space.

Typology of African and Caribbean Pentecostalism in Britain

Previous scholarship has contributed to the historiographies of African and Caribbean Pentecostal churches in Britain (Olofinaja 2013; Adedibu 2012; Aldred 2006; Sturge 2005). Moreover, some of these authors also examined the ritual practices and idiosyncrasies of African and Caribbean Pentecostalism in Africa and its diaspora, flowing from Africa and the Caribbean; liturgical practices in Britain; the influence of African and Caribbean cosmologies in addressing the challenges of their adherents in the British context; critique of the missionary enterprise in relation to claims of re-evangelization and the growing brands of Pentecostal spirituality which is distinct from the historic denominations in the British Isles.

Osgood (p. 110) identifies five major strategies of church planting prevalent among African Pentecostal denominations in Britain:

1 Constrained to plant – which Osgood associates with mostly West African church planters through the initiatives of students who travelled with their religious subscriptions to plant churches to meet the sociocultural and religious needs of their members in the diaspora.
2 Sent to plant – one of the missionary initiatives from African churches to re-evangelize Britain due to the declining fortunes of Christianity by sending missionaries to the British Isles.
3 Transferred to plant – this describes the fissiparous nature of Pentecostalism in general, copious fragmentation and schism among its leadership mostly leading to the emergence of new denominations.
4 Trained to plant – to a large extent, this strategy seems not to be as prevalent in comparison to others among many African and Caribbean Pentecostal church leaders as this category of church plant undergoes theological training in Britain with the primary objective of church planting in the diaspora.
5 Called to plant – the personal initiative of Christians responding to a call to ministry (sometimes without formal theological training), to embark on church planting or without any denominational support.

By whatever means they are established, African and Caribbean Pentecostal churches have a significant presence in British cities. The urbanization of this strand of Christian faith has seen the appropriation of public spaces resacralized for religious use, such as London, Manchester, Birmingham, Bristol, Edinburgh and a host of others that have large immigrant populations. For instance, in the Southwark Borough of south-east London, Rogers observes that the 'Old Kent Road has become something of a shop window for their growth, proclaiming the globalization of Christianity' (Rogers, p. 17). However, it is common in these cities to see most African and Caribbean Pentecostal churches located in post-industrial areas. In comparison with historic denominations, most African and Caribbean Pentecostal churches in Britain are migratory in nature; they have to obtain planning permission for the conversion or outright purchase of their own buildings, which is seemingly a herculean task.

African Pentecostal churches, like their Caribbean counterparts, have made their presence felt in Europe, particularly in Britain and North America, but the largest and most widespread are Nigerian and Ghanaian Christian initiatives. Other less visible Christian communities are Zimbabwean, Congolese, Zairian, Cameroonian, Kenyan and Sierra Leonean immigrants (Adogame, p. 62). Due to limitations of space and research, it is practically impossible to give a detailed historical trajectory of the emergence and proliferation of African and Caribbean Pentecostalism in Britain, yet its historicization is essential to understanding its distinctiveness and perspectives. The next section examines the contributions of various scholars to mapping the religious geographies of African and Caribbean Pentecostal churches in Britain.

Mapping Religious Geographies

The First Modern Pentecostal Preacher from Africa

The first Black Pentecostal church in modern Britain was already in existence prior to British Pentecostalism's emergence in 1907. The first black-led church, led by Thomas Brem-Wilson, was (like the William Seymour Azusa Pentecostal movement) characterized by glossolalia and charismata; its local identity evolved over time to be similar to the Pentecostal phenomenon. Ireson, a protégé of Brem-Wilson, noted that Sumner Road Chapel was also known as the 'House of God'. He further affirmed that Brem-Wilson was 'a powerful evangelist and being black, was somewhat of an attraction in those days, when one saw few coloured folk in London'. Moreover, Brem-Wilson was a transcultural leader, an ecumenist, a philanthropist and an evangelist whose ministry across the British Isles was characterized by signs and wonders (Adedibu 2018). In furtherance of the Pentecostal missionary enterprise of his era, Brem-Wilson's church contributed to the raising and deployment of missionaries to Europe and Australia.

Peter Van der Woude was among the second generation of Dutch Pentecostals, which included Piet Klaver (1890–1970) and Nico Vetter (1890–1945). He was ordained as an Assistant Pastor in 1929 and migrated to Holland in 1934 after the death of Brem-Wilson. Van der Woude was pivotal in the initiation of Pentecostalism in Rotterdam under the auspices of the Assembly of God (Gemeente Gods). Cecil Ireson, a member of Sumner Road Chapel from 1923 to 1926, was also a missionary to Australia, New Zealand and China. Thus, Sumner Chapel and Brem-Wilson contributed to reinforcing the global spread of Pentecostalism. However, due to the affiliation of Sumner Chapel with the Apostolic Church of Great Britain before the death of Brem-Wilson on 29 March 1929 at the age of 62 years, his contribution to the Pentecostal movement is yet to be acknowledged by most scholars and African church leaders. (Sumner Chapel, pioneered by Brem-Wilson, is now known as Sureway International Christian Ministries and is situated at Higgs Industrial Estate, Herne Hill Road, London.)

Modern Missionary Initiative from Africa

The city of Liverpool was a major transit route for ships during the transatlantic slave trade. During World War One, Liverpool was recognized as being socially polarized as a result of immigration, particularly by African Americans. Daniel Ekarte, a Nigerian migrant and a disciple of Mary Slessor at Calabar, obtained a seaman's certificate and migrated to Liverpool on 1 January 1915 with the intention of learning more about Jesus (Adedibu 2012, p. 31). However, Daniel was disillusioned on arrival in England due to the prevailing social and amoral nature of his new context in which he soon participated before his reconversion to the Christian faith after seven years in England. Daniel was the founder of the African Churches Mission (ACM) in Toxteth, Liverpool in 1931; between 1945 and 1949 he took in 'brown babies' – the offspring of affairs between black American men and white Liverpool women. The orphanage was situated at 122/124 Hill Street, Liverpool 8, and was right in the heart of the local immigrant community. Although there was no legal basis for segregation in Liverpool, the prevailing subtle and organized social segregation was noted by Wilson:

Regrettably, many of these agencies possessed and expounded racist, paternalistic ideology which viewed blacks as a problem. Blacks were seen as people of naturally inferior ability and morals who needed special aid in order to survive in a foreign, white and competitive society. These agencies believed their approach to providing desperately needed services for indigent black was beneficial. (Wilson, p. 57)

Daniel Ekarte preached to the diasporic community of Africans in Liverpool and members of his orphanage, but he was also involved in the campaign against discriminatory wages and racial equality between Africans and their British counterparts who worked for the Elder Dempster Shipping Company. Ekarte's contributions to racial justice and the upholding of the dignity of black people in Liverpool was commended by Dr Harold Moody of the League of Coloured People and the Pan African Congress held in Manchester in 1945 (Wilson, p. 67). Despite the commitment of Ekarte and his contributions to social cohesion, his orphanage was closed down as a result of government policy when the National Health Service was established in England; his orphanage was shut down by the City Council and the children were forcibly removed to other orphanages in Liverpool, many of them ending up in Fazakerley Cottage Homes, in the Liverpool 10 area of the city.

The ministry of Ekarte was holistic as it had its prophetic elements in speaking the truth to power and highlighting the racial and economic plight of diaspora Africans. Interestingly, the urban church planting model followed by Brem-Wilson and Daniel Ekarte is still the most widespread approach adopted by African and Caribbean Pentecostal churches, as most of these churches are situated in cities with a large immigrant population; most church plants are homogenous in composition. A similar urban approach seems to be a transatlantic phenomenon as observed in Pentecostal Assemblies of the World as 'cities [in the USA such as Baltimore and New York] became the central focus of independent Black Apostolic churches' (Gerloff, p. 108).

The Windrush Effect and the Emergence of Caribbean Pentecostal Churches in Britain

The immigration history and socio-religious dynamics of Britain changed with the docking of the *Empire Windrush* passenger ship at Tilbury from Jamaica on 22 June 1948. The event eventually heralded a new phase in the history of post-war migration to Britain with the arrival of over 500 Caribbean immigrants settling in London mostly from Jamaica, while others were from several Caribbean countries including Trinidad, Guyana and Bermuda (Sturge, p. 82). The effects of the American policy after World War Two to limit migration from the Caribbean to America was accentuated by Commonwealth ties and a shortage of the middlemen required to rejuvenate the British economy being geared toward industrialization. Paradoxically, the declining fortunes of the economies of the Caribbean were a major push factor to seekers of economic well-being in Britain even if for a short while before returning to their home country. Moreover, there were imperialistic notions of 'Britannia rules' – a dominant philosophy as Britain was presented in the colonies as the centre of decency, of civilization and absolute loyalty to the Crown with the fostering of the Union Jack as a symbol of dominance and imperialistic notions. This permeated every sphere of life in the colonies, including British ethnocentricity even in the educational sector (Sewell, pp. 1–20). Despite the legitimacy of being Commonwealth citizens with the right to migrate to the mother country, the Windrush Generation endured racial, social and economic ostracism in Britain (Aldred, pp. 1–30; Sturge, pp. 1–20); even though '24% of the migrants had management or professional training, 46% were skilled workers, 5% were semi-skilled and only 13% unskilled workers' (Sewell, p. 35).

The failure of the communicant's card of the members of the historic denominations from Caribbean countries to integrate holders into their respective denominations in England due to racism contributed to the emergence of Caribbean Pentecostal churches in Britain. Migrants travelled with their religious backpacks, ritual and religious idiosyncrasies to the motherland. Thus, many moved to deprived inner-city areas like Brixton, Moss Side, Wolverhampton and Handsworth, Birmingham. The Church of God in Christ held its first public meeting in 1952 after the first Pentecostal conference was held in London (Gerloff, p. 56). The New Testament Church of God held its first service at the YMCA Centre, Stafford Street, Wolverhampton, the morning of Sunday 20 September 1953 under the direction of Bishop Oliver A. Lyseight and Bishop Herman D. Brown and on the same day, Bishop G. A. Johnson, Revd Enos Gordon and other believers began a fellowship in Handsworth, Birmingham. The same year, the Church of God of Prophecy was established in Britain. The racial and discriminatory undertones also militated against the new Pentecostal churches led by Caribbeans as they held services in living rooms, kitchens and church halls which were unconventional church planting approaches. However, the fledging denominations provided not only a sacred space for religious rituals, but also social and cultural spaces to foster unity and dignity of Caribbean diasporans as well as providing a familiar socio-religious interpretive framework to cope with the racial challenges in the new context.

Many people migrated to England during the Windrush era for a variety of reasons including missiological (Arnold, p. 21). The Caribbean Pentecostal churches in the 1950s and 1960s were characterized by Pentecostal hermeneutics of warm experientialism and pious affection which heralded the genesis of the development of relevant theology which embraces their dual heritage as people of Caribbean descent and as Christians, succinctly documented by Aldred (2006). In the 1960s and 1970s, Black Pentecostal growth in Britain was mainly identifiable as Caribbean, but from the 1990s this changed with the proliferation of Pentecostal churches from Africa, particularly Nigeria and Ghana. However, the Caribbean Pentecostal churches were forerunners that paved the way for a more culturally sensitive disposition that African Pentecostal churches profited from. Nevertheless, the 1980s witnessed the gradual waning of the growth of Caribbean Pentecostal churches in England, partly as a by-product of visionary and dynamic church planting strategies by some of the leading African Pentecostal denominations and as some of the key leaders of the Windrush era left England. Another factor was the challenge of second-generation youths that opted for Rastafarianism in their search for selfhood, validation and the acceptance within Britain of their Caribbean roots.

Interestingly, there have emerged second-generation Caribbean Pentecostal and Charismatic leaders who are more contextual, visionary and astute entrepreneurs attracting a lot of followers in Britain. Typical examples include Bishop John Francis, the founder and pastor of Ruach City Church as well as the presiding bishop of Ruach Network of Churches. He was consecrated as a bishop on Sunday 7 June 1998 and now has a Ruach City Church membership of over 5,000, satellite TV and radio stations and is a sought-after preacher at conferences across England, America and elsewhere. He is the son of a first-generation Holiness preacher in London from the Caribbean, as is Bishop Wayne Malcolm, founder and Bishop of Christian Life City, the Head of International Christ Ambassadors Network (iCAN). The organization is composed of a church network, a business school and a global network of aspirational believers with a holistic ministry that facilitates drug rehabilitation and youth advocacy. His church membership is about 3,000. Francis and Malcolm represent an emerging second wave of Caribbean British-led churches since the 1990s that are growing while their antecedents wane.

The African Initiated Churches Phase

The British Christian space witnessed diversity with the emergence and proliferation of another stream that is pneumatic and strongly Afrocentric known as the Aladura (Owners of Prayers) Churches as a result of the migration of West Africans, especially Nigerians, Ghanaians and Sierra Leoneans mainly for further studies in Britain. Sometimes called the 'African Initiated Church' (AIC), Cherubim and Seraphim, Nigeria was pioneered in London by S. A. Abidoye with 14 other members all from Nigeria without any ecclesiastical mandate or theological education (Ludwig, p. 346). African churches include the Cherubim and Seraphim, the Celestial Church of Christ, the Divine Prayer Society or the Church of Universal Prayer Fellowship, and the Musama Disco Christo Church or Army of the Church of Christ (MDCC). There are various doctrinal convergences between Aladura churches and Pentecostal churches which make the differences between the two fluid. These include emphasis on divine healing, prophecy, dream interpretation, miracles, glossolalia, the baptism of the Holy Spirit and exorcism. The Aladura churches, like Pentecostal churches, are still engaged in the 'ubiquitous Yoruba search for spiritual power' and regard the Spirit as the ultimate source of worldly success (Harris, pp. 223–34). Many AICs straddled the typological divide and recast themselves as Pentecostal churches affirming and manifesting the gifts, or charismata (Meyer, p. 3). The proliferation of the Aladura pneumatic churches in Britain was largely influenced by a missionary motive, the exclusionary racial climate of the host context in the 1950s and 1960s and the dearth of pastoral care for Aladura adherents in the diaspora. Osun believed the proliferation of AICs was due to openness to ecumenism and ecumenical challenge, the fluidity of schism within the church hierarchy, inherent leadership structure from Nigeria and transferred membership (Adedibu 2002, p. 69).

Neo-Pentecostal Churches from West Africa

The implosion and public visibility of Pentecostalism in Britain has been accentuated by the emergence and proliferation of Pentecostal churches from West Africa on the British church scene. The new emerging trend among this stream of Pentecostalism in Britain in comparison to the Caribbean Pentecostal churches in the 1950s and 1960s was that these neo-Pentecostal churches did not have the classical notions of world-rejecting and puritan roots of their British Pentecostal counterparts; they were strongly influenced by the American prosperity gospel yet deeply rooted in African cosmologies as they appropriated cultural sensibilities which had previously been associated with AICs. The emergence of African neo-Pentecostal churches offered a new phase for the future of Black Pentecostalism in Britain at a time when the classical Pentecostal – including those of older Caribbean tradition – and the predominantly white middle class independent denominational Charismatic churches have generally stagnated or declined. They have a distinctive entrepreneurial drive, visionary and aggressive church planting strategies, and are success-oriented which marks them out from the Caribbean Pentecostal churches established in the 1950s, 1960s and 1970s (Adedibu 2012, p. 69).

African-led Pentecostal churches are the most visible variety among the different genres of new African Christianities that have burgeoned in Britain as well as in North America, especially since 1980. These churches have emerged in two ways. The first has been through churches in the diaspora that have branches and parishes of mother churches with headquarters in Africa. A typical example among several others is the Redeemed Christian Church of God, London. The second way has been through churches founded by African immigrants in the United States and Europe. Pentecostal churches that fall in this second category have their headquarters in the diaspora, and from there they expand back to Africa and other parts of the world. A typical example is the Kingsway International Christian Centre (KICC) with satellite churches in Nigeria, Ghana and South Africa. The success of the Nigerian Pentecostal movement seems not limited to Nigeria but extends to diaspora such as Europe and North America (Asamoah-Gyadu, pp. 74–96).

The first Nigerian neo-Pentecostal church to send a church-planter to Britain was Deeper Life Bible Church, whose pastor, Pre Ovia, in 1985 started a church at the Rockingham Estate Community Hall at Elephant and Castle (Osgood, p. 94). Later that year, the Four Square Gospel Church, a Pentecostal denomination with a rather different genesis, followed suit by sending Matthew Ashimolowo. However, Ashimolowo subsequently left the Four Square Gospel Church to pioneer another independent Pentecostal church named Kingsway International Christian Centre established in September 1992; he and 300 members rented a hall at Holloway Boys School, north London to birth the new church (www.kicc.org.uk). New Covenant Church, led by Revd Paul Jinadu, registered its presence in London through the late Bishop Titus David in 1986. Bishop David left the New Covenant Church in 1988 to pioneer the Christ Family Church on 16 October 1988.

The Redeemed Christian Church of God (RCCG), a transnational independent Pentecostal denomination started at Ebute-Metta as a prayer group – Egbe Ogo-Oluwa (Fellowship of Glory of God) – led and founded by the late Revd Josiah Akindayomi with 12 men as pioneering members. When Akindayomi died on 2 November 1980 at the age of 71, Pastor Enoch Adejare Adeboye was consecrated as the General Overseer of RCCG on 21 January 1981. The change in leadership heralded a new era in organizational structure, changes in some doctrinal positions and globalization of the RCCG brand. RCCG started in Britain as a London-based house fellowship in 1988 by four Nigerians who migrated to the United Kingdom for further studies with the General Overseer, Pastor E. A. Adeboye, in attendance. The RCCG is the fastest growing Pentecostal denomination in Britain; Peter Brierley estimates that RCCG will grow to 156,000 adherents by 2020, but as their 2017 estimated membership was about 62,000 this may represent an overly optimistic view of RCCG's likely growth (Gledhill 2014).

Undoubtedly RCCG is now among the largest Pentecostal denominations in the country on a par with Elim and Assemblies of God which in 2013 had 64,000 and 57,000 followers respectively, hitherto the two largest Pentecostal denominations. The only other large Pentecostal denomination is the New Testament Church of God with about 30,000 followers, but a membership of only 12,000. The phenomenal growth of RCCG is a transatlantic phenomenon as a similar growth trajectory has been observed in the United States. In the light of the global missionary enterprise of the RCCG, scholars have examined aspects of its missionary enterprise, ritual and idiosyncrasies in Britain and beyond (Ukah, pp. 104–32; Burgess 2008, pp. 39–63; Adeboye 2007, pp. 24–58; Adogame 2013, pp. 25–48). Time will tell if other Pentecostals will adopt any of the philosophies of RCCG to stimulate similar growth patterns.

Several smaller African-led churches have emerged in recent times. Harmony Christian Ministries, led by Adewale Olulana, started in 2000 under the umbrella of Revd George Adegboye, founder and Presiding Pastor, Rhema Chapel International Churches with headquarters at Ilorin, Nigeria. Likewise, the Victorious Pentecostal Assembly founded and led by Pastor Alex Omokudu. The Nigerian Pentecostal scene in London is diverse and includes churches that are Pentecostal but are committed to maintaining ethnic distinctives such as the use of the vernacular in their services, including Apata Irapada, a parish of the Redeemed Christian Church of God situated at Peckham, London. Likewise, Mount Zion Ministries (popularly referred to as Freedom Arena), located in Plumstead, London, led by Pastor Debo Adegoke.

One of the prominent Ghanaian Pentecostal churches in Britain is the Church of Pentecost which initially started in 1988 at an Elim

Pentecostal church in Finsbury Park, London. The pioneering team were committed to forming an association as a prelude to a Pentecostal church in the UK, and their Pentecostal Association of UK and Eire metamorphosed into Elim Church of Pentecost; in 2008 it attained charitable status and became a fully-fledged member of the Church of Pentecost. COP was founded by Pastor James Mckeown (1900–89), an Irish missionary sent by the Apostolic Church, Bradford, UK, to the then Gold Coast (now Ghana) in 1937. On the Gold Coast's attainment of independence in 1957 and its adoption of the name Ghana, the Gold Coast Apostolic Church was renamed the Ghana Apostolic Church. The church later adopted the name 'The Church of Pentecost' on 1 August 1962. However, due to the fissiparous nature of Pentecostal churches, the proliferation of these churches might continue in the foreseeable future. While the fortunes of African-led Pentecostalism can further be negatively affected by leadership ineptitude, progress can be accentuated by renewal movements within this stream of the Christian faith as well as visionary leadership committed to the missionary enterprise.

Concluding Remarks

Karla Poewe (1994) observes emphatically the links between nodes and networks of Pentecostalism across class, national and ethnic boundaries. Indeed, scholars agree that there is no single shared habitus of Pentecostal idiosyncrasies of beliefs and practices that are transposed from one context to another. Instead they promote the notion that the peculiar ideas, persons and sacred identities cross borders. Transnational linkages between places of departure and host countries or the new context that Pentecostal adherents adopt as their home characterized by cultural flows of goods, religious iconographies, worship and materials, inevitably leads to the emergence of various hybrid expressions of the Pentecostal movement.

In light of the hybridity that has emerged in the Pentecostal movement, particularly in Britain, some scholars have criticized the movement's pecuniary notions. A typical example is Smith and Campos who observed the creativity of some Pentecostal leaders. They assert that:

The great innovation of the Neo-Pentecostal media preachers has been to simplify the message even further, eliminating doctrine and reducing the message to a commercial transaction of symbolic goods. They have deepened and more effectively individualized the emotive content of religious television. 'Do you want hope? Do you long for forgiveness and liberation? Do you need healing, wealth and power? Demonstrate your faith by entrusting your offering to me, the intermediary with mystery, the channel of transcendence. In exchange, I grant your desire in God's name! Furthermore, I give you the symbol of the sacred; a rose, a vial of holy water, a few drops of healing oil. Use the sacred substance … resolve your problems.' (Smith and Campos, p. 61)

Nevertheless, it is important to note that Smith and Campos' perspective describes the action of some Pentecostal leaders. Indeed the emerging commercialization of sacred articles as well as the dexterity in the use of media technologies by some Pentecostal denominations might be repositioning parts of these movements with similar exploitative traits to the history that led to the emergence of Martin Luther's Reformation. Some African and Caribbean Pentecostal churches and individuals in Britain have had sanctions placed on them by the Charity Commission of England and Wales, the Metropolitan Police and the British criminal justice system due to various financial and moral misdemeanours; there is an urgent need for the leadership of the movement to exercise probity and accountability not only in terms of compliance with the dictates of the Charity Commission but also seek to be in a position of good-standing before their congregants, in biblical terms, 'without any blemish'.

It is impossible to know the numerical strength of African and Caribbean Pentecostal churches in Britain. The proliferation and growth of African Pentecostal and Caribbean churches might have assuaged the declining fortunes of Christianity in Britain through increased attendance and impact on statistics over the years. For instance, in the London Borough of Southwark Rogers (2013) notes that the London Church Census is likely to be the best indirect measure of London black majority churches' (BMC) growth at present, reporting a 58 per cent increase in total Pentecostal congregations in Southwark across 2005–12 and a 44 per cent rise across Greater London. It is, thus, imperative to note that this growth is primarily a by-product of immigrants from Africa into Britain or transferred growth and not a product of conversion from the indigenous Caucasian population; much of the claimed reverse mission is mere rhetoric. These churches are best described as migrant sanctuaries (Ukah, pp. 104–32) due to a lack of indigenous Caucasians among their members. There exists an urgent need for the initiation and sustenance of missiological reflection to enable the movement to develop appropriate contextual tools and strategies to evangelize postmodern Britain.

These churches do seem to be more socially connected with their communities as they identify and prescribe solutions to some of the contextual challenges where they are situated, thereby contributing to social cohesion and community development. Some of these community initiatives include after school clubs, nurseries, youth academies, counselling and skill acquisition centres. Across Britain, various community initiatives have received accolades from the government and communities. Initiatives include Street Pastors led by Revd Les Isaacs, a Peace Alliance led by Pastor Nims Obunge and a host of others too numerous to mention. However, social concerns are mainly targeted at the symptoms of social malaise leaving the urgent need to develop appropriate strategies to engage social policies and governmental constructs including youth and criminal justice and economic structures that perpetuate systemic inequalities against ethnic minorities, including some members of African and Caribbean Pentecostal churches who are at the margins of society. African and Caribbean Pentecostal churches in Britain have contributed to the redrawing of the political map of national and world Christianity. They have done so mainly as agencies addressing the challenges experienced by African and Caribbean people in Britain through exorcism and belief in the Spirit, opening up a new vista of opportunity for the redefinition of world Christianity from a holistic perspective that addresses all facets of human needs.

References

Adeboye, Olufunke, 2007, *Arrowhead of Nigerian Pentecostalism: The RCCG*, Leiden: E. J. Brill, Pneuma, Vol. 29 Issue 1.

Adedibu, Babatunde, 2012, *Coat of Many Colours: Origin, Growth, Distinctiveness and Contributions of Black Majority Churches to British Christianity.* Gloucester: The Choir Press.

Adedibu, Babatunde, 2013, 'Reverse Mission or Migrant Sanctuaries? Rhetoric's Symbolic Mapping and Missionary Challenges of Britain's Black Majority Churches', *Pneuma: The Journal of the Society for Pentecostal Studies*, Vol. 35 Issue 1.

Adedibu, Babatunde, 2016, 'The Missional History and Growth of the Redeemed Christian Church of God in the United Kingdom to date (2015)', *Journal of the European Pentecostal Theological Association*, Vol. 36 Issue 1.

Adedibu, Babatunde, 2018a, 'Mission out of Africa: The Urbanisation of the Redeemed Christian Church of God in the United Kingdom and its Missional Implications', *Interkulturelle Theologie: Zeitschrift für Missionswissenschaft)*, Issue 1.

Adedibu, Babatunde, 2018b, 'Thomas Kwao Brem-Wilson', in *Dictionary of African Christian Biography*, https://dacb.org/stories/ghana/brem-wilson/

Adogame, Afe, 2013, *The African Diaspora: New Currents and Emerging Trends in World Christianity*. London: Bloomsbury.

Adogame, A., 2004, 'Contesting the Ambivalences of Modernity in a Global Context: The RCCG, North America', *Studies in World Christianity*, Vol. 10 Issue 1.

Aldred, Joe, 2006, *Respect: Understanding Caribbean British Christianity*. Peterborough: Epworth.

Arnold, S., 1992, *From Skepticism to Hope: One Black-led Church's Response to Social Responsibility*. Nottingham: Grove Books.

Asamoah-Gyadu, J. K., 2010, 'Spirit, Mission and Transnational Influence: Nigerian-led Pentecostalism in Eastern Europe', *PentecoStudies*, Vol. 9 Issue 1.

Burgess, R., 2008, 'Nigerian Pentecostal Theology in Global Perspective', *PentecoStudies*, Vol. 7 No. 2.

Cox, Harvey, 1996, *Fire From Heaven: The Rise of Pentecostal Spirituality and the Reshaping of Religion in the Twenty-first Century*. London: Cassell.

Gerloff, Roswith, 1992, *A Plea for British Black Theologies: The Black Church Movement in Britain in its Transatlantic Cultural and Theological Interaction with Special References to the Pentecostal Oneness (Apostolic) and Sabbatarian Movements*. Frankfurt: Peter Lang.

Gledhill, Ruth, 2014, 'How Reverse Missionaries Built the UK's Fastest-growing Church', www.christiantoday.com/article/how-reverse-missionaries-built-the-uks-fastest-growing-church/37894.htm accessed 10 November 2018.

Harris, Hermione, 2006, *Yoruba in Diaspora: An African Church in London*. New York: Palgrave Macmillan.

Kwiyani, Harvey, 2014, *Sent Forth: African Missionary Work in the West*. American Society of Missiology Series. Maryknoll, NY: Orbis.

Ludwig, F., 2005, *The Proliferation of Cherubim and Seraphim Congregation in Britain*, in A. Adogame and C. Weisskopel (eds), *Religion in the Context of African Migration*. Bayreuth African Studies Series, No. 75. Bayreuth: Breitinger.

Maxwell, D., 2001, 'Sacred History, Social History: Traditions and Texts in the Making of a Southern African Transnational Religious Movement', *Comparative Studies in Society and History*, Vol. 43 No. 3.

Meyer, Brigit, 1999, *Translating the Devil: Religion and Modernity Among the Ewe in Ghana*. Trenton, NJ: Africa World Press.

Olofinjana, Israel, 2013, *Turning The Tables on Mission: Stories of Christians from the Global South in the UK*. London: Instant Apostle.

Osgood, Hugh, 2012, 'The Rise of Black Churches', in David Goodhews (ed.), *Church Growth in Britain 1980 to the Present*. Ashgate Contemporary Ecclesiology Series. Farnham: Ashgate.

Osun, C., 1981, *Christ Apostolic Church of Nigeria: A Suggested Pentecostal Consideration of its Historical, Organizational and Theological Developments, 1918–1975*, PhD dissertation, Exeter: University of Exeter.

Poewe, Karla (ed.), 1994, *Charismatic Christianity as a Global Culture*. Columbia: University of South Carolina.

Rogers, Andrew, 2013, *Being Built Together: A Story of New Black Majority Churches in the London Borough of Southwark, Final Report*. London: University of Roehampton.

Sewell, T., 1999, *Keep on Moving: The Windrush legacy.* London: Voice Enterprises.

Smith, D. A. and L. S. Campos, 2005, 'Christianity and Television in Guatemala and Brazil: The Pentecostal Experience', *Studies in World Christianity*, Vol. 11 Issue 1.

Sturge, M., 2005, *Look what the Lord has Done! An Exploration of Black Christian Faith in Britain Today.* Bletchley: Scripture Union.

Ukah, A., 2009, 'Reverse Mission or Asylum Christianity: A Nigerian Church in Europe', in Falola, T. and A. Agwuele (eds), *Africans and Politics of Popular Cultures.* Rochester, NY: University of Rochester Press.

Wilson, C., 1992, 'Racism and Private Assistance: The Support of West Indian and African Missions Liverpool, During the Interwar Years', *African Studies Review*, Vol. 35 No. 2.

3

The Rise of the Charismatic Movement in the UK

ROGER FORSTER

In the 1960s and 70s, British society passed through a huge transformation, even revolution, of sexual liberation and anti-establishment
protest. Ancient and traditional values were discarded. Loyalty was
replaced by the mantra 'be yourself'; all else was considered hypocrisy
and the number of adherents of Christianity, reducing since 1916,
accelerated in its decline. Yet at the same time there arose a second
wave of Pentecostal/Charismatic upsurge among the British churches.
The first wave was in 1905–06 followed by the rise of the Pentecostal
denominations, much ignored by the mainline historic churches, and
the second, in the 1960s, was known as the Charismatic Awakening,
emphasizing again supernatural Christianity but this time affecting the
whole church; not only those with conservative evangelical theology,
but Liberals, High Church, Broad Church, Roman Catholics, Free
Churches and Traditionalists.

This account is one man's observations; I lived through this time, and
was partly shaped by it. My wife and I planted the first Ichthus congregation in the early 1970s. I must plead the indulgence of my readers
on two accounts. First, this is a record of my lived experiences during
this time, rather than a conglomeration of research and books others
have written. Second, I have tried to reduce lists of names of significant
players in this bit of history and have possibly neglected those who
were the most influential in others' experience.

I have written of the Charismatic Renewal as a river forged and fed
by ten tributaries which flowed into a single flood and seen more clearly
as such when looked at from a distance of around 50 years. The same
one Spirit was breaking out in at least ten springs. It is hoped that
this modest record will help keep alive the longing for supernatural
Christianity. (Is there any genuine Christianity which is not supernatural?) I have constructed this history under ten main headings.

The Brethren Stream

It was in the late 1950s when I received a mysterious phone call suggesting a meeting with a complete stranger, outside – notice not inside – St Paul's Cathedral. The caller, a certain David Lillie, would be happy to treat me to lunch. Although there was a definite whiff of conspiracy in this invitation, it was too good an opportunity for a young evangelist 'living by faith', as they would say, to refuse. So I went. The outcome was an invitation to join a group of men who, under the leadership of Arthur Wallis, were seeking to rediscover the tangible power of God to re-evangelize the UK. Some of the group were, like Arthur, from the West Country, and they were planning to advance this longing of theirs by a conference, which became the first of three significant prayer gatherings. These were at Exmouth, Mamhead Park and Herne Bay.

I had met Arthur, a Brethren evangelist and Bible teacher, some few years previously and had invited him to speak at a meeting of airmen on the RAF station at Locking, near Weston-super-Mare. Arthur had just published his book on revival, *In the Day of Thy Power* (Wallis 1956). The RAF camp meeting had been the nearest thing I had yet witnessed to revival as airmen were turning to Christ. I was stationed there while doing my national service. Arthur had recently spent time in the Hebrides where a few years earlier there had been reports of unusual stirrings of God's Spirit. His book, later to be renamed and revised as *Rain from Heaven* (Wallis 1979), was sparking interest throughout the British churches, in particular those of a conservative evangelical tradition in which indeed Arthur himself had been reared. Dr Martyn Lloyd-Jones, who had a large following of disciples and was influential in that section of the church which had a Reformed fundamental puritan background, had an increasing interest in the work of the Holy Spirit and revival, and had requested a visit from Arthur to discuss the need of the British churches to experience the Spirit, and the biblical basis for revival as presented in Arthur's book.

It was now two or three years since my release from the Air Force and I had, in my youthful zeal for Christ, planted five house churches. All but one passed into oblivion – the remaining one became part of our Ichthus movement in the late 70s. It was possibly this unsought reputation for collapsing churches and evangelistic fervour which led to my being favoured with the aforementioned phone call, and the honour of addressing these revival-seeking senior brothers about the nature of the true church which would receive, promote and release God's Spirit-power in the UK. I took the challenge and spoke very fast for almost two hours. The transcript was so long it could not fit in with the other three addresses when the fruits of the conference were published. We still hadn't received revival! That was the Exmouth Conference 1958. Two more conventions were called, in 1962 and 1965, at Mamhead Park and Herne Bay Court, while more were planned and spontaneous gatherings arose.

The Herne Bay Court Convention invited Willy Burton, who had planted around a thousand churches in the Congo. He first went out into the African mission field from a Brethren Assembly but returned as a Pentecostal. This was the model of many who attended these conferences. While of course many men and women began to be challenged from nearly all denominations in the UK, a large number from the Brethren assemblies as they were known – leaders, evangelists and members – were being drawn into the ranks of the New Charismatics. A few, like Willy Burton, found their way into the already established support structures of the Pentecostal denominations and brought a fresh influx into these 60-year-old streams. Most at first tried to influence their original churches and if they found the flow of the gifts they were experiencing unacceptable to these Brethren assemblies, they often became spiritual gypsies travelling round different churches of spiritual notoriety or reputation. A simple distinction arose between those influenced by Charismatic expressions only, and those wishing to found churches more amenable and fitted for such gifts.

One of my earliest mentors/teachers after my conversion was a well-known, controversial, Brethren preacher, George H. Lang. I later found that he had been similarly influential on Arthur Wallis, who also drank from the springs of Andrew Murray and R. A. Torrey. Lang taught that there was a second work of the Spirit distinct from the New Birth namely the filling or baptism in the Spirit. He was not overly impressed with 'speaking in tongues' as the only evidence of the baptism but pointed me to his biography of a nineteenth-century Indian convert of the Brethren missionary A. N. Groves, an Indian evangelist named Aroolappen who spontaneously spoke in tongues during the 1860 Tinnevelly revival (Lang 1939). Lang also directed me to the earliest foundational teachers of the Brethren movement earlier in the nineteenth century, Darby, Kelly and Mackintosh, all of whom taught that receiving the Spirit was distinct from the New Birth. Lang's careful biblical exegesis and fatherly interest helped resolve many issues and encouraged me and many of the younger Brethren preachers to be open to the Spirit's power which was being manifested at the time. Oscar Panero (a friend of Arthur Wallis), Len Adams (an ex-Brethren missionary) and Dennis Clark were all influences and so were many others whom I would have loved to name. This stream, largely from a Brethren background, began to teach in spontaneous home groups.

It was not long before these home groups, enriched by many hungry believers from all denominations, began to meet not just for the 'special' Charismatic speakers, but regularly; so the house church movement of Charismatic free churches began drawing adherents from all denominations and theological persuasions. Again, without necessarily a commitment to the House Church Movement (as it was beginning to be called), more broad-hearted Brethren speakers from home and abroad such as Campbell McAlpine and Dennis Clark began to minister to these new house meetings.

The Pentecostal Stream

The traditional Pentecostals were by this time, the early 1960s, well established in the UK. However a major influence coming from the Pentecostal Church, worldwide in its impact, was the publication in 1962 of a North American Pentecostal pastor's book, *The Cross and the Switchblade* (Wilkinson 1962). David Wilkinson's story of a ministry among street gangs in New York, with its record of the conversion of Nicky Cruz, made a huge impact on many of the tired non-supernaturalistic churches everywhere as it was translated into many languages. It would be too strong to say that the rejection of Spirit-power and gifts was overcome by this one book but certainly the negative attitudes in Britain, and more particularly Germany and Japan where Spirit gifts were regarded as worse than heretical, began to be diffused. Many traditional believers in UK churches welcomed the growing interest in Charismatic gifts and experiences and fanned this fire into a furnace, even throwing their lot in with the new house church movement. Cecil Cousens, an erstwhile Apostolic Church pastor, was in the Arthur Wallis crowd and much appreciated as one with a long-time acquaintance with Pentecostal phenomena. My long-time friend Eldin Corsie, who for a time had been the Elim President and pastored the flourishing Kensington Temple church, made room for the 'new' Charismatics while continuing his traditional Pentecostal ministry. Eldin has always appeared to me as the example of Pentecostal holiness and humility in life and ministry from which others and I benefitted. Others of Pentecostal persuasion were more critical of the new stream and kept their distance. As my own work began to grow I had to learn to let go and be pleased if some of our converts left us for Eldin's more established work! I had already benefitted from other traditional

Pentecostals such as Principal Percy Parker and Pastor Dyer of Long Ashton; Faith, my wife, had received the 'baptism in the Spirit' under a godly Assemblies of God Pentecostal pastor in West London.

Arthur's group was well disposed to receive Pentecostals Bryn and Keri Jones. Bryn had returned from exceptional ministry in the Caribbean and Guyana. The two brothers threw their lot in with the Arthur Wallis group and gave considerable strength to the newly planted Charismatic churches. Bryn's inspiration led to the formation of the Dales Convention in the North, and the Capel Convention became the Downs Week in the South of England. A smaller and later Charismatic week was started in Wales with Phil Rees, an Anglican clergyman of Free Church disposition, who had worked with me in London. He built on the work of Don Werner and David Watson and 50 other clergy influenced by them. These 'weeks' of ministry and fellowship were attended by thousands from all denominations and became the expressions of Charismatic revival for which the church in the UK was clearly hungry. While many remained in their inherited denominations with a desire to see them open the door to more evident Holy Spirit activity, hosts of others swelled the work of the house churches, which became known later as the 'new' churches since they were too big to get into the average-sized front room. However, like our own history, the home or house groups are a fundamental and essential part of our structure, providing real eye-to-eye relationships and saving us from virtual reality and imagined social media-tweaked existence, which were later to arrive on the scene!

The 'new' churches began to grow or link together for fellowship, shared ministries, church order and discipline and new leaders emerged with their followers. Attempts to hold these 'streams' led by their 'apostles' proved to be impossible. Unfortunate titles began to emerge in the Reconstructionist streams. Reconstructionists are those of the renewal who wanted a total reformation of the church for a scriptural church order – not just a church manifesting the gifts. Such movements have originated in every century of the Church. Certain leaders got together to form a coherent body, calling themselves the Magnificent Seven and later, as they extended, the Fabulous Fourteen. Sadly, difficulties and disagreements arose and it soon broke up as they fell out with each other. I will name some of these men, not to criticize but to acknowledge them in their desire to honour God and be faithful to what he was doing at this time, even if this attempt at structural unity was unsuccessful. The year was 1972. Of course there was Arthur Wallis and Bryn Jones his running mate – or was this relationship now running the other way round? There was Hugh Thompson, an ex-Brethren evangelist; Peter Lyne, who later having planted in the UK moved to New Zealand and continued in the new church streams; Graham Perrins who was perhaps the most theologically equipped among them; David Mansell; John Noble; Gerald Coates; Terry Virgo; and Barney Coombes. Later the Fabulous Fourteen extended to a large group including Stuart Bell and the new churches flourished in the 1970s to 1990s as these leaders, including myself, exercised apostolic ministries in the church and nation, as well as overseas.

However, to return to the Pentecostal stream from which Bryn and others had been drawn, it must be recognized that the experience of God's presence in Bonnie Brae Street, Los Angeles, the miraculous gift of worshipful singing, the feeling of the love of God within a quarter of a mile of the Azuza Street building to which Pastor William Seymour's small group had moved, had some considerable impact in creating the UK situation of the 1950s to 1970s where many believers were longing for a similar visitation from God. However, I had never consciously met a Pentecostal while a student at Cambridge, where I first in 1951 put my faith in Christ, and then in 1953 was baptized in the Spirit. Faith, my wife, was baptized in the Spirit in 1958 and a certain Spirit-filled minister, Edgar Trout, came into our lives while we were seeking in the mid-1960s to run our home as a spiritual 'rescue shop' for people in need. Edgar's wisdom and Charismatic ministry was exceptionally helpful to us along with many others. This was particularly in the case of the exercise of deliverance ministry. The rapidly declining moral and spiritual state of the country was requiring more Spirit-power than many true believers had experienced. Those such as Edgar were preparing and heightening the expectation of a new Pentecost, and the defeat of the spirit-powers. Finally, South African David Du Plessis, General Director of the World Pentecostal Movement, was challenging denomination leaders, even the Pope. Smith Wigglesworth had earlier prophesied Du Plessis' significant role in the Charismatic worldwide renewal in the mid-century through all denominations.

The Black-led Stream

Bryn Jones knew Philip Mohabir while he had ministered in Guyana. Philip already had a reputation as a church leader in a growing number of countries. He was a godly black preacher. Through Bryn he ministered into the restoration streams and had also set up his own. It was a privilege to have one of his daughters on our year's training programme and to benefit from her musical worship ability. She symbolizes for me the tremendous influence that has come from the Caribbean and later from African churches. If the Windrush Generation from the 1950s and onwards had been more warmly received in the UK their contribution to renewal would have been even greater. As it was, they gradually changed the worship style of the British church. Through their lively worship style, worship became more accessible and so acceptable to a larger number of people. In fact, such a worship medium is now named Charismatic worship and most churches use it at some point in their activities. Black/white fellowship in churches has still some way to go, but the impact and changing style of worship – more open to the expectation and use of Holy Spirit gifts – is a factor in the changing scene in the church in the UK making room for the deepening and widening interest in the filling of the Holy Spirit.

The Windrush Generation brought with them in the late 1950s and early 1960s a charismatically oriented worship form. This was irrespective of which denomination they came from. Later on John Stott was reported as saying, when warned that the Anglican church in which he was going to preach was inclined to Charismatic worship and theology, 'I thought all churches were a little charismatically inclined these days.' Whether this was so or not, it was clearly now generally accepted that the style of worship had considerably changed and this worship has facilitated the spread of the revival message in the UK. This should not surprise us since the same feature was seen in Wesley's day during the Great Awakening. Charles Wesley's 8,500 songs backing up his brother John's unflagging preaching made an incalculable contribution to awakening a people to God. Graham Kendrick – known throughout much of the Christian world as a songwriter and worship leader – has for many years worked with very gifted black musicians such as Steve and Velveta Thompson, which again highlights the immense contribution made by African Caribbeans to the Charismatic Renewal. Graham's years with Ichthus Christian Fellowship were a great blessing to us and significantly contributed to our growth.

From the beginning of the influx of non-white preachers into the British scene I was aware of their calling from God, which was to awaken the British churches from their spiritual stupor. Often I would say as much to our predominantly white churches. Despite the inhospitable lack of welcome we gave our brothers and sisters in the beginning, things have changed more than 60 years later with a black Charismatic Archbishop of York and many fervent black preachers in the ranks of the historic churches. The impact of Joel Edwards as (former) Director of the Evangelical Alliance and the wonderfully changed atmosphere in Churches Together in England with the strength and spirituality of the black-led denominations, have been a great stimulus to the theological study and reality of the supernatural in the British scene. However, this is a long way down the line from the late 1960s and early 1970s, where in the initial rise in Charismatic Renewal it was largely, though not exhaustively, the impact on worship of the African Caribbean style which contributed to the movement's advance. Add to this element the many black preachers like Philip Mohabir and scores of others; the black-led churches were contributing to fervent preaching again. One of the cherished comments in those days when I was younger and my voice was stronger, was when I was complimented in a black-led church with 'He preaches like a black man'! Incidentally, fervent preaching was one of the six necessary characteristics sought after by the Pietist movement which influenced Britain in the seventeenth and eighteenth centuries.

The Reformed/Puritan Stream

Martyn Lloyd-Jones influenced, taught and pastored a large number of followers. His Friday night Bible studies at Westminster Chapel were renowned and packed out. I had at this time of my spiritual journey requested a couple of appointments with the 'Doctor', as he was affectionately known, to discuss the doctrine of the Holy Spirit, its baptism or seal and the place of renewal in the Christian experience. He was very kind, humble and encouraging. His insistence and fervour inspired me, and his injunction 'to pursue the Lord' did not go unheeded. He entrusted me with his books of Puritans who had experienced the Spirit of God in their personal lives and ministries and seen revival on local levels. I loaned him two books of mine. It certainly encouraged me to run hard after God. As the spiritual renewal movement began to manifest itself, many of this particular theological persuasion found what they were longing for in Martyn Lloyd-Jones' fervent Welsh preaching. It needs to be said that John Calvin, to whom many paid respects, clearly taught that the gifts of the Spirit had ceased to be given after the first century. Many were now experiencing more than their theology allowed. I like to think that many believers I love and respect are better than their theology. The 'Doctor' himself was clearly sidelined by many in his theological tradition, while many of his admirers found their way into the new churches which were arising. Yet others have retained a place in their ecclesiology for the Spirit's manifestations and revival theology.

The North Circular

This title might sound a little trite and so play down what was in reality a significant contribution or stream into the Charismatic Renewal of the 1950s to 1970s. Pastor George V. North (1913–2003) had a long and Spirit-filled ministry. His later years were marked by a large number of churches, at home and overseas, in which spiritual gifts were encouraged. One or two of my earliest young converts, whom I had either baptized or encouraged, found their way into their strong dis-cipling structure, eventually carrying responsibility in their ministry. Chief among these was perhaps Norman Meeton. I'll not forget his long journey to encourage me when I landed up in hospital after a car crash which had given me a broken femur. Norman had been an Angli-can trained curate whom I had impressed with the obedience of water baptism while ministering in Liverpool in the early 1960s. After George North was taken to glory, Norman's ministry became all important. Of course the somewhat trivial-sounding title is really an affectionate description of the churches George North regularly visited. George (or 'Wally' – again an affectionate designation by those who loved him) had a largely Wesleyan (plus Quaker) background and theology, inheriting from them a strong holiness motivation and a developed 'two-experiences' teaching, or second blessing – which North coalesced into one baptism in the Spirit. This stream flowed in preparing many for the renewal as well as contributing necessary elements of faith, holi-ness and discipleship. The use of Charles Wesley's hymns was a regular feature of these meetings.

The Chard Movement

A Brethren couple, Sid and Mill Purse, using their farm and guest house in South Chard, Somerset, after contact with ladies from Elim and Assemblies of God, ministered in the early 1960s and 1970s to large numbers of visitors who came because of the reputation of long worship meetings, including healings and deliverances. Their minister-ing was largely in worship, out of which everything else flowed. Many small house groups emerged under their inspiration. Little systematic teaching from scripture was given, but emphasis on the Holy Spirit's filling and gifting were predominant. The presence of God at this time in both Chard and its offshoots was intense and self-evident. So many well-known names today attended Chard or one of the offshoots, or had hands laid on them from Sid and Mill or one of their spiritual offspring. The healing evangelists Ian Andrews and Don Double came from this movement, as later did Jonathan Conrathe. Harry Greenwood was also a preacher from this movement. Our much-loved songwriter Graham Kendrick had hands laid on him at a Chard offshoot to receive the Spirit and is pleased to acknowledge the blessing it was even though it was only once and he never went again. This was a familiar story.

My old contemporary from our Cambridge University days, David Watson, who became one of the Church of England's most renowned evangelists, similarly had hands laid on him there for ministry. His colleagues – also from our Cambridge days – David McKinnis and Michael Harper, both also Anglican clergy with a later Charismatic history, were similarly affected by Chard. Something of this impact with the Anglican Church I will recall later. This sort of contact and subsequent continual blessing, following on to the end of the twentieth century, could be reported by so many in all denominations at the time even though Uncle Sid and Auntie Mill had served their generation and 'fallen asleep'. This movement was perhaps one of the most obvious tributaries flowing into the river of Charismatic blessing in the 1960s and 1970s.

The Anglican Church Contribution

If you thought from the previous section that high on the list of bene-ficiaries from contact with Chard were Anglican Christians and clergy in particular you probably would be right. Outside the house churches, now new churches, who were seeking total radical reconstruction of English Christianity, the most obviously affected were those of the Church of England. They had no desire to leave the denomination but many clergy had become hungry for God. Of course there were many godly men and women who saw the state Church as essential for the continuance of 'Christian England'. This may have been a mistaken view but was held sincerely. They loved the Church, its history, rituals and practices, its status and privileges, but also loved and longed for more of God. One such clergyman, who was a Charismatic precursor to the Charismatic Renewal, was Trevor Deering, whose deliverance ministry became well known. Colin Urquhart, an Anglican priest, early in the renewal received the Spirit and a healing ministry, later forming his own stream.

When Billy Graham was invited to the UK, I heard criticism and even saw tears that the Church of England had to turn to an American to stop the persistent decline it had experienced since 1916. Haringey

1954 was so successful it changed a lot of the British feeling of superiority over US Christianity: now there was a willingness to learn. Although the renewal had already begun, Dennis Bennett's book *Nine o'clock in the Morning* (1970) had a worldwide impact, opening up even established Anglican clergy and laity alike. Dennis was born in England and was an Episcopalian priest. The impact of his best-selling book with its testimony to receiving the Holy Spirit – selling the idea of supernatural Christianity and the power of the Spirit's enabling – was enormous. He visited the UK with his message a few times. A further significant ministry not only to Anglicans but throughout the UK for years was that of Jean Darnall. Hundreds if not thousands received the Spirit through her preaching and ministry. She was and is much loved, although she and her husband Elmer returned to the States after many years here.

Probably the most well-known ministry in the 1980s was again from America, namely that of John Wimber. John had become involved with the Jesus People Movement. His preaching, healing and ministry of the baptism in the Spirit filled and inspired many conservative believers in the Church of England. Clergy like 'Teddy' Saunders, David Watson, David McKinnis, Sandy Miller of Holy Trinity Brompton – which as HTB later became a large resource church for the Charismatic movement – and many others, invited John Wimber to England, and a wide range of ministries and denominations received blessing. Much has changed now in many Anglican churches. John was a loving and loveable man with his generous-hearted wife, Carol. The Vineyard movement of churches is an ongoing memorial to him throughout the world, and notably here in the UK.

The Charismatic Renewal has changed a large part of the Church in England; the life, activities and service of the state Church. Many are content to serve within its renewed walls, while the radicals of the Charismatic Renewal are not. However the work and experience of the Holy Spirit have brought about a Spirit-ecumenism which no committees could ever have done (Ephesians 4.3). Missions in universities all over the UK were enhanced by many assistant missioners being Spirit-filled clergy, together with converted pop stars like Barry McGuire who not only sang people into the Kingdom but would also hug them in with a huge bear hug and prayer, a style rather new to us 'Brits'!

The Jesus People Movement (JPM)

Barry and others like him came from the Jesus People, a movement from the States, in particular California and the West Coast. The JPM was looked upon, at first, as a part of the anti-establishment hippie culture for disaffected young people, but the misunderstanding was soon lost. This fundamentalist, moral crusading Christian movement was working largely among the poor, the destitute, outcasts of society, evangelizing beach boys and dropouts, and thus invading the drink and drug scene. Love, it is true, was high on their programme, but love as it is seen in Christ thus creating a brotherhood – including equally sisters. Shared goods and rescue houses for the afflicted became a hallmark of their care and concern for all people irrespective of race or gender. It was said that there were three affirmations these radical followers of Christ were to live by: don't sin, love God and declare the Son of God has come. On the West Coast of the States, Chuck Smith and Calvary Chapel became a roof over the heads of the otherwise open-air activities of seeking the lost and worshipping al fresco. John Wimber, a former evangelical Quaker, found himself drawn to the movement and discovered his gift of healing; Arthur Blessit carried his wooden cross throughout the world, and in such ways and with many stories of recovered lives the movement's influence spread.

Some of the early JPM preachers reached London and other places in the UK. One businessman in particular, a certain Kenneth Frampton, was moved to give them time and his property. He came originally from the Exclusive Brethren, but his generous heart and admiration for any biblical fundamental work meant he would help as far as he could. Imagine my surprise on Christmas morning to receive his phone call. Exclusive Brethren shun the church calendar but feel they celebrate the incarnation every day of the year. His phone call was about two hours long while my family was not too pleased waiting for Christmas dinner, but he urgently wished to hear what I thought of the Jesus People. Mr Frampton of course was no longer confined to the Exclusives but embraced the Spirit as so many were doing at this time. He later with his family served the UK church in many ways, not least in the Deo Gloria Trust. Of course there were dangers in the JPM and certain leaders left the straight and narrow through their unaccountability. However, it must be said there were no more excesses than in many of the more-accountable movements.

It is also worthy of note that the theological stable from which Frampton came was strictly separate from any of the emphases, both liberal and conservative, found at this time in popular and academic areas of historic churches. In particular, the then current recognition among a growing number of believers was the obvious neglect of the doctrine of the Holy Spirit to the degree that some theologians would even talk as though the history of church creeds and statements had been Binitarian rather than Trinitarian and perhaps this was the time to rectify this. Strangely, the Exclusive Brethren, with little contact with any from outside, began in the 1930s to make assertions about the dishonouring neglect of the third person of the Godhead. This must be rectified they said, and the Spirit glorified along with the Father and Son. It is impossible in the New Testament to find where the Holy Spirit is addressed or worshipped. By using the Old Testament in a very typological fashion, which they do, two Old Testament passages were claimed to authenticate their glorifying the Spirit in worship and addressing the Spirit of God. The first text was Numbers 21.17, 'Spring up, O well! – Sing to it!'. Second, a favourite of Pentecostals, Ezekiel 37.9, where 'breath' is the word for Spirit in Hebrew, and is worshipped and prophesied to.

The impact of the JPM in the UK is hard to assess. There was no outward structure of a new denomination or rescue work. However, the overall influence was a challenge to the younger believers to step out with God and expect the gospel to work in the least likely places. Much social action was stimulated which led to more dependence on the Holy Spirit to be effective. Cooperative living was not widely adopted, but had already been practised in the UK by some communities. There is little doubt that the outstanding success of the JPM was partly due to the failure of other anti-establishment societies in San Francisco to be fulfilling, satisfying and liveable.

The Power Ministers

In the 1940s there were some exceptional and very powerful ministries which arose in the United States and moved around all parts of the world until the 1970s to 1980s. It is hard to know what contribution these made in the UK but the reputations and extreme experiences were recounted and stimulated people's desire for revival. Some of these Charismatic preachers made great claims, some were questionable, some possibly fraudulent but others demonstrated miraculous words of knowledge and prophecies. Many believers were careful not to commit themselves too closely to these ministries on account of Jesus' warnings about false prophets being known by their fruits.

With all of the above in mind it is worth noting that some of these appeared on the scene and ministered to many of the streams mentioned. One name was Paul Cain, one of the youngest of the 1940s power ministers who resurfaced working with John Wimber in the 1980s and 90s. Many took prophecy seriously because of him, some coming from the influential levels of our society. Paul even visited and prophetically ministered to Saddam Hussein when that Iraqi leader was at the pinnacle of his career. Sadly many were hurt when Paul himself needed help morally. Ern Baxter had a lovely biblically saturated ministry and I enjoyed sitting at his feet and listening to his stories. In his earlier ministry he travelled with William Branham. Bob Mumford was in the same group. These two, along with Derek Prince, Don Basham and Charles Simpson, became known as the Fort Lauderdale Five, who promoted 'Heavy Shepherding' – a form of discipling one another. This was discredited and Bob Mumford later apologized for their unnecessary controlling. The Fort Lauderdale Five tried to take over the Fabulous Fourteen, but thankfully were resisted by some. Bob, though, was delightful to share a platform with. There were others no doubt preparing the ground for Charismatic awakening that must be glanced at for completeness' sake and to honour our brothers and sisters in their sincere attempts to please our Lord and glorify him with their service. These prophets and their ministries left you expecting more from God than we yet knew and stimulated the rising Charismatic outbreak in the 1960s and 1970s.

Miscellaneous Rivulets

If you have read through all of the above you will realize that the manifestation of the Charismatic gifts and renewed interest in the Holy Spirit was by no means a central fountainhead, neither was it a stately flowing of a well-channelled flow of God's river of experience which could be easily identified with particular spots of the UK, or with a particular denomination or one gifted ministry. It was an outburst of springs all over the country, better described as a huge underground source or reservoir bursting up in a multiplicity of spouts from the one Spirit. It is because of this that having identified many major movements and ministries there are indeed a host of individual contributions from outstanding ministries as yet unnamed. With the fear of leaving some significant personalities out of my lists, I have gathered names from history, particularly my history, for your consideration and hopefully blessing and emulation.

Derek Prince was a scholarly Pentecostal Baptist who prepared the ground intellectually for renewal. David Pawson's biblical preaching contributed to Charismatic gifts' acceptability to evangelicals. Ian Petit and Peter Hocken broke down prejudice concerning Catholicism. Peter visited me to talk about theology and one of my publications and we had sweet fellowship in Jesus for one and a half hours in my study before I realized he was a Roman Catholic priest in mufti. The Methodists have a renewal group called 'Dunamis', led by Charles Clarke. The United Reformed Church pastor Bob Gordon championed renewal in his denomination and beyond, while Scotland had David Black at Bishopbriggs leading the way into spiritual gifts. One other great preacher from the earlier part of the twentieth century was T. Austin-Sparks, whose spiritual interpretation of scripture enabled him to make much of Jesus. He taught 'follow the anointing' – he himself did not speak in tongues, but he did awaken many to the spiritual world and influenced many who later served the Charismatic upsurge.

In conclusion, the Charismatic Renewal rooted in British Christianity in the 1950s to 1970s has changed British churches in a number of beneficial ways:

- Christians are closer to each other in the unity of love and the Spirit.
- The supernatural nature and calling of the Church is being recovered from unbelief.
- Christians have in general become more aware of spiritual warfare, the occult and the tangible presence of evil.
- The gifts of the Spirit are recognized in all denominations as never before.
- The British Church can no longer be seen as Binitarian rather than Trinitarian.
- The Person of the Holy Spirit is recognized and honoured.

References

Bennett, Dennis, 1970, *Nine O'clock in the Morning*. Plainfield, NJ: Logos International.

Enroth, Ronald M., Edward E. Ericson Jr and C. Breckinridge Peters, 1972, *The Story of the Jesus People: A Factual Survey*. Exeter: Paternoster Press.

Hocken, Peter, 1986, *Streams of Renewal: The Origins and Early Development of the Charismatic Movement in Great Britain*. Exeter: Paternoster Press.

Lang, George H., 1939, *The History and Diaries of an Indian Christian, J. C. Aroolappen*. London: Thynne & Co.

Lang, George H., 1949, *Anthony Norris Groves, Saint and Pioneer*. London: Paternoster Press.

Turner, Ralph, 2014, *57 Years of Restorationism in the UK: Ongoing Legacy or 57 Varieties?* UK: Mattersey Hall in association with the University of Chester.

Wallis, Arthur, 1956, *In the Day of Thy Power*. London: Christian Literature Crusade.

Wallis, Arthur, 1979, *Rain from Heaven*. London: Hodder & Stoughton.

Wilkinson, David, 1962, *The Cross and the Switchblade*. Goring-by-Sea: Pyramid Books.

Recommended Reading

Bebbington, D. W., 1989, *Evangelicals in Modern Britain: A History from the 1730s to the 1980s*. London: Unwin.

North, G. W., 1976, *The True Evidence of Baptism in the Spirit*. Exeter: Short Run Press.

Pawson, David, 1989, *The Normal Christian Birth*. London: Hodder and Stoughton.

Raistrick, Judith, 2010, *The Story of G. W. North: a 20th Century Preacher*, Greenville, SC: Ambassador International.

Riss, Richard M., 1982, 'The Latter Rain Movement of 1948', *Pneuma*, Vol. 4, Spring.

Synan, Vinson, 1997, *The Holiness-Pentecostal Tradition: Charismatic Movements in the Twentieth Century*. Grand Rapids, MI: Eerdmans.

Thurman, Joyce V., 1982, *New Wineskins: A Study of the House Church Movement*. Frankfurt: Peter Lang.

Walker, Andrew, 1998, *Restoring the Kingdom: The Radical Christianity of the House Church Movement*. Guildford: Eagle.

Wallis, Jonathan, 1991, *Arthur Wallis: Radical Christian*. Eastbourne: Kingsway.

Wimber, John, 1990, *The Dynamics of Spiritual Growth*. London: Hodder and Stoughton.

Part Two

Pentecostal and Charismatic Diversity

4

Marks of British Pentecostal and Charismatic Churches

WILLIAM K. KAY

Pentecostal and Charismatic churches in the UK are diverse. They vary in their history, to some extent in their doctrine, in their ecclesiology, in their practice and social attitudes and in their resources. Their congregations range from small and struggling start-ups to powerful megachurches. This chapter will provide an overview, beginning with their history and origins and then following them through the twentieth century to the present time.

Beginnings

Three classical indigenous Pentecostal denominations can date their beginnings to the years of, or just after, World War One. Essentially, they came out of the revivalist events at the start of the century. The Welsh revival of 1904–05 was a well documented series of meetings taking place for the most part in the numerous chapels dotted across Wales. It was not centred around expository or evangelistic preaching, but more rooted in an upsurge in repentance and spontaneous singing and coupled with appeals to surrender to the pleadings of the Holy Spirit. Evan Roberts, its most famous speaker, had prayed 'bend the church and save the world' and it was the 'bending' of the church which was his passion. Approximately 100,000 people were added to the churches in what was a nominally Christian society where almost everybody had attended Sunday school and knew Welsh hymns and Bible stories from infancy (Jones, pp. 1–9).

When the revival burned out in the autumn of 1905 passions subsided but in 1907, a train journey away in Sunderland, a new spiritual outpouring occurred in the Anglican parish of Revd Alexander Boddy (1854–1930) (Wakefield 2007). He had invited T. B. Barratt (1862–1940), a Methodist from Norway, to speak. Barratt had received a spiritual baptism in New York after travelling there to raise money for his evangelistic mission in Oslo. The fundraising aspect of his trip was a failure but, while in New York, he had heard of the Azusa Street revival taking place in Los Angeles and become convinced of its reality and the spiritual experiences associated with it. As a result he spoke in tongues. Returning to Norway he initiated fiery revival at his city mission which Boddy, an inveterate traveller, had taken the trouble to witness at first hand. So, responding to an invitation, Barratt sailed over to bring his spiritual fervour to Sunderland and spread the doctrine and experience of speaking in tongues.

A year later Alexander Boddy called a convention on Pentecostal topics. Men and women came from different parts of Britain, including those who had been touched by the Welsh revival, and listened to preaching, discussed Pentecostal and Charismatic gifts, and began to reach a consensus on the meaning of these spiritual experiences. The Sunderland Convention was held annually until 1914 and all the major leaders who emerged within the Pentecostal movement attended during one year or another and reached a broad understanding of how Pentecostalism should either be incorporated into existing churches or made the basis for new evangelism and ecclesiology.

The first Pentecostal denomination to be formed was the Apostolic Faith Church in Bournemouth in 1908 and this included a number of Welsh congregations which, in January 1916 (Thomas, p. 16), broke free from the parent body to form their own Apostolic Church which continues until this day. They fully embraced the Pentecostal and Charismatic gifts of the Spirit but also believed that the government of local churches should be by apostles and prophets, often with the prophets providing some kind of utterance which would be expounded by the apostle. In the governmental use of spiritual gifts and in the high place they gave to apostles and prophets operating in combination, the Apostolic Church differed from the two other classical Pentecostal groups that emerged about this time.

George Jeffreys founded the Elim Pentecostal Church in Ireland in 1915. Originally called the Elim Evangelistic Band, it changed its structure and name as it grew (Kay 2017). Jeffreys had been converted during the Welsh revival and had had dealings with the Apostolic Faith Church at a very early stage in his ministry but he came to reject its doctrines and practices and so established his own denomination with pastors in charge of congregations and his own ministry of evangelism and church planting eventually publicly acknowledged as apostolic, but apostolic in the sense of the function of the apostle rather than as a description of a form of government. The Elim church transferred to England in 1921 and, although it went through various complex constitutional changes, became essentially a nationwide set of churches governed through a ministerial conference, at least until 1939.

Independently and separately of both these denominations, a collection of independent congregations of various types and origins came together in 1924 as the Assemblies of God. They were those congregations which disputed the theology of the Apostolic Church and resisted the centralizing tendencies of George Jeffreys and his powerful spearhead ministry. The Assemblies of God were, from the beginning, democratic in outlook – indeed they were almost trade unionist in their conference practices. Both Assemblies of God and Elim, however, were fundamentally democratic in their polity, allowing ministers who represented congregations a chance to debate and vote for any collective decision made during the annual conference. Elim became more democratic after George Jeffreys left, and the Assemblies of God remained democratic until about 2004.

Progress

These three Pentecostal groupings would not have called themselves denominations – though, sociologically speaking, that is exactly what they were. They each adhered to their own explicit statements of faith, regulated their affairs constitutionally, began to own property, circulated their churches with magazines that helped to build identity and protect doctrine, ordained their own ministers, sent out missionaries and held their own annual conferences – though with slightly different balances of power between leaders and led. The Apostolics and Elim were largely founded by recognized and dominant individuals, the Williams brothers (Apostolics) and George Jeffreys (Elim), whereas the Assemblies of God (AoG) had no such founder. It is true John Nelson Parr (1886–1976) had called the original meeting that gave rise to AoG but he had not planted all the churches and, indeed, pastored only one congregation all his life.

During the 1920s and 1930s the Assemblies of God and Elim grew remarkably by holding campaigns and crusades and other outward-looking evangelistic events. The Jeffreys meetings were the most stunning, regularly reported in the national and local press and attracting huge crowds including, each year from 1926 until 1939, one that filled the Royal Albert Hall and, for several years, the Crystal Palace with a capacity of 20,000. While they were zealously evangelistic, these Pentecostal groupings were also critical of other churches and therefore effectively sectarian. They were outside the mainstream of theological debate and had little or no influence on Anglicans, Baptists, Methodists, Congregationalists and other long-established denominations. And, by keeping themselves separate, their distinctive beliefs in baptism in the Holy Spirit and divine healing were more or less unchallenged. They avoided the liberal/fundamentalist debates of the 1920s and 1930s though Jeffreys preached strongly against modernist theology or any attempt to deny the miraculous content of the gospel. In respect of the divisive issue of war and peace, the Assemblies of God took a pacifist position while accepting that church members were free to put on a uniform to fight if they felt in their conscience that this was right. Elim was less pacifist in orientation. Both these denominations and the Apostolics, however, were opposed to the rise of the cinema and none ever bothered with football or great sporting events and in their own lifestyle would have been keen to observe Sunday as a day of rest and worship.

War and Beyond

So determined were the Pentecostal churches to grow that they rarely paid attention to social and economic circumstances. Revival was the cure to all ills and the churches had no interest in a 'social gospel'. As a second war loomed on the European horizon, the Pentecostal churches felt eschatological forebodings. When war was declared, pacifism was more acceptable than it had been in 1914. Even so, many younger Pentecostals went overseas to fight while bombs fell at home. Evangelism was almost impossible due to petrol shortages and electricity outages, and Sunday school was hampered by the evacuation of many children from the cities. Instead of evangelism Pentecostals prayed, and their annual conferences were noted for unity and sober hope.

Once the war was over, military conscripts were released back into civilian life, but social attitudes were now different. Churchgoing habits, particularly among ex-servicemen, had been eroded and, though Pentecostals looked round for another national evangelist to hold gigantic divine healing crusades, they were unable to find anyone of the stature of Jeffreys. Instead Billy Graham made exploratory visits to Britain in the late 1940s and began to build effective inter-church and ecumenical cooperation with his evangelistic – but not Pentecostal – campaigns. London in 1954 was the first high point and huge crowds attended, quite eclipsing anything the Pentecostals might have hoped to achieve. Converts were directed to all kinds of evangelical churches with the result that Anglican, Baptist and other churches were swelled.

In 1952 the World Pentecostal Conference came to London. This coincided with the beginnings of post-war immigration from the Caribbean to Britain. Oliver Lyseight (1920–2006) arrived from Jamaica in 1951 and attempted to find a spiritual home in the existing Pentecostal churches but felt rebuffed and so set out to establish congregations that would be attractive to the newcomers ('Oliver Lyseight; Obituary'). The New Testament Church of God was able to begin its operations and by 1957 could count 150 members in five churches, with the one in the Handsworth area of Birmingham being the largest. Although Elim gave serious consideration to formal affiliation with the Church of God in the United States, the necessary 75 per cent vote in favour was not quite attained and a similar shortfall in 1956 at the British Pentecostal Fellowship prevented the integration of black congregations within the existing Pentecostal denominations. Consequently, the scene was set for main classical Pentecostal denominations to coexist amicably side-by-side. None was prepared for what happened next.

The Charismatic Movement

During the 1960s the mainline denominations began to experience Charismatic or Pentecostal phenomena – speaking in tongues, healings, visions, prophecies, words of knowledge, prostration under the power of the Spirit – that took them, and the Pentecostals, completely by surprise (Hocken 2002). Initial publicity focused on the West Coast of the United States and the Episcopalian Dennis Bennett whose dying congregation was revitalized to the extent that he attracted the attention of *Time* magazine. Rapidly crossing the Atlantic, the movement gained a foothold within British churches and was supported by the founding, in 1964, of the Fountain Trust, an interdenominational agency intended to support, by conferences and a magazine, the spread of the Charismatic Awakening. The Anglican Michael Harper (1930–2010), who founded the Fountain Trust, edited *Renewal* magazine. With the Charismatic Awakening came a loosening in ecclesiastical formalities and a warming of relationships. Worship began to be spontaneous and less tied to an ancient prayer book. Lay people began to speak publicly, to lead meetings, to preach and in this way the clergy/lay divide began to blur. While all this was happening in the churches, rapid social change was occurring across the Western world. Liberalization of sexual mores was accompanied by the appearance of youthful, often musical, celebrities whose promotion of drugs or unconventional morality – the so-called new morality is too often the old immorality – only added to the psychedelic aspects of the 1960s.

The churches adjusted themselves to the sight of vicars leading worship from guitars or house meetings where prayer for the sick was commonplace, and women now began to feel confident in the exercise of their own charismata, whether in prayer for healing or speaking in tongues or prophesying. So the 1960s were a period of spiritual revitalization within the churches without any attempt to reform the ecclesiastical structures by which the churches were led and governed. The process came to be called 'renewal' and was distinct from what followed it, 'restoration', which from the 1970s onwards was an altogether more radical perspective on church life. While Charismatic Christians remained within their denominations seeking to change them gently from within, the restorationists wanted a radical solution that would involve leaving mainline churches and starting afresh with what were first called house churches, then new churches and finally apostolic or neo-Pentecostal networks.

The Charismatic movement bemused the classical Pentecostal churches. Assemblies of God and Elim, now led by an ageing first generation of stalwarts, reacted slowly and with puzzlement to what was happening. Some pastors expected the Charismatics to be thrown out of their mainline denominations, but this did not happen. The renewalists found the Pentecostals old-fashioned and were rarely attracted by their down-to-earth lifestyles and, in truth, there was something of the class divide between the middle class renewalists and the working-class Pentecostals, between the piano in the Pentecostal hall and the pipe organ in the dignified stone church.

The 1970s and Onwards

A radical group within the Charismatic movement delighted in renewal but was unsatisfied at the failure to reform the ecclesiology and governance systems of the mainline churches. This radical group eventually struck out on a restorationist path. There may have been as many as 15 new networks which started up in the early 1970s (the dates of their trust deeds can be tracked on the Charity Commission website). The story has been told in Andrew Walker's excellent *Restoring the Kingdom* (1998) and, more recently, in my own *Apostolic Networks in Britain* (Kay 2007). It is a story of brave and pioneering people who started meetings in their homes or hired halls and avoided all the machinery and paraphernalia of traditional denominations. They wanted to emphasize apostles who appointed elders and to simplify all structural and governmental functions into a basic relational model. Churches were either 'in relationship' with the apostolic figure or they were not. There was little else holding the new groups together; at the start anyway, many of them were relatively small and amounted to only a few congregations. Only as time went on did they become quite substantial: when, in about 2010, Terry Virgo stepped down as the apostle of New Frontiers, there were something like 240 congregations associated with him in the UK, and many more overseas.

Each of these networks was different. Some were more like service organizations while others were determined to evangelize by church planting. Some were ecumenically inclined, like Ichthus with Roger Forster, but others were sectarian in orientation, like Covenant Ministries International with Bryn Jones (Kay 2007, p. 340). They all shared a Protestant belief in the authority of the Bible and welcomed Charismatic gifts within their churches as well as the Ephesians 4 ministry gifts of the apostles, prophets, evangelists, pastors and teachers. Many of the networks stressed relational mission which meant they sent people unsystematically overseas to work with like-minded Christians wherever opportunities beckoned; others, like New Frontiers, focused on church planting and, in this sense, contrasted with traditional mission which had usually performed a supporting role on the field but stopped short of actually establishing new indigenous congregations. There were, of course, exceptions to the traditional pattern as when W. F. P. Burton established hundreds of congregations in the Congo in the years after 1915 (Ewen Robertson 2015). Where the emphasis was on church planting there was also an emphasis upon strong expository preaching but not to the extent of excluding humanitarian work in the UK or elsewhere.

The apostolic networks made an impact out of all proportion to their size, through the spread of their ideas and practices. During the 1980s and 1990s they were the trendsetters among British churches in their music, in their ethos and occasionally in their theology. They replaced the old pessimistic eschatology of the Pentecostal churches waiting for the tribulation by an optimistic eschatology anticipating the global influence of the gospel and the Spirit. It was they who dispensed with 'dressing up to go to church' by introducing smart-casual clothing even for preachers. They were family oriented, really believed that the 'churches are people not the building' and they stripped away the mystique surrounding apostles. Pastors were often called by their first names and churches would want to 'have fun together' in their meetings, or on holiday. The emphasis on relationships was genuine and reduced the social distance between church members and each other or between church members and their ministers. Many of these subtle shifts in church life made their way by osmosis across the ecclesiastical spectrum. This was brought home to me when I heard a junior Anglican bishop speak at a conference. He had often attended new church events and was dressed in trainers and with a t-shirt and sounded just like one of the neo-Charismatics, with the same preoccupations and way of talking.

The networks were established during the 1980s when Britain was enjoying an economic upturn and when the pound was strong. Desktop computers were coming into vogue by the 1990s and the internet had become ubiquitous by about 2000. Young people who attended universities were attracted to the Christian Unions that were often the largest societies on the campus. These had been undergirded by evangelical travelling secretaries that gradually became more open to the Charismatic movement. Some of the new churches such as Trent Vineyard, and Southampton Community Church, were formed with a large contingent of students from the nearby university. They knew how to attract the young – and the young, with their degrees, were equipped for the job market.

The networks, after becoming established, began to reach out with big events like March for Jesus and to infuse confidence through their triumphal music, the first of which was in London in 1986 with Graham Kendrick's compositions much in evidence. Before long the networks joined the Evangelical Alliance to which they brought new faith and vision while, inevitably and over time, they endured the usual cycle of splits and losses. They ran large conferences and, because of the strength of the pound and the declining price of air travel, were able to widen their perspectives with short-term mission. Conferences allowed networks to draw in new people and to promulgate their teachings. When the numbers of churches affiliated to each network are examined, the figures between 2007 and 2017 show steady growth in some instances, such as New Frontiers; there was decline in other instances and relative stasis in yet others (Brierley (ed.) 2002, 2017). And, although the networks had come into existence in a variety of ways – Vineyard was not initially a church planting movement – and with or without megachurches – the more successful networks soon acquired at least one, they were remarkably similar.

It is true that some networks were ecumenical and others sectarian in attitude and some accepted female leadership and others did not, and it is perhaps the case that those with female leadership tended to be less focused on targets and goals. The acquisition of property, especially outside London, followed and it was not uncommon to find churches erecting barn-like structures on commercial estates with open interior spaces for worship, a coffee shop and offices and plenty of parking. Theologically the networks remained committed to Charismatic gifts and a direct personal encounter with God through the Spirit was always desired and, indeed, high quality and newly written music in worship was directed to precisely this end. By 2010 New Frontiers was reconfiguring itself to become six 'spheres' led by new and younger leaders with the same values and goals they had learned under Terry Virgo (https://newfrontierstogether.org). Between 1989 and 2016 it grew 29 congregations in London (Jeffery and Kay 2018). By 2016 Vineyard was focusing upon a fresh phase of church planting accompanied by the training of church planters (www.vineyardchurches.org.uk/articles/the-next-chapter/). By 2017 Kingdom Faith was seeking to convert its northern and outlying churches into apostolic hubs from which new congregational plants could be pioneered (www.kingdomfaith.com/podcast/video-4691-clive-urquhart-vision-2018.aspx). A fresh expansionist purpose, often connected with a transition to the second generation of network leaders, was becoming visible. Restorationist theology was giving way to Charismatic evangelicalism.

An Unexpected Turn of Events

Huge shifts in the world's population occurred after 1945. Migratory flows, charted by the United Nations, were predominantly from the global South to the global North (www.un.org/en/development/desa/population/migration/index.shtml). As far as Britain was concerned, its Commonwealth fostered links between countries that had originally been within the British Empire and therefore provided schooling through the medium of English and prepared pupils for examinations devised for the British educational system. This meant that large numbers of Nigerians and Ghanaians spoke English and had acquired qualifications that were recognized in the UK. After independence both Nigeria and Ghana passed through periods of military dictatorship. There were military juntas in charge of Nigeria from 1983 to 1998 and similar periods of civic destabilization in Ghana. Because of Commonwealth connections, visa restrictions for Ghanaians and Nigerians before 1988 were practically non-existent with the result that a wave of aspiring or educated men and women made their way to Britain. Some came as students and others as doctors, nurses, lawyers or accountants and the like and began to establish congregations.

Church formation passed through a series of phases (Osgood 2012). Sometimes professional people began the church in their spare time and in other cases prayer groups became churches. In yet other cases denominations based in West Africa sent church planters to Britain. And in yet other cases churches formed in Britain established connections with West Africa. People and money flowed in both directions. According to one set of statistics the African population in Britain in 1971 stood at 75,000 but by 2001 this had risen to 500,000 (Coleman 2003). Moreover, there were ethnic, but not necessarily cultural, connections between the arrivals from West Africa and the much earlier arrivals from the Caribbean. The Caribbean churches, without migratory assistance, also grew by 20 per cent between 1975 and 1979 (Osgood, p. 108). Without any clear government plan or conscious international strategy, people movements of high significance to the religious life of Britain occurred: many migrating Africans saw themselves as travelling to the 'prodigal continent' on a journey of 'reverse mission'. Without exploring the multi-dimensional complexities of this phenomenon, the consequence was visible to all: black majority churches began to burgeon (Kalu 2010).

Although the Cherubim and Seraphim Church had started in Britain in 1965, many others date from the 1970s: the Aladura International Church (1970), the Celestial Church of Christ (1974), Christ Apostolic Church Mount Bethel (1974), the Church of Jesus Christ Apostolic (1975) and Christ Apostolic Church of Great Britain (1976) (Osgood, p. 109). The surge of activity was sustained in the 1980s with the planting of the Church of Pentecost's first UK congregation in 1988, the same year as the Redeemed Christian Church of God (RCCG) (Osgood, p. 112; Burgess, p. 129). Others also arrived including the Deeper Life Bible Church (1985), the Foursquare Gospel Church (1985) and the New Covenant Church (1986); Universal Prayer Group Ministries (UPG) opened its first church in 1988 (Burgess, p. 129). The 1990s saw the trend continue. Matthew Ashimolowo left Foursquare to start Kingsway International Christian Centre (KICC) in 1992, at a time when Nigerian immigration was on the increase: statistics give 47,201 migrants in 1991 and 88,380 in 2001 and about 80 per cent were resident in London (Burgess, p. 129).

By 2017 the Church of Pentecost had 132 congregations in the UK, the RCCG an astonishing 864 and Kingsway International, pursuing a strategy through its new 24-acre site in Dartford, attracts 10,000 people in just two congregations (Brierley 2017; www.kicc.org.uk/church/our-history/). The Church of Pentecost from very humble beginnings dating back to the dedicated ministry of Pastor James Mckeown

(1900–89), an Irish Missionary sent by the Apostolic Church, Bradford, UK, to the then Gold Coast (now Ghana) in 1937 (http://thecophq. org/overview.php?id=4&&amps;BRIEF+HISTORY), became part of the Elim Church in 1994 but amicably demerged in 2010 – a fine example of inter-church cooperation that gave the newer denomination an opportunity to find its feet and adjust to British charity law. Now, like many of the African churches, it has to deal with the full transition into British culture. On the one hand it has older congregations that worship comfortably only in an African language and, on the other, it has younger Anglicized congregations with different problems from their parents or the first generation of migrants.

The story of the RCCG in Britain begins with four Nigerian students who formed a house fellowship in London in 1988. The fellowship became a church and was registered as a charity in 1990 in Marylebone and later moved to the Angel, Islington. A second parish started in Greenwich in 1992 and shortly afterwards the Agape Fellowship in the Elephant and Castle area was merged. Further expansion occurred a year later with Tony Rapu's vision to plant a large congregation 'to complement the multiplication of parishes that is the standard RCCG approach' (Adedibu 2016). Jesus House was formed with an emphasis on innovative leadership, vibrant worship and excellence and it soon grew to 400 people and then 3,000. The basic plan of RCCG was to establish a parish model allowing members to reach a church situated close by. It is this that has led to the multiplication of congregations. The parish model was accompanied by the shift from the Yoruba language to English and from older to contemporary music as well as by bringing teachings on personal development, motivation and prosperity. Apostolic teams were used to mobilize the laity and more recently RCCG has set up a training establishment in the UK and sought to develop missional communities with 'key leaders who are transcultural mediators' with the ability to contextualize preaching and understand cultural shifts. Prayer (sometimes for whole nights), fasting (sometimes for weeks), spiritual warfare and adventist convictions are energetically pursued.

KICC expanded rapidly in 1993 acquiring a large building in east London but by 1995 this building had been outgrown. The congregation topped 3,000 and began to mobilize technology to broadcast church services worldwide as well as expanding into career and legal counselling. By the mid-1990s further services were necessary in the London area using the Hackney Empire theatre and the congregation had added another thousand people. A large £2.7 million property with an 8-acre site was acquired in east London to allow for the erection of a 4,000-seat building, but by 2006 KICC had to surrender the land for redevelopment associated with the Olympic Games in 2012. After much searching a 24-acre site was acquired in Chatham, Kent.

KICC and many other churches of its kind are strong on prosperity teaching and pastors work hard to build up the self-esteem of members and give them the capacity to succeed entrepreneurially. The preaching is fiery and praise-filled and there is frequent interaction between the congregation and the man or woman in the pulpit, with 'say after me ...' a frequent prompt. These churches are frequently co-pastored by a husband and wife team, which gives the pastor's family enormous influence within the church while putting high expectations on their children, and it is not uncommon for family members to be appointed to junior ministerial roles.

The high-profile Nigerian and Ghanaian churches with their prosperity and success message stirred the Caribbean churches which had for a long time been engaged in humanitarian work as well as gospel preaching. The New Testament Church of God had a strong holiness ethos, manifested in the ceremony of foot-washing, for example, and was part of the worldwide fellowship with its own bishops and national leadership who dovetailed into the wider international leadership that met in Cleveland, Tennessee, USA. To bring the African and Caribbean churches together despite their contrasting styles and theological emphases, Oliver Lyseight of the New Testament Church of God helped to establish the Afro West Indian United Council of Churches in 1977 that was superseded by the Afro-Caribbean Evangelical Alliance in 1989, itself later named the African and Caribbean Evangelical Alliance before closing down in 2009 ('Oliver Lyseight; Obituary'; Osgood, p. 115).

Mainstream Charismatics

While restorationists left their churches in the 1970s to set up new congregations outside existing denominational parameters, many others remained and worked from within their home denominations. Among those was David Pytches (Pytches 2002), an Anglican missionary bishop who helped to set up the New Wine network that now comprises over 2,000 congregations and offers a range of advice, ministry, help and inspiration through its regional conferences and summer events (www.new-wine.org). There is assistance for congregations within the network that wish to plant new churches; there are mission and youth activities and many other supporting departments. Its United event each summer attracts large numbers as does Soul Survivor, aimed more at youth (https://soulsurvivor.com/summer/). This is a light-touch organization – now in 14 countries and across many denominations – that partners with the Holy Spirit without the authoritarianism found in other churches on the Pentecostal/Charismatic spectrum.

Holy Trinity Brompton (HTB) is an Anglican church strongly affected by the Charismatic movement in a fashionable part of London. Under its previous vicar, Sandy Millar (1985–2005), the church launched the Alpha course, a programme of teaching based around key questions and with a specific introduction to Charismatic Christianity, as well as a marriage course designed to prepare people for marriage or enrich existing marriages, and started planting congregations in dying parishes. Nicky Gumbel, who organized and wrote much of the Alpha course, took over in 2005 and the church has continued to expand as a Charismatic centre seeking to contribute to evangelization of the nations and the transformation of society. Its Alpha course has been adapted for use with young people or in prisons and in many countries while its church-planting activities, unusual in Anglicanism, have continued to revitalize evangelical Christianity in London and beyond. There are now about 25 churches planted through HTB and its leadership conferences can fill the Royal Albert Hall. When an overall assessment of the Charismatic movement among ministers in the Anglican Church in the UK is attempted, one reaches a figure showing about a quarter (24 per cent) are 'attracted to the Charismatic movement' according to an unpublished paper by Leslie J. Francis, Andy Village and David Voas using data collected from a large survey in 2013.

Hillsong originally grew in the ecosystem of Australian Assemblies of God which passed through renewalist transformations in the 1970s and 1980s (Clifton 2009; Crouch 2016; Riches and Wagner 2017; https://freshstreams.net/about-us/). It also emerged as a movement or brand in its own right. Analyses of its appeal have focused upon its ability to use electronic media to embody and convey its sense of the presence of God. Its music and worship style became identified with an experiential Christianity and its preaching is also direct, relevant and aimed at the digitally literate young. Its preachers become celebrities and people are emotionally and intellectually connected through periodic sermons streamed throughout the family of churches to provide underlying unity of purpose. Its deliberate targeting of major world cities made London an obvious destination in the 1990s and, from there, congregations have been established in Tonbridge, Oxford and Newcastle with plants in Birmingham and Edinburgh. While not always welcomed by other Charismatic groups, it has nevertheless powered its way forward and rapidly achieved a London megachurch and other growing congregations.

Fresh Streams, the Baptist Charismatic network, runs conferences and provides leadership to some 350 connected congregations, some of which are also members of New Wine (https://freshstreams.net/about-us/). Operating in their own sphere, Roman Catholic Charismatics are a vital group within the 5 million people in the UK describing themselves as Catholics. Of these about 1 million are regular church attenders. It is estimated that about 5 per cent of these churchgoers have experienced baptism in the Holy Spirit, with an estimated 20,000 regularly involved with the Charismatic Renewal in prayer meetings, conferences, special ministries, communities, youth ministry, worship groups, evangelization, etc. The influence of these 20,000 on the life of the UK Catholic Church is considerable, as they are mostly very active in their parishes and serve in all kinds of routine and creative ways in the day to day running of their churches. The church also contributes to the arts, communities, renewal, discipleship, evangelization, intercession, seminars, lay movements and ecclesial communities, retreats, conferences, pilgrimages and more.

A recent study of Pentecostal and Charismatic churches in a British town found their eschatology was predominantly restorationist/Latter Rain while accepting the kingdom of God as both now-and-not-yet (Jeanes 2017). So, healing does occur as an in-breaking of the kingdom of God as part of a great restoration of the Charismatic gifts lost to the Church after the first few centuries although often it is theologically understood that healing and all the benefits of atonement will only finally be realized at the return of Christ. Healing beliefs are significantly shaped by popular teaching rather than by sharp-edged exegesis of scripture.

Classical Pentecostal Denominations

The turbulent and exciting events taking place in Britain after 1970 impacted the old classical Pentecostals. Assemblies of God attempted to reform itself in the 1970s by simplifying its constitution and streamlining its decision-making process. It continued to gather its ministers together at an annual conference where collective decisions were made after debate and voting. There were those within AoG who wanted to get rid of both these things to allow 'leaders to lead' and over about ten years the decision-making machinery was gradually changed to give the General Conference less authority and a small group of leaders more authority. By 2008 constitutional transformation had taken place with the result that British AoG, unlike AoG in many other parts of the world, was hardly democratic at all. By 2017 it was possible to see the results of the change of governance, and they were not pretty. At least 100 churches had been lost and many ministers had left and denominational income dropped by at least 25 per cent in a few years. Power had been concentrated into the hands of a small number of men who claimed apostolic authority, where this authority was managerial and legal rather than relational since the board of AoG Inc. were also the national leaders of Assemblies of God. The board's powers were legal under company and charity law.

Regarding the Elim Pentecostal Church, the governmental structure has remained largely unchanged in recent years though periodically its national leadership team has become assertive. The emphasis in the 1990s was on church growth but, when John Glass took over as General Superintendent, the emphasis was on 'building bigger people' until, in about 2010 through what was called TBC (The Big Centenary Ask), there was a reprioritization toward the planting of new churches. The effects of these initiatives have not been empirically scrutinized but the impression given is of a Pentecostal denomination in good health. According to Peter Brierley's figures, Elim has grown from 501 churches in 2012 to 538 in 2017 (Brierley (ed.) 2017).

There was also doctrinal revision in 1993 and three changes might be highlighted. Of these the most obvious was the broadening of the outlook so as to cover a wider range of doctrines so that there were statements of faith rather than statements of distinctive Pentecostal beliefs. The explicit doctrine of healing, which was bound up with Elim's campaigning years from 1915 to 1936, was removed but without any change in the implicit belief that Jesus Christ heals today. The change appears to have been pastoral, presumably because some people remain unhealed. For slightly different reasons the premillennial framework in which belief in the Second Coming was set was stripped away and Elim simply asserted its belief in 'the personal, physical and visible return of the Lord Jesus Christ to reign in power and glory' (www.elim.org.uk/Articles/417857/Our_Beliefs.aspx).

The New Testament Church of God having been established in the 1950s and grown steadily now plans to become more cosmopolitan so as to reflect more closely the locations of its congregation (https://ntcg.org.uk/wp-content/uploads/2016/03/mmcc-vision-document.pdf). In this way, it is hoped, the congregations will become more varied and diverse with regard to ethnicity and socio-economic strata. Second, the church is bringing its voice into the public sphere by engaging with national, interdenominational and humanitarian agencies. Third, the church is intentionally engaged in theological conversations through, for example, the Oliver Lyseight Lectures (https://ntcg.org.uk/education/events/dr-oliver-lyseight-annual-lecture/); and, fourth, it is keen to raise the standards of leadership within its churches and, to this end, inaugurated the Leadership Training Centre that normally operates out of its headquarters in Northampton (https://ntcg.org.uk/education/). Multiplication of congregations has continued at about 5 per cent per year, reaching 138 in 2017 (Brierley 2017).

Megachurches

No study of Pentecostal and Charismatic churches within the UK would be complete without reference to megachurches. These are usually defined as congregations comprising 2,000 or more. Of these there are 12 in the UK of which only one, All Souls, Langham Place, is unequivocally un-Pentecostal; others are Hillsong, Kingsway International Christian Centre, Kensington Temple, Holy Trinity Brompton, Ruach Ministries, Winner's Chapel, Glory House Plaistow, Jesus House Brent Cross Network Church, New Wine Church and Renewal Christian Centre. In some instances the congregation is the flagship of a denomination but others are independent or at the centre of their own ring of satellite congregations, and sometimes both. The size and resources available to megachurches are translated into significant potential for social action, broadcasting (especially over the web, which is largely free), publication, overseas mission, training or education as well as access to local politicians. Even when the congregations are part of a denomination, they may function quasi-independently because denominational leaders will want to avoid any confrontation with their powerful pastors.

Megachurches provide first-rate preaching and music of a professional standard and, during the week, will break down into numerous small groups with their own leaders organized in various configurations, perhaps by language, interest group or locality; it is often in the small groups, rather than the big public meetings, that Charismatic gifts are allowed to flourish. The church becomes a social centre for its people and will often offer a wide range of activities to its members designed to match its particular emphasis. Comparisons between the small shop and the shopping mall may be made: the small local church with few activities and amenities and the megachurch offering a comprehensive range of ministries, specialities and opportunities under one large roof.

Conclusion

Huge variety is evident from this survey of Pentecostal and Charismatic churches in Britain but it is reasonable to anticipate there will be elements of convergence between them over time. The specifically African churches are likely to become fully indigenized while the classical Pentecostal churches are likely to become more culture-friendly than previously and more willing to engage in humanitarian ministry and social action. Worship styles are likely to converge as music is shared digitally. Against the trends toward similarity, there are also bound to be differences and new theological divides may surface. Already there are some differences between Pentecostals who permit elements of democratic governance and those that forbid it. Equally, there are differences between Pentecostal groups that welcome the ministry of women and others that suppress it. Challenges raised by LGBTI gender politics can hardly be avoided either. And it is possible to suppose emphasis upon the miraculous may also become divisive as some Pentecostal and Charismatic churches give prominence to the Holy Spirit's dynamism and so license unpredictable behaviour. But a movement that has survived the terrors and temptations of the twentieth century will surely surmount the challenges of the twenty-first.

References

Adedibu, Babatunde, 2016, 'Missional History and the Growth of the Redeemed Christian Church of God in the United Kingdom 1988–2015', *Journal of the European Pentecostal Theological Association*, Vol. 37 Issue 1, pp. 80–93.

Brierley, Peter (ed.), 2002, *Religious Trends no 3*. London: Christian Research.

Brierley, Peter (ed.), 2017, *UK Church Statistics no 3: 2018 edition*. Tonbridge: ADBC.

Burgess, Richard, 2012, 'African Pentecostal Growth: the Redeemed Christian Church of God in Britain', in Goodhew, D. (ed.), *Church Growth in Britain: 1980 to the Present*. Aldershot: Ashgate.

Clifton, Shane, 2009, *Pentecostal Churches in Transition: Analysing the Developing Ecclesiology of the Assemblies of God in Australia*. Leiden: Brill.

Crouch, Dona, 2016, *Hillsong Church's Contribution to the ACC*. Unpublished.

Coleman, D., 2003, 'The Demographic Consequences of Immigration to Britain', in H. Disney (ed.), *Work in Progress: Migration, Integration and the European Labour Market*, pp. 9–40. London: Institute for the Study of Civil Society.

Ewen Robertson, A., 2015, 'The Distinctive Missiology of the New Churches: an Analysis and Evaluation', *Journal of the European Pentecostal Theological Association*, Vol. 35 Issue 2, pp. 144–61.

Hocken, Peter D., 2002, 'Charismatic Movement', in Stanley M. Burgess and Eduard M. van der Maas (eds), *The New International Dictionary of*

Pentecostal Charismatic Movements, revised and expanded edition, pp. 477–519. Grand Rapids, MI: Zondervan.

Jeanes, Matthew, 2017, *An Empirical Study of Pentecostal and Charismatic Understanding of Healing and Suffering*. Unpublished MA dissertation for the University of Chester at Regents Theological College.

Jeffery, Sam and William K. Kay, 2018, 'The Growth of London's New Churches: the Example of the Newfrontiers Network', in David Goodhew and Anthony-Paul Cooper (eds), *The Desecularisation of the City: London's Churches, 1980 to the Present*. London: Routledge.

Jones, R. Tudur, 2004, *Faith and the Crisis of a Nation: Wales 1890–1914*. Cardiff: University of Wales Press.

Kalu, Ogbu U., 2010, 'African Pentecostalism in Diaspora', *PentecoStudies*, Vol. 9 No. 1, pp. 9–34.

Kay, William K., 2007, *Apostolic Networks in Britain: New Ways of Being Church*. Milton Keynes: Paternoster.

Kay, William K., 2017, *George Jeffreys: Pentecostal Apostle and Revivalist*. Cleveland, TN: CPT Press.

'Oliver Lyseight; Obituary', 2006, in *The Times*, 19 April, p. 61, www.thetimes.co.uk/article/oliver-lyseight-8xrkh6fpscp accessed January 2018.

Osgood, Hugh, 2012, 'The Rise of Black Churches', in D. Goodhew (ed.), *Church Growth in Britain: 1980 to the Present*, pp. 107–26. Aldershot: Ashgate.

Pytches, David, 2002, *Living at the Edge: the Autobiography of David Pytches*. Bath: Arcadia.

Riches, Tanya and Tom Wagner, 2017, *The Hillsong Movement Examined: You Call Me Out Upon the Waters*. London: Palgrave Macmillan.

Wakefield, Gavin, 2007, *Alexander Boddy: Pentecostal Anglican Pioneer*. Milton Keynes: Authentic Media.

Walker, Andrew, 1998, *Restoring the Kingdom*, Guildford: Eagle.

Websites

http://thecophq.org/overview.php?id=4&&amps;BRIEF+HISTORY
www.kingdomfaith.com/podcast/video-4691-clive-urquhart-vision-2018.aspx
www.un.org/en/development/desa/population/migration/index.shtml
www.vineyardchurches.org.uk/articles/the-next-chapter/
https://freshstreams.net/about-us/
https://newfrontierstogether.org
https://ntcg.org.uk/education/
https://ntcg.org.uk/education/events/dr-oliver-lyseight-annual-lecture/
https://ntcg.org.uk/wp-content/uploads/2016/03/mmcc-vision-document.pdf
https://soulsurvivor.com/summer/
www.elim.org.uk/Articles/417857/Our_Beliefs.aspx
www.kicc.org.uk/church/our-history/
www.new-wine.org

5

Pentecostal Diversity in England and the Wider UK

DANIEL AKHAZEMEA

Diversity announced the birth of the Pentecostal movement on the day of Pentecost as evidenced by the nationalities of spectators and languages spoken by the disciples. This appears reinforced by diversity of spiritual gifts and manifestations. Pentecostalism today defies definition; as there is no homogeneity in theology, worship practices, missiology or biblical understandings. Even during the apostolic age, there was divergence in beliefs and practices. Attempts to engage in homogenous expression was, and still is, a major source of conflict. This chapter argues that homogeneity is neither biblical nor expedient. The various strands within the Pentecostal movement must embrace the challenges of diversity and, through education and creativity, walk in Christian love and unity. This diversity presents great opportunities for dialogue, reflection and mutual understanding among practitioners. The biblical call is unity in diversity.

The descent of the Holy Spirit on believers on the day of Pentecost came in the birth-robe of diversity. Babatunde Adedibu is of the opinion that the 'Pentecostal movement has its origin in the Judaic-Christian church which started in Jerusalem on the day of Pentecost at Jerusalem in AD 33' (Adedibu, p. 3). As was recorded for us by Luke the Evangelist in Acts:

Parthians, Medes, Elamites, and residents of Mesopotamia, Judea and Cappadocia, Pontus and Asia, Phrygia and Pamphylia, Egypt and the parts of Libya belonging to Cyrene, and visitors from Rome, both Jews and proselytes, Cretans and Arabs – in our own languages we hear them speaking about God's deeds of power. (Acts 2.9–11)

The growth of biblical Christianity after Pentecost was never homogenous. There quickly arose differences in expression when non-Jews became believers. While the Jerusalem believers embraced some aspects of Judaism, syncretism of a sort, the Antioch believers expressed their faith differently by depending on revelations received from the Holy Spirit and teachings of Paul and other apostles. The Epistles attest the cultural flare to their worship and beliefs. Disputes naturally arose between these expressions that required resolution by the Jerusalem conference as recorded in Acts 15. Even among Gentile believers differences existed reflecting their cultural preferences.

Pentecostalism or the Pentecostal movement arose from the rediscovery of the baptism of the Holy Spirit with evidence of speaking in tongues and the manifestation of the gifts of the Holy Spirit in the late nineteenth and early twentieth centuries. As Pentecostalism places special emphasis on a direct personal experience of God through the baptism with the Holy Spirit and the manifestation of his gifts, much dependence is placed on the leading of the Holy Spirit. This presents grounds for diversity with regard to interpretation and situational application. Diversity in Pentecostal faith expressions has grown over the years. William Kay sees Pentecostalism as probably the most vibrant and rapidly growing religious movement of the twentieth century (Kay 2011). He reckons that it started as a revivalist and renewal movement within Christianity that encircled the globe in less than 25 years and grew in North America and then in other parts of the world with the highest birth rates (Kay 2011).

During the apostolic age, there were divergent beliefs and practices. Paul in Galatians 2 explained how there was sharp disagreement between Peter and himself over diversity of expressions of the faith. The attempt to engage in homogenous expression was a major source of disagreement with, and indeed persecution, of Paul and his ministerial team. This he expressed strongly in his letter to the Philippians. Suspicion among Pentecostals has continued till now regarding the best expression of the Pentecostal faith.

It appears evident in scripture that diversity was generally accepted by the majority of the believers during the biblical era and indeed during the early church. In Peter's defence before the Jerusalem Council Luke records Peter as saying:

> 'If then God gave them the same gift that he gave us when we believed in the Lord Jesus Christ, who was I that I could hinder God?' When they heard this, they were silenced. And they praised God, saying, 'Then God has given even to the Gentiles the repentance that leads to life.' (Acts 11.17–18)

It would also appear that the persecution of the early believers left little room for a desire for uniformity of faith expressions. The meeting of Paul with the Jerusalem Council and the resultant letter to the Gentile saints further explains the view of the early church:

> 'We have decided unanimously to choose representatives and send them to you, along with our beloved Barnabas and Paul, who have risked their lives for the sake of our Lord Jesus Christ. We have therefore sent Judas and Silas, who themselves will tell you the same things by word of mouth. For it has seemed good to the Holy Spirit and to us to impose on you no further burden than these essentials: that you abstain from what has been sacrificed to idols and from blood and from what is strangled and from fornication. If you keep yourselves from these, you will do well. Farewell.' (Acts 15.25–29)

Pentecostalism appears to encourage cultural diversity as the Holy Spirit works through different cultures. One of the obvious evidences of the revelation of the Pentecostal movement in 1906 was the fact that people of different colours and races worshipped God together under the black preacher William Joseph Seymour. The services were not controlled and people expressed themselves as they felt led by the Holy Spirit. Paul encouraged freedom of spiritual expression in worship, a liberty that lends itself to spontaneity and creativity in the worship experience. Such creativity invariably results in differences in the way worship is conducted. Some characteristics of Pentecostalism include speaking in tongues, healing, miracles and freedom in the operation of gifts of the Spirit in worship.

Argument is often raised as to whether the Holy Spirit is the author of confusion, a view strongly expressed by John MacArthur Jr in his books, *Charismatic Chaos* (1992) and *Strange Fire* (2013). It must be understood, however, that diversity is part of God's creativity. It is God's idea. The Babel rebellion was a human attempt at homogeneity that was quickly judged by God (Genesis 11). The Bible robustly describes this diversity in relation to the variety of gifts available in the church (1 Corinthians 12 and 14). The liberty within the body must never become a basis for confusion.

Historical Reflections

Essential characteristics of the Pentecostal faith appeared to have diminished and even became unknown till the nineteenth and early twentieth century. Baptism in the Holy Spirit, speaking in tongues and the manifestation of the gifts of the Spirit got relegated to the background. Even so, there does not appear to be a definitive definition of Pentecostalism. Scholars have given some descriptions that may possibly hold true for most Pentecostal expressions. Alan Anderson, for example, reflects that 'Pentecostal and Charismatic renewal movements are concerned primarily with the experience of the baptism in the Holy Spirit accompanied by gifts of the Holy Spirit especially speaking in tongues, prophecy and healing' (Anderson 2016). Walter Hollenweger proposes that we think of Pentecostalism as a way of doing theology related to experience, that is open to oral rather than literary forms of transmission, ecumenical in its plurality and expressing itself in the category of pneumatology (Hollenweger 1997). William Kay thinks Pentecostalism should be looked at as a type of Christianity that does not depend on liturgies, prayer books, creeds and a highly educated clergy, but rather on the testimony of lay people communicating their intense relationship with a personal God (Kay 2009).

In modern discussions, Pentecostalism and her sister, the Charismatic movement, present similar features. Allan Anderson in discussing the characteristics of identifying Pentecostals and Charismatics argues that the initial distinguishing features between the early or classical Pentecostals, the Charismatics and the neo-Pentecostals have all but disappeared and that discussions about contemporary Pentecostalism would better be expanded to cover the various strands in Pentecostalism and Charismatic movements and their variants (Anderson 2004). This is the view of this chapter.

Strong support for this position is the fact that the Charismatic Renewal movement arose from the penetration of Pentecostalism into the mainline Protestant and Catholic churches with the aim of renewing and reviving the historic churches. Neo-Pentecostals include churches who prefer to see themselves in the Third Wave of the Spirit movement originating from Fuller Theological Seminary in 1981 under the teaching ministry of John Wimber, and the various new churches that have no direct affiliation to the mainstream Pentecostal denominations are also here recognized within the broad description of Pentecostalism.

Pentecostal Diversity

The early Pentecostal movement in Britain mirrored the American expression of what is now termed 'classical Pentecostalism'. These generally subscribe to the initial evidence theory that speaking in tongues is evidence of the baptism in the Spirit. The movement did not express itself univocally. Allan Anderson (2016) suggests that 'classical Pentecostals are themselves divided into various types, which are as distinct as other divisions within Protestantism'. Within classical Pentecostalism there were evident differences in their theologies and worship practices. Henry Lederle identified three major streams: the Wesleyan Holiness Pentecostals, the Baptist Pentecostals and the Oneness Pentecostals (Lederle 1988), with differences in their beliefs.

The early Pentecostal movement was not without challenges. While virtually all Pentecostal denominations trace their origins to Azusa Street, the movement has experienced a variety of divisions and controversies. An early dispute centred on challenges to the doctrine of the Trinity resulting in some holding the traditional Trinitarian position and the others moving into the Oneness or non-Trinitarian position – known also as 'Jesus-only'. Within the non-Trinitarian camp, Father, Son and Holy Spirit are seen as different designations for the one God (Bernard 1993). Oneness Pentecostals reject the doctrine of the Trinity, viewing it as pagan and unscriptural, and invoke only the name of Jesus in baptism.

Vinson Synan argues that allowance should be made for diversity within the Pentecostal movement (http://web.oru.edu/library/holyspirit/pentorg1.html). He reasons that all Pentecostals agree on the presence and demonstration of the charismata, spiritual gifts, in the modern church but that beyond this common agreement there is much diversity, as in all the other branches of Christianity. Walter Hollenweger argued for what he called 'responsible syncretism' when considering churches to be classified as Pentecostals (Hollenweger 1997). William Kay views Pentecostalism outside the Western world as often assimilating features of traditional culture combined with Pentecostal distinctives (Kay 2009). He emphasizes that over the last one hundred years Pentecostalism has been diversifying with the result that definitions must now stretch to include every variation.

Steven Land draws attention to the fact that two thirds of Pentecostalism is now a Third World movement, and only a quarter of its members are white (Land 1993). There are therefore many movements throughout the world, like thousands of African-initiated churches, which may be described as Pentecostals but have developed a form of Christianity quite different from Western Pentecostalism. It is often argued that Pentecostalism has taken on quite different characteristics in different parts of the world largely because 'freedom in the Spirit' tends to allow adherents to be more flexible in developing their own culturally relevant forms of worship expression.

Mark Sturge was helpful in pointing out that the theologies of the early African and Caribbean churches were brought to the UK from the Pentecostal traditions in the USA influenced by their respective cultures and divided between Trinitarians and Oneness (Sturge 2005).

Churches describing themselves as Pentecostals today in the UK therefore are diverse in their theologies and worship practices. Several factors contribute to this reality:

- Indigenous Pentecostals have their roots in North American Pentecostal expressions, which in themselves were not homogeneous.
- African and Caribbean Pentecostals came with their culturally influenced expressions of Pentecostalism.
- Immigrants from other continents of Asia and Latin America came with their own cultural influences.
- Neo-Pentecostal variations were brought to the fore by, for example, the 'Toronto' blessing which focused less on speaking in tongues as evidence of the Spirit baptism but rather embraced total immersion in the Holy Spirit, or soaking, and other spiritual manifestations which may include speaking in tongues.

Doctrinal Differences

It is difficult to define Pentecostal theology. There does not appear to be a homogenous theology agreed upon by all Pentecostals. There are however some distinguishing features that can make Pentecostalism recognizable. William Kay suggests that glossolalia, healing, prosperity and spiritual warfare illustrate how Pentecostalism's openness to religious experience has facilitated its malleability (Kay 2011). His suggestion that the criterion of speaking in tongues, or glossolalia, reduced the range of revivalist phenomena that congregations or preachers were looking for in their quest for spiritual power or holiness does not appear to reflect modern Pentecostal thinking. While for many Pentecostals speaking in tongues is an essential part of Pentecostalism, it does not define the essence of it.

Walter Hollenweger classified Pentecostalism into three groups

– classical Pentecostals; the Charismatic renewal movement; and 'Pentecostal-like' indigenous churches in the Third World (Hollenweger 1996). Added to these are the Third Wave or new churches. Some of these churches have departed quite significantly in some respects from the classical position, as can be said of the Catholic Charismatics, part of the renewal movement, that retain their allegiance to Rome. Pentecostalism must therefore be seen as a movement that has many widely divergent forms, rather than as homogenous. Robert Anderson is of the view that whereas Western classical Pentecostals usually define themselves in terms of the doctrine of initial evidence, the Pentecostal movement must be more correctly seen in a much broader context – as a movement concerned primarily with the experience of the working of the Holy Spirit and the practice of spiritual gifts (Anderson 1979).

Even though the Pentecostal movement is said to have had its beginnings in the United States, it appears to owe much of its basic theology to earlier British perfectionist and Charismatic movements of the eighteenth and nineteenth centuries. Vinson Synan (2016) argues that at least three of these movements – the Methodist/Holiness movement, the Catholic Apostolic movement of Edward Irving and the British Keswick 'Higher Life' movement – prepared the way for what appeared to be a spontaneous outpouring of the Holy Spirit in America. The theology of early Pentecostalism therefore drew largely from the theology of the Methodist/Holiness movement. Vinson Synan summarized these as follows:

- Emphasis on a second blessing called the 'baptism in the Holy Spirit' with various interpretations concerning the content and results of the experience.
- An emphasis on divine healing 'as in the atonement' and the premillennial rapture of the church.
- Overwhelmingly Arminian in their basic theology and strongly perfectionistic in their spirituality and lifestyle.
- The Keswick emphasis that stressed the Pentecostal aspects of the second blessings, some calling the experience 'Pentecostal sanctification'.
- The second blessing as both a cleansing and an enduement of power.
- Teaching of a 'third blessing' baptism of fire after the experience of being born again and sanctification.

Arguably, the Holiness movement in America produced the first Pentecostal churches in the world. Although these were not described as Pentecostals before 1901, they retained most of their perfectionistic teachings which had been formed as a 'second blessing' after becoming Pentecostals. Such holiness denominations simply added to their theology the baptism in the Holy Spirit with glossolalia as initial evidence of a 'third blessing'. It may be safely said then that Pentecostalism, at least in America, was born in a Holiness cradle.

Another area of doctrinal difference is the mode of baptism. Allan Anderson explains that most classical Pentecostals in the USA practise adult baptism by immersion but that this is not necessarily the same in other parts of the world. He stressed that Pentecostalism takes on many forms quite different from those of North America, and in a global context the North American types are not really meaningful (Anderson 2004). The Methodist Pentecostal Church, for example, practises infant baptism and follows some Methodist liturgy. Many Pentecostal groups, including some of the largest Pentecostal churches in Europe and many in the Charismatic movement, do not insist on the initial evidence of tongues (Lederle 1988). Some groups, particularly older African-initiated Pentecostal churches, use ritual symbolism in their liturgy. This perhaps informs Anderson's suggestion that it may be very difficult to conclude what is meant by 'Pentecostal' today, but perhaps the term should best be understood as referring to those movements with an emphasis on the experience of the power of the Holy Spirit with accompanying manifestations of the immanent presence of God (Anderson 2016).

Theology of Missions

While Pentecostals are known for productive and widespread mission work, theological reflection has not kept up with praxis. A number of leading Pentecostal theologians have in recent years engaged in robust reflection on key issues they consider as underlying motifs and distinguishing features as well as urgent challenges facing Pentecostal mission. Grant McClung provides a contemporary conception of Pentecostal theology of mission. He describes the characteristic theology as including five main features:

- It is biblical because it is marked by an affirmation of exactness or a literal interpretation.
- It is passionate as it regards passive spirituality as neither acceptable nor normative.
- It must be carried out in the power of the Holy Spirit emphasizing that the Holy Spirit is personally and powerfully present with

believers to orchestrate the continuing redemptive ministry of Jesus Christ to the uttermost parts of the earth.

- It is Christocentric because doctrines or experiences are considered normative only if they are Christ centred.
- It is spurred by divine urgency of the soon return of Christ. (McClung 1986, pp.1–22)

This eschatological urgency appears to be at the heart of understanding the theology of Pentecostal missions. It therefore emerges that the foundation of Pentecostal theology of missions stands on a tripod of the emphasis on the power of the Holy Spirit to sanctify, empower and release urgency for the preaching of the gospel in view of the soon coming of Christ.

A very important consideration of Pentecostal missiology is the emphasis on supernatural empowerment for world evangelization. Byron D. Klaus succinctly captured this when he emphasized:

A sense of participation in a story of eschatological significance, supported by the supernatural Spirit empowerment(s) creates a strong sense of destiny in the Pentecostal identity. Only the divine intrusion of the Spirit of God is viewed as adequate for the eternal resource for end time harvest. (Klaus, pp. 325–8)

However, while this general understanding underlies Pentecostal theology of missions, wide diversity exists in the way this is done among various strands of the Pentecostal movement in Britain. William Kay expresses the view that the simplicity and flexibility of Pentecostalism and its characteristic parallels facilitated their spread and adoption even when the religious space in society was limited (Kay 2011). For example, although classical Pentecostalism favours power evangelism, some modern Pentecostals focus more on presence evangelism or intrusion into the secular space. New churches also engage more in relationship evangelism making good use of sociological principles. As the attractional mode of evangelism is not proving effective in reaching the people for God, more closely knit groups are now thought to provide the key to effective evangelism.

Worship

One of the distinguishing features of Pentecostalism is its mode of worship. Vinson Synan explains that the Azusa Street movement seems to have been a merger of white American holiness religion with worship styles derived from the African American Christian tradition which had developed since the days of chattel slavery in the South (Synan 2016). According to him expressive worship and praise at Azusa Street, which included shouting and dancing, had been common among Appalachian whites as well as Southern blacks. It would appear that the admixture of tongues and other charisms with black music and worship styles created a new and indigenous form of Pentecostalism that was to prove extremely attractive to disinherited and deprived people, both in America and in other nations of the world.

In its pioneering days in Azuza Street, the worship was mainly spontaneous, free and not necessarily organized or controlled by people as the Spirit was allowed freedom to lead worshippers. Although modern Pentecostal worship services are somewhat controlled, the freedom of the Spirit to direct and lead is given priority. Much Pentecostal worship is designed to bring about an experience of God's presence, and to this end the atmosphere and music encourage openness to the presence of the Holy Spirit. The gifts of the Spirit are often demonstrated during church services. It is generally understood within Pentecostal churches that worship is both a lifestyle and an event or an experience. However, the focal point of Pentecostal worship is the corporate event or experience, as what happens during the corporate potentially enables the worshipper to enjoy a fulfilled walk with God outside the event.

The influence of African American spirituality was evident in early Pentecostalism. Walter Hollenweger considers the main features of this African American spirituality to be an oral liturgy, narrative theology and witness, the maximum participation of the whole community in worship and service, the inclusion of visions and dreams into public worship, and understanding the relationship between body and mind manifested by healing through prayer (Hollenweger 1986). Iain MacRobert includes rhythmic hand clapping, the antiphonal participation of the congregation in the sermon, the immediacy of God in the services and baptism by immersion as part of 'Africanisms' (MacRobert 1988). These expressions were fundamental to early Pentecostalism and remain in the movement to this day.

Pentecostals believe that central to the purpose of the formal worship event is enabling Christians to draw near to God both individually and corporately to offer sacrifices of praise in the expectation that God's blessings, including his active presence, will follow. In most African and Caribbean churches in Britain worship usually includes a lot of ecstatic singing, dancing, clapping and sometimes loud exclamations extolling the great acts of God and his relationship with the believer. However, worship appears more controlled among the indigenous

Pentecostals in Britain. It is generally believed that as God's people worship him wholeheartedly, he becomes active in a special way. That is, God's Spirit is 'poured out' and therefore God comes and moves and works in the midst of his people.

The expression of this general worship is exhibited in different forms. It would appear that these forms have cultural influences. Some sections of the Pentecostal movement follow an order in their services while others are more spontaneous and have unpredictable but controlled expressions in their worship. The classical Pentecostals of the Western world and the immigrants from the Caribbean, Africa and Asia express their worship differently. There is no homogeneity even among the African Pentecostal worship where rituals are common. Practices that are indigenous to their native worship are sometimes imported into the Christian worship. This provides a wide range of variety in their worship expressions. The growth in Britain of the immigrant expression or the independent churches from Latin America, Africa, Asia or the Caribbean place the stamp of their culture on their mode of worship. A visit to different Pentecostal churches in London on a typical Sunday, for example, reveals obvious diversity in worship styles, content and expression.

Hugh Osgood, Co-Chair of the UK Charismatic and Pentecostal Leaders Conference, in a briefing for Churches Together in England's Pentecostal Leaders Forum identifies five 'constituencies' within the Pentecostal Movement in Britain with diverse worship modes (Osgood 2017). These are:

- Britain's indigenous Pentecostal churches that came into being at the time of the Pentecostal movement's initial impact in Britain. Among these early denominations are the Assemblies of God and the Elim Pentecostal Church.
- The Caribbean diaspora Pentecostal churches that arose from immigration of people from the Caribbean in the 1950s and 1960s.
- The indigenous Charismatic churches with an openness to the manifestation of the gifts of the Holy Spirit formed throughout Britain from the 1960s better known as the 'new churches' movement.
- The African diaspora Pentecostal churches – mainly African independent churches established by migrants from Africa from the 1960s established primarily to provide the kind of Pentecostal worship experience enjoyed in their home nations to the immigrants and also perhaps form a basis for evangelizing people of other cultures.
- Other diaspora Pentecostal churches including migrants from nations principally from South American, Far East Asian and many other diaspora groups.

Each of these constituencies has certain peculiarities in the way they worship. Some of the Caribbean churches came with their native way of worship while the Africans came with diverse cultural emphases in worship. The principles of the centrality of the baptism of the Holy Spirit with the evidence of speaking in tongues, strong reliance on the authority of the Bible, the manifestation of the gifts of the Spirit, and to some extent the theology of prosperity are central in these immigrant churches. One differentiating feature of these immigrant churches from the indigenous British Pentecostal churches is their understanding of the theology of prosperity and liberation.

Challenges and Opportunities

There is fluidity in the discussion about what constitutes Pentecostalism in Britain today. From the classical Pentecostals like Assemblies of God, to the African Independent churches like the Redeemed Christian Church of God, to the Third Wave churches like the Vineyard, and the more recent 'new churches' like Hillsong or C2, diversity is clearly evident. Within the African-initiated churches, there appear to be vast differences in theology, worship and mission. Three main subsections appear clearly identifiable – those from English-speaking West Africa, those from the Francophone African nations and the Southern African nations. Theologies of deliverance practices, missions and prosperity are varied. They are largely influenced by the American prosperity theology that does not appear to sit well with either the classical indigenous Pentecostals or the new churches. The new churches' emphasis is on personal relationship with God and intimate spiritual fellowship with the Father leading to the demonstration of the power of God. Diversity is not definable by geography but by ideology and theology. Each strand seeks to spread its influence across Britain.

There are challenges in the level of variation in Pentecostal practices in Britain. From wrong interpretation of the scriptures to support unbiblical practices to 'cult-like' practices that often invite bad press, practitioners within the Pentecostal movement are sometimes misrepresented or misunderstood. Syncretism appears common in the immigrant congregations, which is ultimately self-defeating. Although not many today see themselves as classical Pentecostals, the value of orthodoxy in beliefs and practices would ensure that Pentecostalism endures through the changing times ahead. This is already very evident in the theology of missions of the new churches as they engage a culture that may not be conducive to the beliefs and practices of classical

Pentecostalism. For example, the healing campaigns of North American Pentecostalism, which contributed to the growth of Western forms of Pentecostalism in many parts of the world, reached their peak in the 1950s and are no longer a common feature in today's Pentecostalism.

Another area of challenge is theological education. As many Pentecostals focus on dependence on the Holy Spirit they easily play down the importance of theological education. This is particularly true of immigrant churches. This is a major concern, as theological reflection does not appear to match praxis. Diversity could also present great opportunities for dialogue, reflection and mutual understanding among practitioners. It also provides a plethora of choices to seekers. It provides a platform for different expressions suited to the plurality of the British population. It is of utmost importance that the British Pentecostals maintain a high view of scripture, engage in relevant mission expressions and embrace basic evangelical doctrines.

Conclusion

It can be safely said that diversity has been a common phenomenon from biblical times to modern engagement with the working of the Holy Spirit. It has its challenges that have continued to result in controversies and divisions. The multiplicity of denominations and independent churches is traceable to the leading of the Holy Spirit. It is not clear if it is the intention of God to allow for the level of diversity currently evident in the Pentecostal movement. In this era of social media and television dominance, any religious phenomenon can take a global shape. Before the advent of the frightening currency of news and information, a religious phenomenon could remain local for a season. This does not apply today. It could be safely said that variety is a gift from God and freedom in the Spirit has contributed greatly to the spread of the gospel in the twentieth and twenty-first centuries.

What is called for is an understanding among the various strands of British Pentecostals. It is important to stress the areas of agreement, strengthening relationships even as we seek to better understand areas where we may have divergent views on theology or practice. In this way the movement would continue to be a major influence in Christianity in Britain. Both classical and neo-Pentecostal beliefs and practices need to be accommodated within the larger definition of Pentecostalism. Diversity can indeed be a great blessing to the body. And this should be celebrated.

References

Adedibu, B., 2012, *Coats of Many Colours*. London: Wisdom Summit.

Anderson, Allan, 2004, *An Introduction to Pentecostalism*. Cambridge, UK: Cambridge University Press.

Anderson, Allan, 2016, 'The Origins, Growth and Significance of the Pentecostal Movements in the Third World', www.artsweb.bham.ac.uk/aanderson/publications/origins.htm

Anderson, Robert M., 1979, *Vision of the Disinherited: The Making of American Pentecostalism*. New York: Oxford University Press.

Bernard, David K., 1983, *The Oneness of God*. Series in Pentecostal Theology, Vol. 1. Hazelwood, MO: Word Aflame Press.

Cauchi, Tony, 2016, 'British Pentecostal Pioneers', www.revivallibrary.org/pensketches/engpp_menu.php

Hollenweger, Walter J., 1986, 'After Twenty Years Research on Pentecostalism', *International Review of Mission*, Vol. 75 Issue 297.

Hollenwenger, Walter J., 1996, 'The Black Roots of Pentecostalism.' Unpublished paper, Selly Oak Colleges, Birmingham.

Hollenwenger, Walter J., 1997, *Pentecostalism: Origins and Development Worldwide*. Peabody, MA: Hendrickson.

Kay, Willian K., 2009, *Pentecostalism*. London: SCM Press.

Kay, William K., 2011, *Pentecostalism: A Very Short Introduction*. New York: Oxford University Press.

Klaus, Byron D., 'The Holy Spirit and Mission in Eschatological Perspective: A Pentecostal Perspective', *PNEUMA*, Vol. 27 No. 7.

Land, Steven J., 1993, *Pentecostal Spirituality: a passion for the Kingdom*. Sheffield, England: Sheffield Academic Press.

Lederle, Henry I., 1988, *Treasures Old and New: Interpretations of Spirit Baptism in the Charismatic Renewal Movement*. Peabody, MA: Hendrickson.

MacArthur John F., 1992, *Charismatic Chaos*. Grand Rapids, MI: Zondervan.

MacArthur John F., 2013, *Strange Fire: The Danger of Offending the Holy Spirit with Counterfeit Worship*. Nashville, TN: Nelson Books.

McClung, L. Grant, Jr (ed.), 1986, *Azusa Street and Beyond: Pentecostal Missions and Church Growth in the Twentieth Century*. South Plainfield, NJ: Bridge Publishing.

MacRobert, Iain, 1988, *The Black Roots and White Racism of Early Pentecostalism in the USA*. Basingstoke: Macmillan.

Osgood, Hugh, 2017, *The Pentecostal and Charismatic Constituency within the British Church*, www.cte.org.uk/Groups/248695/Home/Resources/Pentecostal_and_Multicultural/The_Pentecostal_and/The_Pentecostal_and.aspx

Sturge, Mark, 2005, *Look What the Lord has Done! An Exploration of Black Christian Faith in Britain*. Bletchley: Scripture Union.

Synan, Vinson, 2016, 'The Origins of the Pentecostal Movement', Oral Roberts University, http://web.oru.edu/library/holyspirit/pentorg1.html

6

Women in Ministry and British Pentecostalism

DIONNE LAMONT

Women are endowed with a plethora of gifts and the Pentecostal Church is the poorer when these are not recognized, developed and released. From its inception the Pentecostal movement has benefitted from the significant contributions made by women despite gender discrimination (including unreasonable demands such as adherence to modesty rules). The tremendous growth of the Pentecostal movement in Britain and around the world continues to benefit from women's contributions in a church and a world that still is largely operated from the perspectives of men. We can but imagine the benefits to the kingdom of God in the world were women empowered fully to occupy their God-ordained place free from obstructive and oppressive patriarchal privilege. This chapter explores actualities and possibilities concerning women in ministry in Pentecostal churches; it celebrates gains while highlighting some challenges that remain for a church that is truly equal for male and female made in the image of God and empowered by the Holy Spirit to serve together to the glory of God.

Pentecostals believe in the baptism of the Holy Spirit, whose descent is recorded in the book of Acts, and whose accompanying gifts are recorded in 1 Corinthians: knowledge, wisdom, prophecy, faith, healings, miracles, discerning of spirits, speaking in tongues and the interpretation of tongues. The exercise of these and other gifts has been foundational in ensuring the sustenance and growth of the Church over generations. Crucially, these Spirit gifts are self-evidently gender neutral. Despite this, in classical Pentecostalism the involvement of women in the Church has been limited, leaving women without an equal chance to contribute to the running of the Church or even expressing their views on the various issues facing the Church.

Patriarchal Dominance

According to Matthias Deininger, many women have been silenced while others have given up in their quest for a fairer Pentecostal church (Deininger, p. 120). While challenging the status quo has been a fairly difficult task for Pentecostal women, they have made important contributions to the development of the Church. Pentecostalism is the fastest growing Christian group in Britain and other parts of the world (Brierley 2014), and women members have played an important role in the formation of major Pentecostal denominations (Walsh, p. 13).

Revd Beverley Thomas, speaking at a conference by Pentecostals to mark the 500th anniversary of the Reformation, reminded us that women's struggle for inclusion and recognition in the Church has a long history. 'It is usually the case that the contribution of women in church history is written separately,' she said. Acknowledging the Anabaptist tradition as an antecedent of Pentecostalism, Thomas pointed to the contributions and treatment of women in the sixteenth century, providing insight into Mennonite women doing theology, sacrificing and contributing alongside their male counterparts (Thomas 2017). For example, in a time of religious persecution, Katherina Hutter of Switzerland, together with her husband, led groups of refugees across the countryside after being removed from their homes. They moved from one safe house to the next, baptizing and encouraging demoralized believers. Katherina was imprisoned in 1535 in the castle of Branzoll above Klausen. A more terrible fate met the Dutch Mennonite Maria van Beckum, who was executed by fire only a few hours before her sister-in-law, Ursula van Breckum, was also burned at the stake. Anna Jansz of Rotterdam, the mother of a young boy – Isaiah – was also executed in 1685. As she was led away to her execution, she called out to the onlookers for someone to raise her child. A local baker stepped out of the crowd and promised to raise the boy as his own. These women, and others, have suffered for their faith, yet have had their contributions ignored or underplayed and undervalued (Snyder and Hecht 1996).

Just like Mennonite women, Pentecostal women have lived in a system of patriarchy from the early years of the Church. In this system, exclusively male elders had the power to choose who they wanted to lead or oversee and almost always chose in their own male image. The Pentecostal churches inherited the patriarchal values that dominated Christian societies for much of church history. This has included the manner in which God has been portrayed artistically and verbally exclusively as a male figure. Portraying God as a man has not only given validity to men running the church, but has given permission to some husbands to view their role in the family as rulers who are entitled to dominate their wives and children. Arguably, some still do, based on my experience as a pastor. Women who suffer abuse from their male spouses and seek refuge in the church find male dominance there too and with nowhere to turn find that marital conflicts can get worse (Lux-Sterritt and Mangion, p. 78).

When God is understood as a gender neutral Spirit, women can feel a stronger association with the church, as well as loved, cared for and protected within the religious environment. Joining and participating in the Church also gives women the power and energy to deal with challenges, particularly gender-based ones, that face them outside the Church. This is particularly helpful when women lack access to therapists and other professionals who deal with such cases (Robeck and Yong, p. 52). When women feel comfortable in their religious space they are likely to invite others to attend church. It is reasonable to suppose that while Pentecostal churches have done well by women playing their part in unsatisfactory situations, churches can benefit and grow even more by making women feel welcomed and respected.

Some commentators see women in the Roman Catholic Church, for example, as relegated to nunneries because they cannot be ordained and appear to have little or no major role in running the Church's affairs (Ruth, p. 55). While the full picture of women in the Catholic Church is wider than the nunnery/ordained ministry binary, the same has been said about Pentecostal churches where women were not ordained but were left with menial tasks like cleaning the church, decorating and arranging the seats – important as these are (Coleman, p. 46). The inferiorization of women to men in the Pentecostal churches echoes the wider Church down the centuries. However, this has been challenged on theological grounds since God has placed the gifts of the Spirit in the Church and women are full members, as are men. Women have historically found ways to subvert male dominance and thereby ameliorate their marginalization. Much better though is when women and their gifts are recognized and embraced as legitimate members of the whole body of Christ, contributing to the accelerated growth of Pentecostal churches. Advances have been made, but this never seems to be achieved without facing down challenges from those who are not convinced that women's involvement benefits the well-being of the Church, or put the principle of fixed gender roles above any benefit that may be gained (Hinds, p. 50).

Examples of Women in Leadership

Women have been great advocates of social and gender equality and some Pentecostal churches have provided the context within which their voices have been heard. While the traditional doctrinal/ethical positions of the Church have sidelined women, advocates for equality have gradually produced a shift in attitudes and the Pentecostal movement has gradually started to embrace gender equality, though not universally as yet. The Church, though principally theocratic, has become more democratic in its functions and members are now encouraged to contribute and voice their opinions on pertinent matters regarding the Church. Women have taken advantage of this and have sought to correct the gender injustices that have been there for ages. By making others know the effects that gender injustices have had on their growth and well-being, women have been the driving force toward the search for change (Kay, pp. 35–7) and many practices considered a norm among traditional Pentecostals are no longer accepted.

In Britain, women have faced major challenges among widespread patriarchy in ensuring that their voices and their efforts bear fruit. African and Caribbean women who came to Britain as immigrants brought their beliefs and values with them and have established these practices and cultural mores in a new land (Beckford, p. 95). High on their list has been the value they place on matriarchy as a key component in society and how their leadership can create better opportunities for themselves, their families and their communities, including the church (Toulis, p. 55). Tough challenges were met with a fighting spirit and determination to be incorporated in the full life of the Church and society in Britain. This maternal spiritual and practical presence has accompanied the transition from traditional old Pentecostal practices to the newer strand of Pentecostalism. The struggle for gender equality in the Pentecostal Church has been at the forefront of women's activities with many advocates prepared to fight inequality and gender segregation particularly in the areas of decision making and recognition.

The struggle for recognition of women's great contribution has been a worldwide phenomenon. There has been no lack of women attempting to and playing their part in spreading and enhancing a Pentecostal gospel of Christianity. Joyce Lee and Glenn Gohr (1999) highlight several women who have made major contributions to the Church. Among them is Rachel Sizelove, who lived in a small town in Missouri, United States, and was the first to establish a Pentecostal church in her town. She had a vision of a 'sparkling fountain' rising up from Springfield and flowing to the ends of the earth. Later, the Assemblies of God started to operate in Springfield, from where the message of the Church was sent all over the world.

An important contribution also came from Carrie Judd Montgomery, born in Buffalo, United States, in 1858. Carrie is known for her travels around the world and written documentation of the Pentecostal movement. Her publications, such as the journal *Triumphs of Faith*, played an important role in disseminating Pentecostal ideas. Another woman who spread the Pentecostal message was Maria Woodworth-Etter. Her evangelistic ministry began in the 1880s and she travelled across the United States with messages of salvation, attracting thousands of believers and contributing to the growth of the Church. Rachel Sizelove, Carrie Judd Montgomery, and Maria Woodworth-Etter were all white women and represent some of the many women who have contributed to the growth of the Church. Unfortunately, just as in the case of black women, the activity of white women in the Pentecostal Church is not well documented.

Today, the role of women in the Church has changed considerably, as in most organizations, and it has become possible for women to hold positions that are equal to their male counterparts. This achievement is the result of women maintaining a strong stance regarding their involvement in the Church. They have put male dominance under scrutiny by highlighting and demonstrating that women can make key decisions in running the Church. This, of course, did not always get a positive reception from all the men (Kay, p. 22). Now, women can fulfil church functions that were previously reserved for men. Women now serve as apostles, bishops, pastors, evangelists, and departmental leaders in their local, regional, national and international church organizations. As a consequence, women can take part in activities such as baptism and other important church ceremonies (Cho, p. 19).

Aware that gains can be subtly taken away, the need to protect and nurture women leaders' right to lead has led to discussion groups consisting solely of women becoming common within Pentecostal churches. These groups are used as a 'safe space' where women can discuss the issues that affect them as well as deliberate on the various solutions to the problems that they face, including political, social, economic, spiritual and ecclesial matters. More so, these groups seek to ensure that the welfare of women, children and disadvantaged people in the community are addressed.

Further examples of the contributions of women to the Pentecostal Church may provide additional insights into the role that women have played in Pentecostalism. Below I identify a random group of women Pentecostals who, like me, come from the African and Caribbean

Pentecostal community and I give brief summaries of their contributions. Equivalents can be found in white Pentecostal communities too.

Pastor Yemisi Ashimolowo is the 'First Lady' and resident pastor of Kingsway International Christian Centre (KICC), one of the largest and fastest growing churches in Western Europe. Through KICC's Winning Women Ministry, she oversees the spiritual lives of more than 5,000 women: married women, single women, pregnant women, women who want to bear children, single mothers and mature women of God. She equips women with the necessary knowledge that helps them reach their potential in Christ. All over the UK, Europe, the USA and Africa, she has delivered speeches that have impacted thousands of women from different backgrounds. She has freed women from their personal and environmental limitations and has continued to inspire more women to become the best they can spiritually and otherwise.

Bishop Dr Esme Beswick MBE has been influential within Pentecostalism in Britain over decades. She is President and a founding member of the Joint Council of Churches for All Nations. She has long history as a pastor and is currently Senior Pastor of Nebaioth Ministries in Brixton and Stockwell in the London Borough of Lambeth. Bishop Esme was the first black woman to become President of Churches Together in England and in 2002 was co-signatory to the first CTE Presidents' Covenant committing English Church Leaders to work together, in the presence of Her Majesty the Queen, at a Golden Jubilee Service at Windsor Castle. She has been Chair of the Brixton Council of Churches, Borough Dean of Lambeth, agenda committee member of the British Council of Churches, and steering committee member of Churches Together in Britain and Ireland. She has served on the government's (now defunct) Inner Cities Religious Council. Her achievements have impacted people in several parts of the world as she has travelled to countries including America, Israel, Nigeria, Jamaica, Italy, Greece, Russia, France, St Vincent and Finland. A source of inspiration for many young Christian women who aspire to achieve spiritual and secular growth, Bishop Beswick is a classic example of a woman who refuses to take 'no' for an answer when it comes to the issue of gender equality in the Pentecostal Church.

Pastor Yvonne Elizabeth Brooks is the First Assistant Pastor of New Jerusalem Apostolic Church, based in Aston, Birmingham, and is passionate about seeing people delivered and healed through the power of God and released into their life's vocation or ministry. She is the founder and President of Women of Purpose Ministries, an organization that seeks to spread the gospel to women. Through this foundation, she has greatly helped women to change the course of their lives and to become more productive both spiritually and economically. Pastor Yvonne has received several awards for her ministerial work in the UK and other parts of the world. Awards include one from the Association of Jamaican Nationals for being a local community hero, a Women of Excellence Trailblazer award, and one of the Wise Women Awards in 2013. She produces audiobooks that help young Christians to learn how to pray and live successfully in a challenging world.

Pastor Celia Collins is a prophetic preacher, motivational speaker and founder of Rehoboth Foundation. She was cited by *Keep the Faith* magazine as one of Britain's most influential women. Her Foundation offers leadership vision development consultancy, motivational and mentoring programmes, executive coaching and business strategy services. She also offers practical training for effective leadership and success of both individual destiny and corporate objectives. Pastor Celia runs a leader's mentoring programme to coach young upcoming leaders, equipping and motivating them for the tasks they will undertake. She trains pastoral leaders to help strengthen ministries and equip them for community transformation. Pastor Collins travels the world imparting her inspired wisdom among various cultures, in religious and secular settings; while in the UK she serves on several boards. Her work has been a great contributor to the progress and respectability of Pentecostalism in Britain, with many young leaders around the world under her tutelage. Pastor Celia serves also as director for Operation Mobilisation, is a vice-president for Tearfund, a steering committee member of the National Church Leaders Forum, a director for Churches in Communities International, and is an Advisory Council Member of Cinnamon Network.

Pastor Mary Eniolu served for several years at the New Wine Church in London; she is now a senior pastor with her husband, Pastor Julius Eniolu, at Lighthouse Christian Centre, Maidstone, Kent. She is also a public speaker, a biblical and theological teacher, a music minister, an entrepreneur and a mentor to many. She is passionate about her love for the power of God being demonstrated and spreads the message of love and hope to the people in her church and beyond.

Revd Marjorie Esomowei is an ordained minister and co-pastor of Triumphant Church International, London, England. She has apostolic oversight of churches in Europe, South Africa and Nigeria. A resourceful woman, her teachings about Christianity have reached people through television, radio and print media. Marjorie started her ministry in the early 1980s and works with the help of her husband, Revd Clem Esomowei, inspiring especially Christian women in her role as a prophetic intercessor. She is the president and founder of Wisdom for

Women International and founder of the Wise Women Awards and the Comfort Home Orphanage.

Penny Francis is the co-pastor and wife of Bishop John Francis, as the founders of Ruach City Church UK, based in five locations: Brixton, Kilburn and Walthamstow in London; Birmingham, England; and Philadelphia, USA. She has been of great help to women in Europe through her seminars and lectures that shed light on many of the issues affecting them. She has lectured at First Born Church Seminary School, and runs the 'I Do' seminars for engaged couples contemplating marriage, and various life topics. Pastor Penny reaches out empathetically to other women since she understands the trials that they go through from her own background.

Abbiih Oloyede is a pastor at City Chapel, a multicultural church in east London, and host of the television programme Womenz World on OHTV. She empowers women through her organization, Womenz World. The areas she focuses on are spiritual and emotional well-being, physical well-being, business and career development. Her organization has the vision of teaching, touching, connecting and transforming the lives of aspiring women, inspiring them to maximize their skills, abilities, talents and networks by providing pertinent resources, platforms and experiences. Abbiih's mission is equipping and resourcing women toward achieving independence, financial freedom and excelling in their life choices through practical skills programmes, seminars and events.

Dionne Gravesande is the head of Church Advocacy at Christian Aid. Her role entails developing relationships with church leaders and organizations throughout the world. She is also a member of the New Testament Church of God and currently serves on the board of National Youth and Christian Education where she leads in the area of training and development. She has been a mentor to a large number of young Christians whose spiritual life she has helped to mould. She has also helped to raise funds across the UK to support various projects across the countries where Christian Aid operates.

The nine black women identified above represent only a sample of the many women involved in leadership across the denominations and streams of Pentecostalism. Much more could be said about each and all of them; for example I have not mentioned academic achievements. Their varying roles and responsibilities represent a clear example of how, in spite of historic and contemporary barriers, Pentecostal women now play invaluable roles inside and outside the Church.

A majority of the people who go to church are women. This may be because more men are losing interest in church. Women are actively taking part in ensuring that the number of men who leave the Church reduces significantly by creating groups whose roles are to convince more men to join the Church and to ensure that those who attend it are not influenced negatively by those who don't. This and similar activities and actions are highlighted in research into church attendance in the UK carried out by the Christian international aid agency Tearfund (Ashworth and Farthing 2007). Women's involvement in Pentecostal churches range from the office of bishop to helping children understand their faith. In a recent study aiming to find out the roles of parents in shaping the religious culture of their children, it was shown that 75 per cent of the millennials interviewed said that their mother played a bigger role than their father in introducing them to the faith and church (May, p. 73).

In a society that has actively promoted male dominance, participating in the affairs of the Pentecostal Church can give women a feeling of being valued, thereby deepening their sense of self-worth and creating environments conducive to growth, not only of women but of the entire community. When equal opportunity of participation is ensured women expand their learning and spirituality and add value to their communities. When this is not the case women experience alienation, exclusion and feelings of being undervalued. There can be few if any reasons why gender should play a determining role in whether a person has a say in the ordering of financial committees and other key decisions where aptitude and competency should be the qualifying grounds.

The Role of Feminism

Part of the success of Pentecostal women, especially the younger generation, concerns the love of and involvement in music as a form of worship. This has facilitated numerous women finding music as a form of self-expression. It has become commonplace to see young women leading and being part of gospel choirs, playing instruments that once were the preserve of men, from drums to the bass guitar. This form of young women's power is akin to a feminist revolution in Pentecostal churches. A growing number of women are emerging as composers, producers and presenters of music that is used to encourage and strengthen people in their faith. This includes praise and worship songs that are sung in churches during worship services (Robeck and Yong, p. 25). Women skilfully compose songs that are sung and taught to young children to educate them about Christianity and life in general from a young age. Music, being a universal language, helps communicate to the Christian believers and unbelievers about religion and belief (May, p. 65). These activities are relevant at a time when some young people are tempted to get involved in crime, drug and substance abuse, and promiscuous sexual activities that can lead to unwanted pregnancies and other consequences.

Pentecostal women have often started initiatives such as engaging in fundraising activities. Such activities help to create job opportunities for people engaged in project-based enterprises. Some fundraising efforts also help in the setting up of facilities for people with disabilities, terminal illnesses, orphaned children and more. In some cases, Pentecostal women provide help in the form of scholarships for bright students from less fortunate families. Pentecostal women form effective fundraising or lobbying or prayer units based on interests or geography. Unlike former times, Pentecostal churches nowadays consist of smaller units and divisions in addition to major denominations in the Church (Robeck and Yong, p. 35). By forming these smaller groups, sometimes called cells, women are able to directly nurture new converts. Moreover, by effectively operating cell groups Pentecostal women remain in touch with other like-minded women and with those in community with needs that can so easily go unmet by institutional services. If feminism is essentially about female self-determination then feminism is alive and well in Pentecostal churches.

Sarah Bessey (2013) shows that in the early days women were treated as equal to men. She argues that Jesus himself was a feminist. Sarah feels that the Church should be in the frontline in fighting for equality between men and women especially in the Church (Bessey, p. 12). Bessey argues that Christ treated men and women with equal respect and the Church should copy his example. She gives various instances from the Bible that show how much Jesus respected women. This respect has gradually been eroded over the years by male chauvinists who feel that being male makes them superior to women. According to her, the line between being male and being female should be completely eliminated, and the Church should function as a single unit without any gender barriers (Bessey, p. 42).

Empowered women in the Church can contribute to a positive development of society. Social injustices such as forced prostitution through human trafficking, domestic violence, discrimination and other social ills that affect women to a higher degree may stand a better chance of improvement if women's intuition and loving care are brought to bear. Some of the problems faced by Britain right now, from trouble in the boardroom to trouble in the home, may be attributable to a lack of power that women need in order to influence others through the worldview that they have developed from being women in a world that seeks to define them. It is not unrealistic to believe that as women feel more accommodated in the Church, the number of people who are involved in drug and substance abuse may reduce significantly under female influence. Empowered mothers within the Church may seize the opportunity in partnership with their husbands to raise their children and those in community in the Christian faith and therefore to instil good morals and virtues in these children from a very young age (Hinds, p. 54). Doing this will have a very positive impact on society in the long term. One commentator suggests that since some people, male and female, naturally feel closer to women, it will be easier for them to listen to women rather than men (Beckford, p. 101). The social problems that are plaguing our communities cannot be dealt with solely by legal frameworks, the heavy sometimes brutal hand of the law; they can be more sensitively addressed by empowered women with religious motivation. With women taking a lead on a par with men, the Church can be involved in conflict resolutions and in helping with the reformation of offenders.

In conclusion, women are part of God's creation including the Church and therefore including Pentecostalism. Ideally, women and men should coexist on a basis of divinely given equality. However, as I have been arguing, equality in the Pentecostal Church has had to be fought for by women. While progress has been made, the battle is not won, as some Pentecostal women may still experience the legacy of patriarchy. For instance, while full equality in places of worship has not been fully achieved, there have been very important and crucial changes in the Church, notably the possibility for women to serve as evangelists, bishops, apostles, pastors and leaders within the Church. The efforts made by women, great or small, have helped create the religious environment that is now enjoyed by many in Britain. With more of such women standing up for this equality and against injustices, the progress of the Pentecostal Church in Britain will continue to be a positive one and the benefits of this will be enjoyed by generations to come.

References

Ashworth, Jacinta and Ian Farthing, 2007, *Churchgoing in the UK: a Research Report form Tearfund on Church Attendance in the UK*, Teddington: Tearfund, http://news.bbc.co.uk/1/shared/bsp/hi/pdfs/03_04_07_tearfundchurch.pdf

Beckford, R., 2011, *Dread and Pentecostal: A Political Theology for the Black Church in Britain*. Eugene, OR: Wipf & Stock Publishers.

Bessey, Sarah, 2013, *Jesus Feminist: An Invitation to Revisit the Bible's View of Women*. New York: Howard Books.

Brierley, P. W. (ed.), 2014, *UK Church Statistics 2: 2010–2020*. Tonbridge, Kent: ADBC.

Cho, Kyu-Hyung, 2017, 'Understanding of the Pentecostal Movement as Spirituality of Process through the Case Study of British Pentecostalism', *Journal of Yongsan Theology*, Vol. 42.

Church of England. House of Bishops, 2004, *Women Bishops in the Church of England? A Report of the House of Bishops' Working Party on Women in the Episcopate*. London: Church House Publishing.

Coleman, Simon, 2003, *The Globalization of Charismatic Christianity: Spreading the Gospel of Prosperity*. Cambridge: Cambridge University Press.

Deininger, Matthias, 2014, *Global Pentecostalism: an Inquiry into the Cultural Dimensions of Globalization*. Hamburg: Anchor Academic Publishing.

Fuller Studio, 2018, 'Women in the Pentecostal Movement', https://fullerstudio. fuller.edu/women-in-the-pentecostal-movement/ accessed 16 March 2018.

Gidley, Sophie, 2017, 'Challenges for Women in the Church', BBC News, 21 January, www.bbc.com/news/uk-wales-38660979

Hinds, Kathryn, 2008, *The Church*. New York: Marshall Cavendish Benchmark.

Kay, William K, 2007, *Apostolic Networks of Britain: New Ways of Being Church*. London: Paternoster.

Lee, Joyce and Glenn Gohr, 1999, 'Women in the Pentecostal Movement', *Enrichment Journal*, Fall, http://enrichmentjournal.ag.org/199904/060_women.cfm accessed 28 July 2018.

Lux-Sterritt, L. and C. Mangion (eds), 2010, *Gender, Catholicism and Spirituality: Women and the Roman Catholic Church in Britain and Europe, 1200–1900*. London: Macmillan International Higher Education.

May, Scottie, 2005, *Children Matter: Celebrating Their Place in the Church, Family, and Community*. Grand Rapids, MI: William B. Eerdmans.

Robeck, C. M. Jr and A. Yong (eds), 2014, *The Cambridge Companion to Pentecostalism*. Cambridge: Cambridge University Press.

Ruth, Michael, 2016, *The Catholic Church*. New York: Greenhaven Press.

Snyder, C. Arnold and Linda A. Huebert Hecht (eds), 1996, *Profiles of Anabaptist Women: Sixteenth-Century Reforming Pioneers*. Waterloo, Ontario: Wilfrid Laurier University Press for the Canadian Corporation for Studies in Religion.

Thomas, Bev, 2017, unpublished response paper in Pentecostal/Charismatic response to 500th Anniversary of the Reformation, London: Churches Together in England.

Toulis, N. R., 1997, *Believing Identity: Pentecostalism and the Mediation of Jamaican Ethnicity and Gender in England*. Oxford: Berg.

Walsh, Timothy Bernard, 2012, *To Meet and Satisfy a Very Hungry People: The Origins and Fortunes of English Pentecostalism, 1907–1925*. Milton Keynes: Paternoster.

Yorke, B., 2014, *The Conversion of Britain: Religion, Politics and Society in Britain, 600–800*. London: Routledge.

Part Three

Pentecostal and Charismatic and Mainstream Christianity

7

Ecumenism and Pentecostals in Britain

ANNE DYER

The theme of ecumenism has at times stricken with fear many an evangelical or Pentecostal – at least those brought up in the Britain of the 1960s – and it is those who have been running the churches over the past few decades. There has been a fear of compromise of doctrine, a fear of being forced into uniformity of preceding traditions, even other faith traditions, that leads to a false unity. It has led to Pentecostals being 'aloof' as Dale Irvin said, not daring to explore ecumenism (Irvin 1995). Yet we are in a 'common household', an 'oikos', to steward the things of God as mediating priests for the world to come to know God through Christ. Underlying Pentecostalism there has also run a stream of awareness of the ecumenism of the Spirit but, in ways that differ from some non-Pentecostals. For some, ecumenism is understood as a uniting in interfaith, not just interdenominational relations, as by prevenient grace the Spirit works among all religions, leading to God (Kim 2003, 2009). However, even as an ecumenism of the Spirit among Christians the practicalities did not work out to see it run free as opposition came and exclusivism resulted for a first generation. As we follow the decades through we find a pendulum swing, from an unexpected source.

The Twentieth Century: Roots and Intentions of Original Pentecostalism – for Britain

In 1907 the Anglican Vicar of All Saints, Monkwearmouth, Sunderland, Alexander A. Boddy, invited Thomas Ball Barratt of Norway's Methodist City Mission in Christiana (now known as Oslo) to share what the Lord had been doing in his ministry ever since his return from the USA. Boddy considered it was more marvellous than even the Welsh revival which he had also visited. So, in Sunderland in an Anglican church, Pentecostalism had its British birth. Gifts of the Spirit were evidenced and renewal felt. Independent missions took it on whereas

Anglicanism did not. Its progenitors would not have believed how the movement has fragmented since that time (Lim 2016). At the beginning of the second millennium Burgess and van der Maas (2002) counted 18,810 independent, indigenous and post-denominational groups of global neo-Charismatics, 1,500 intra-denominations in North America and up to 1,500 just in Chile. Classical Pentecostals of the Pentecostal European Fellowship considered 54 denominations as members.

Barratt and Boddy often interacted with many international inter-denominational Pentecostals between 1907 and 1920. As a result of events in Barmen, Germany – where Pentecostal revivalism had become over-enthusiastic and been rejected by the German Lutherans in the 1909 Berlin Declaration – Barratt wrote:

> It is really sad to think that numbers are being prevented in England and elsewhere from seeking the Baptism of Fire because of their terror for counterfeits. This proves satisfactorily to my mind that the way in which some of the leaders of Christian thought in Great Britain have been dealing with the matter has not been a wise one. Surely their efforts ought not to have influenced people to get out of the way of the blessing, but much rather, while guarding the way against the difficulties, to make it as easy as possible for them to get to the blessings the sooner the better.

Gerrit Polman, leader of the Netherlands' early Pentecostal movement, who was a 'sectarian against his will' according to Cornelis van der Laan, commented on Polman and Martha Visser's reports that 'they reveal something of an overwhelming ecumenical spirit in the Pentecostal meetings, not found in the traditional church' – of that decade at least. They felt 'a belonging to the great universal Christian church in 1919', while by the time of writing in 1937 it was missing. Martha replied, 'While in the tiny circle cast away by official Christianity, you experienced something of the great universal Christian church' (van der Laan 2011, p. 269). Polman placed his hopes in 'Divine Unity' and John 17.21 and stated 'The purpose of the Pentecostal revival is not to build up a church, but to build up ALL churches' (van der Laan p. 268).

Boddy (Wakefield, p. 93), as also Seymour in Los Angeles, emphasized the baptism of love. Seymour stated 'Love, faith and unity are our watchwords...' (*Apostolic Faith*, Issue 1:1 (January 1907), p. 2). By Issue 1:5 p.1 he wrote '[God] recognizes no flesh, no colour, no names, Azusa Mission stands for the unity of God's people everywhere. God is uniting his people, baptizing them by one Spirit in one body ...' (Irvin, p. 27). Irvin states they believed that 'Church divisions were a human creation and product of sin ... eradication of sin would accomplish the eradication of the sin of sectarian or denominational divisions' (Irvin, p. 35). Irvin goes on to emphasize that the early Azusa days' use of tongues was a 'freeing sacrament, a wake-up call to encounter the whole oikumene ... a rebirth of the ecumenical (or apostolic) church' (Irvin, p. 42).

Pandita Ramabai of the Mukti Mission, Pune, India, did not emphasize the phenomena of the Pune revival (which included speaking in tongues), but she did emphasize the Holy Spirit bringing a baptism in love. The romance of 'The bridegroom coming' formed the eschatological theme of early twentieth-century articles; Boddy's periodical *Confidence* used it to mean that the new movement was one body, preparing for that event. Throughout Boddy's ministry he sought to promote unity – at least among those receiving a Pentecostal experience (Wakefield, p. 147). Even so their terminology on baptism in the Spirit, and its practical outworking, worked against them.

Historic denominations' officialdom had no say nor interest nor organization in the 'Pentecost' of 1906 Sunderland. The Keswick conference, for which Boddy wrote 'Pentecost for England' (Wakefield, p. 84), included Jesse Penn Lewis – letters survive from Lewis to Boddy in the Donald Gee Archives, Mattersey Hall. Wakefield (p. 94) shows how they rejected the phenomena associated with the literature published on the spiritual gifts by Boddy. The League of Prayer led by Reader Harris rejected it, with Harris dropping 'Pentecostal' from the League's title (Wakefield, pp. 90–3).

The Denominationalizing of Pentecostalism: 1920s–1950

The new Pentecostals of the early to middle of the twentieth century were therefore defensive concerning their experience, which had ramifications for doctrine on both sides (Osgood 2014 CTE). Did their theology come from an experiential epistemology that they then found 'proof' for from scripture? Both sides within a modernist context of reason and apologetics argued their defences. Biblical exposition on the Holy Spirit and the spiritual gifts were paramount in early writings from Pentecostals in periodicals and their articles were turned into books (Gee 1932; *Redemption Tidings*, 1947; Los Angeles, p.12). Only by the 1990s did Pentecostals develop scholarship on hermeneutics or ecclesiology.

Pragmatically, then, the Pentecostals denominationalized themselves despite their own initial thinking that this Pentecostal renewal was a restoration for all the Church. The Apostolic Faith Mission had formed their own networks – one from Bournemouth in 1909 and one from

Pen-y-groes in 1915; their emphasis on Ephesians 4.11 ministry gifts for leadership would prove influential by the later twentieth century across Charismatic groups, but provoked opposition from other Pentecostals in the 1900s. By 1919 Elim had constituted itself as an evangelistic band in Wales/England and 1915 in Ireland; after various negotiations, Assemblies of God was formed in 1924 with a more autonomous congregational ethos. AoG's leaders, Harold Horton, John and Howard Carter and Donald Gee wrote in defence of Pentecostalism.

The first article of the first issue of *Redemption Tidings*, the Assemblies of God publication in July 1924 (probably by editor John Nelson Parr) quotes the hymn 'Judge not!' The implication is that both Pentecostals and non-Pentecostals were judging others – probably negatively. 'Forgive and love' are the penultimate words. That theme continued in the next issue's editorial too, citing Psalm 133, 'How good it is when brethren dwell together in unity' ('With whom?' one might ask). Yet is that not the spirit of ecumenism fostered by the Holy Spirit? It continues with a defence of the baptism of the Spirit copied from the American periodical, *The Pentecostal Evangel* by Smith Wigglesworth. He never actually aligned himself with any denomination after 1907, but was at the service of all churches to invite his ministry. The editorial states:

> Meetings have sprung up in villages, towns, and cities, and these meetings do not recognize denominational bounds – or other sectarian limitations, but being separated from all carnal pleasures and influences, seek to worship the Lord in simplicity and apostolic primitiveness by gathering round 'the Lord's Table'. (Parr, p. 8)

They refused all ordination as being merely of human origin, but recognized the gifts which the 'Great Ordainer', Christ Jesus, has given to the Church (Eph. 4.10–13). So, while denominational bounds were not recognized, all were free to participate in services, the refusal to ordain could also have meant a rejection of the historic denominations' mode of clericalism – countering ecumenical possibilities.

The Evangelicalization of Pentecostalism and the World Council of Churches (WCC): 1950s–1960s

By the time of the second generation of Pentecostalism after World War Two, Pentecostals sought more acceptance. So, in the 1950s, at the Billy Graham campaigns in England the Pentecostals participated as co-workers, being invited to join in the teams of counsellors for Haringey and Wembley. However, this did not commence an evangelicalization of Pentecostalism as happened with Assemblies of God in the USA when in the 1950s Zimmerman (the Vice, and then full, General Superintendent) became President of the American National Association of Evangelicals. Acceptance was sought there but members reacted against the WCC even though they could go along with Bebbington's (1988) evangelical foundation that promoted biblicism, conversionism, crucicentrism and activism.

Ecumenism was being promoted through the new WCC: in 1951 a meeting of the Central Committee of the WCC in Rolle, Switzerland, defined 'ecumenical' as 'properly used to describe everything that relates to the whole task of the whole church to bring the gospel to the whole world' (Sunquist, p. 130) in a summary list of ecumenical conferences and their themes since 1910 Edinburgh. Despite this missionary purpose, few evangelicals were involved and far fewer Pentecostals – just one man, David Du Plessis, who came to be known as 'Mr Pentecost'. By the 1960s, the Evangelical Alliance had welcomed in all denominations – including Pentecostals. On the other hand, this evangelicalization emphasized the distancing of classical Pentecostalism from the newer Charismatic movement.

A long account could be given of 'Mr Pentecost's' involvement with the IMC and then WCC during the 1950s and 1960s among mainstream churches and later the Catholic Church. Du Plessis and Gee were invited to the 1961 conference of the New Delhi International Missionary Council and WCC. The American Assemblies of God (AoG) General Superintendent, Thomas F. Zimmerman, requested them not to attend for the sake of his relationships with the US National Association of Evangelicals of which he was President; Du Plessis went. In effect he was defrocked as a minister of AoG until 1980 for his ecumenism. Meanwhile he worked alongside Pentecostals from as far as Chile, new Charismatics like Anglican Michael Harper or Catholic Charismatics of Notre Dame USA. Du Plessis is reported by Gee to have said,

> I felt the World Council, by this act was demonstrating to the world their recognition of the Pentecostal Revival. Many came to me to get acquainted and to ask detailed information about Pentecostal doctrine and Pentecostal experience. (Gee, p. 17)

Gee quoted a Faculty member of Princeton Theological Seminary in his editorial:

> The ecumenical question is primarily a question of the Holy Spirit … It is disturbing that the World Council of Churches has not dealt with this question as a major theme in any general council … In our

own age the Pentecostals have begun to attract the attention of classical Protestantism. They have been able to move into countries with a flexibility we do not possess, and through their ministry produce the fruits of the Spirit in the lives of men. We who have stifled the fire of the Spirit of God now see it blazing up in other groups as judgement upon us. For God's Spirit refuses to be stifled even by the Church. (Gee, p. 17)

The implications were that the onus was on the historic denominations – of classical Protestantism – not the Pentecostals themselves to stir up 'the fire of the Spirit of God'.

Gee was convinced that there were opportunities open to Pentecostals to move into the historic churches, but the main leaders of Pentecostal denominations of the USA or Europe did not move. Other nations' Pentecostal denominations were left to permeate the world's (WCC-linked) churches. Outright rejection of other denominations was evidenced by Pentecostals in the US and UK: Gee wrote in the same editorial: 'Among Pentecostal denominations there has been determined opposition to the World Council of Churches. Alleged heresy in doctrine and the danger of being enticed into a false unity are emphasized.' Any move toward each other at international to grassroots levels was not going to have a happy time in the 1960s.

New Churches to Britain

In the 1950s, migrant churches, including Pentecostal ones, largely from the Caribbean, were beginning to grow. Many had found English churches not in their style, and indeed often not too welcoming (Trotman, p. 13; Anderson, p. 103), and anecdotally confirmed by a range of black students at Mattersey Hall where I have taught since 2000. As noted above, despite initial feelings of rejection by historic denominations in the 1950s or later, African-Caribbean churches established their original denominations in Britain. These include the New Testament Church of God and the Church of God of Prophecy, which were well established in the Americas and the Caribbean. More recently a host of new African churches have grown in various networks – the Redeemed Christian Church of God, Kingsway Christian Centre and others such as the larger of many West African, or African sub-Saharan networks like the Apostolic Faith Mission. It is these groups who have related across denominations at national leadership levels in groups like Churches Together in England.

The first Meeting of the African and Caribbean churches with the WCC was held in Leeds in 1995. Gerloff had agitated for this meeting, stressing the diversity these churches had from totally opposite styles of backgrounds: black/white; grassroots/analysts; oral/literary (Gerloff 2010). The membership criterion for WCC was a denominational membership of 25,000 (World Council of Churches 2013), and that was not a possibility for the New Testament Church of God UK at that stage though internationally possible (Aldred, pp. 186–7; Aldred and Ogbo). Mutual awareness was at least achieved. Presentations were made on the more cultural aspects – education, resources, identity, as well as mission and evangelism. Theology was not the key concern. Nor was representationalism. However, they can relate to the British Churches Together in England and do so in a far more obvious way than the white Pentecostal churches. Since Gerloff's (2010) initial research of the 1970s to 1990s, there has been great growth and proliferation of churches planted in Britain from many parts of the world, particularly Africa.

With Joel Edwards in the Evangelical Alliance, 1997–2009, and more recently the first appointment of a Pentecostal President to the CTE, Bishop Brown, 2013–17, there is evidently a greater respect for Pentecostals in the wider community. Locally the New Testament Church of God has some examples of cooperative work. The Church has an office in Northampton; and Phyllis Thompson, their key educationalist, has established 'Globe Group' as an ecumenical reading group that includes six traditions – Baptist, Catholic, Quaker, Methodist and Anglican members as well as Pentecostals (personal communication, 2016).

Now the African churches from Ghana, Nigeria, Zimbabwe, etc., aim to be multicultural churches yet are without many white indigenous people. Ebenezer Aryee, an AoG minister, initiated the African Diaspora Mission Network in Leeds in 2016 to facilitate African churches' adaption to reach indigenous English people. Many appear to be more open to relating to other churches now the second generation is developing in leadership roles and are open to discovering a more contextual approach.

The Twenty-first Century: British Pentecostal Denominations and Other Denominations

It seems that in this century there has been a pendulum swing in how Pentecostals of all flavours (classical, Charismatic, neo and African or Asian) stand in relation to other churches. From rejection and exclusivism has come an acceptance, even respect and cooperative work, and Pentecostalism is seen as normal in most places. A postmodern tack might consider relationships of higher value than doctrinal ones. Pastors at grassroots level relate across denominations in city prayer fraternals and for missional purposes. Notably in a book on unity back in 1968, N. B. Cryer and E. N. Goodridge commented on a range of churches working together; none were Pentecostal back then, but their comments concern personalities among ministers (Cryer and Goodridge, p. 129). Without key friendships between ministers the unity among their churches might not have come about.

Fourth- and Fifth-Generation Pentecostalism

Has Pentecostalism come of age? Is it now fully engaged at national levels, having denominational representation? After all, 22 of the 48 Churches Together in England members are Pentecostal/Charismatic, i.e. 46 per cent, and yet involvement with others is left to grassroots willingness. There are Assemblies of God representatives in Churches Together in England and the Evangelical Alliance, but not those with policy-making influence for Assemblies of God itself. During the 1990s Paul Weaver, the General Superintendent of Assemblies of God, worked with the Evangelical Alliance, with Dr David Allen working on the Evangelical Alliance's ACUTE panel for doctrinal issues. By 2000, the Assemblies of God began reorganizing itself governmentally and few churches would have been aware of any ecumenical interest at their national levels; it is at grassroots that some assemblies relate across churches. John Partington, then national leader of Assemblies of God, explained in an interview on 14 October 2016 that as a pastor he related to Anglicans locally but recently he actually withdrew Assemblies of God GB from the Pentecostal European Fellowship, without providing any reasons.

However, Assemblies of God has been relating to its sister church, Elim, better than it did in 1922 in its embryonic form, when its potential group rejected overtures to join Elim. Elim does not insist on speaking in tongues as 'initial evidence' of Spirit baptism, nor as Assemblies of God has termed it, 'the essential biblical evidence' as confirmed in AoG's 2010 National Conference revision of their 12 'fundamentals' teachings, because these terms can be an obstacle. Elim now has more churches than AoG and they are relating to each other at all levels but have no plans to join up (Mandryck, pp. 42–4).

William Atkinson, once principal of Elim's Regents Theological

College, in an email in 2016 related the high involvement of Elim within inter-church organizations but described them as on the 'conservative' wing of evangelicalism. John Glass, Elim's national leader, was confirmed as the Evangelical Alliance's Chair from 2014, which spoke volumes for interdenominational interaction, at least among evangelicals. As for scholars, William Atkinson is now working at the London School of Theology; CARE is led by Lyndon Bowring, another Elim minister; Neil Hudson works within the London Institute of Contemporary Theology. So there is some ad hoc 'ecumenism'.

As for African-Caribbean Pentecostal churches, they are more than ever involved not just in the Evangelical Alliance, but in Churches Together. There may be multifarious groupings among black-led churches but they must have worked hard at seeking relationships across the board; their needs for advocacy sociologically may have triggered this 'better together' practice.

Pneumatological Ecumenism

It is not doctrine or a praxis imperative that brings unity; it is missional action that brings mutual purpose. What can be asked is: What can Pentecostals offer the process of developing ecumenism? I suggest that it lies within pneumatology – a pneumatological ecumenism, not an organizational ecumenism. Paul in Ephesians 4 speaks of walking in unity, humility, patience, etc., due to being in one body and one Spirit, in keeping with Luke's terminology in Acts; this can bring a resolution on definitions of being filled with the Spirit; it is easier terminology for non-Pentecostals than terms like 'baptism' or 'subsequence' theory. Indeed, the Charismatic movement has preferred the verb 'to be filled' with the Spirit and it can offer future consideration. The issues lie in how we mutually understand 'life in the Spirit of God'.

The Charismatic Movement

Since the 1960s, Anglicans, Methodists, Baptists and United Reformed churches have had streams of renewal. There were still some who found the power of the Holy Spirit not conducive to staying within long-term denominations – they are often Reformed and cessationist, or are Brethren churches. Many newly Charismatic churches maintained their independence in becoming restorationists (Hocken 1997; Walker 1998). Advice was even sought for their new experiences from leading preachers. Martin Lloyd-Jones was one such consultant for Terry Virgo who subsequently developed Coastlands in the 1970s and, since 1993, New Frontiers International. According to MacLeod, Lloyd-Jones stopped short of a full Pentecostal package: 'he opposed Keswick Higher Life teaching, removed Spirit baptism from sanctification and perfectionism and yet asserted an experimental "seal of the Spirit"' (McLeod 1988). Subjectivity and objectivity were typically in apposition in the 1960s due to modernist perspectives. Is it fair to say postmodernism can relieve us of that tension and integrates experiential subjectivism with an objective theology?

During the 1970s and 1980s various networks were formed; some, such as Coastlands, were more Reformed in doctrine. Some were Arminian, as with Ichthus under Roger Forster's leadership. Some did not seem to mind either extreme. Kay (2006) gives an account of ten Charismatic networks, including Vineyard as a Third Wave group among apostolic networks exemplifying new ways of being church. Even these 'new ways' are now however being superseded by an 'emerging church' and Fresh Expressions. Some were freer to relate to communities in newer ways. Pioneer, under Gerald Coates, often with Roger Forster or John Noble, would create opportunities for serving the nation, not just communities local to their churches; so, from the Festival of Light in 1973, through Spring Harvest camps, to the Prayer for the Nation in 1999 at Emmanuel Church, Marsham Street, Westminster, many a Christian from all and any denomination would come together. Walker (1998) categorized these new churches as R1 and R2; R1 being more Reformed and conservative, even exclusive; R2 being more forward looking, involved with others while still promoting the infilling of the Spirit. Under Ground Level, with Stuart Bell, Baptists, Methodists, Assemblies of God and others fellowshipped during the early 1980s in a form of ecumenical network. They continue to work with Anglican and Methodist pioneers in creating Fresh Expressions among Ground Level church plants.

Despite the controversies around the Toronto Blessing, 20 years later, many a city has a prayer network across the denominations, with leaders meeting regularly for fellowship and encouragement. So, the interaction of denominations at grass roots level has proved more effective than nationally intentioned ecumenical manoeuvring.

Official Cooperation in Ecumenism – the Debate over Other Church Families

We have seen that in the 1960s there were tensions, Donald Gee stressing commonalities, stymied by colleagues. In the light of New Delhi, Gee wrote:

> As far as the Evangelical Alliance is concerned, our primary object is to draw together all evangelicals, and we welcome to our ranks all those of like precious faith regardless of their attitude toward the Ecumenical Movement, 'in things essential, unity; in things doubtful, liberty; in all things, charity,' is a sound guiding principle. (Du Plessis 1970)

Gee continued, 'Our many (Pentecostal) divisions call for hearty repentance before God ... The Pentecostal Movement has its own confessions to make before it criticizes others, for our divisions are notorious and worldwide.' Both sides had problems. Gee's answer?

> The unity for which our Lord prayed is based on something more fundamental than just another creed and constitution. He revealed the divine method when He said that it is the glory that unites. It is a fact that when Christians wait on God together in prayer and worship there quickly comes flooding into the hearts the love of God for each other. Something of the same 'glory' unites them when they go out together to 'preach the gospel to every creature'. (Gee 1932)

To bring it into the twenty-first century, we can see some attempts at bringing mutual recognition. It is probable that if we look at grassroots churches in different towns – more than national levels – we can see mutual cooperation on different projects as in HOPE and local Churches Together, vastly improving mutual understanding.

Common Stances – or Not?

The five Protestant Reformation 'Sola' points would be agreed upon by Pentecostals – by grace, faith, Christ, scripture and God's glory alone. However, Pentecostals might have to argue that they are insufficient for full practical development of fullness in Christ as the Holy Spirit is not mentioned, if implied. Their pneumatological stance is actually Christological, seen in Christ, but activated by the Spirit. Glossolalia with 'subsequence' theory for the baptism in the Spirit, as a formula for the initial infilling of the Holy Spirit, can be an obstacle across denominations. One, two or three salvific stages – regeneration, sanctification and then baptism for power to witness – have been incessantly debated.

Doctrinal commonalities do not overcome the differences. By the 1960s exclusivity had only been broken with some evangelicals but the Charismatic movement also isolated the classical Pentecostals until perhaps the 1990s, when they became gradually 'Charismaticized' – at least musically! By the 1970s Charismatic (Streams of Renewal, Dales, etc.) songs began to filter into the Pentecostal circles; and even within evangelical streams of the historic churches. Worship was both an answer to a foundational place for working together and a basis for problems with issues within congregations – on age or ethnic variations.

For ecumenical perspectives, Simon Chan and de Koch have worked on a Trinitarian ecclesiology that might map communion as koinonia, while mapping charisms onto ministry as ascension gifts (Vondey 2008; Gros, pp. 291–329). On these grounds there may be room for dialogue from common points extending into a renewed understanding of Pentecostals by others. Surely, as Vondey declares, true ecumenism lies in 'companionship and hospitality' and broadens out 'sacramental perspectives of ecumenical ecclesiology' (Vondey, pp. 292–3). A question comes to mind: are Pentecostals in general even concerned with these challenges?

Ecclesiological Styles

Pentecostalism is ever flexible to new contexts such as among Brazilians or West Africans; so also among twenty-first-century variations on non-cessationists, Pentecostals are pragmatists. Pentecostals prefer to be without a set liturgy. Pentecostals prefer mission and persuasion conversionism, and oppose liberal stances on moral issues. Therefore, there are issues of difference that work out in practical matters, not just church styles of worship. Whatever version of 'Renewalist' – Pentecostals and Charismatics, or Post-Charismatics – they are also infamous for the number of schisms and multiplicity of groups. Statistics are many in variation and taxonomy. Suffice it to say that Caribbean-derived churches have the longest lifespan and biggest size in the UK, now joined by many from West Africa and Southern Africa, all with cultural, episcopal, individualist variations on style and doctrine. 'Renewalist' Charismatics were by far the largest Pentecostal grouping in 2002 at 70 per cent with neo-Charismatics at 25 per cent and classical Pentecostals at 5 per cent (Mandryck, pp. 850–1; Kay 2002, pp. 42–5).

Anglicans, United Reformed, Baptists and so on relate independently with Pentecostal churches on a local basis, particularly if they have absorbed a flavour of Charismatic styles. In England, the Anglicans are perhaps more willing to relate at higher levels. The renewal movement had a strong impact on Anglicans during the 1960s through the Fountain Trust led by Michael Harper. More recently, an Anglican Pentecostal Theological Steering Group co-chaired by the Bishop of Birkenhead Keith Sinclair and CTE Pentecostal President Agu Irwuku has been meeting. Kay sees ecumenical activity as a necessary attempt by Christians to combine 'against the erosion of Christian attitudes, values, institutions, rights and traditions within an increasingly hedonistic, intolerant and sceptical society' (Kay 2014, pp. 160–71).

Doctrine, identity, ethnicity and cultural background can all be overcome within the Pentecostal families. Can they then look beyond, befriending and partnering each other for the purposes of mission, to fulfil the prayer of Jesus that his disciples should all be one (John 17)? As we have seen, some attempts have been made. Beyond Britain these attempts have had more success.

Beyond the UK

Raymond Pfister, writing from his own European experience, wants the Pentecostal Church to change its attitudes and practices – a move from 'owning' spiritual truth to sharing it. Pfister calls for a journey from indoctrination to education, from convention to tradition, from monologue to dialogue, from excluding to belonging, from owning to sharing and finally from stagnation to exploration (Pfister, pp. 133–45).

Jean-Daniel Plüss has established on the European continent a position for European Pentecostals to dialogue with Reformed churches. Mel Robeck of the Assemblies of God, USA, long experienced in ecumenical dialogue with Catholics, has spent a lifetime trying to alleviate the fears of his denomination's leaders. Both Plüss and Robeck have been involved in setting up the Global Christian Forum in which the Pentecostal World Fellowship is a participant body. Now that the 'centre of gravity' of Christian faith is more in the global South, the new churches coming into Europe from across the world may well be the clue to the future, if only schisms and fears can be overcome. Is this leading the pendulum swing from rejection and exclusivism of the early twentieth century to the greater church growth in Britain and worldwide? There may be potential here for mutual cooperation with new perspectives from new generations and ethnic groups.

A Conclusion for Britain?

Within the multiplicity of renewalists, within and outside the historic denominations, the catalyst for changing attitudes may lie with the burgeoning migrant or diaspora churches when they become focused on reaching the indigenous non-Christian British. This along with their good relationships growing through Churches Together in England can provide a catalyst for a united missional perspective in Britain. Benefits of the whole process should lie in friendships, an ease of understanding, prayerfulness for one another, a willingness to improve better self-understanding and working relationships that benefit the kingdom of God in missional perspectives.

The 1906 to 1908 Pentecostals would have wanted to see today's attitudes toward an increasing 'pneumatological ecumenism' enabled by Pentecostals now heading organizations like Churches Together in England, particularly those of the newer groups, and especially black churches. Can 'pneumatological ecumenism' work further – for the world's harmony? Unity in diversity? We should always end with Jesus' desire for his Church to be united (John 17) and make it feasible by forgetting non-essentials, to concentrate upon essentials – love for God, his world and his people.

References

Aldred, Joe, 2001, 'The Black Church in Britain and their Relations with the Ecumenical Movement', in Dahling-Sander, C., et al. (eds), *Pfingstkirchen und Oekumene in Bewegung*. Frankfurt am Main: Verlag Otto Lembeck.

Aldred, Joe and Keno Ogbo, 2010, *The Black Church in the 21st Century*. London: Darton Longman & Todd.

Anderson, A., 2014, *An Introduction to Pentecostalism*, 2nd edn. Cambridge: Cambridge University Press.

Burgess, Stanley M. and Eduard M. van der Maas (eds), 2002, *The New International Dictionary of Pentecostal Charismatic Movements*, revised and expanded edition. Grand Rapids, MI: Zondervan.

Cryer, Neville B. and Ernest N. Goodridge, 1968, *Experiment in Unity*. London: A. R. Mowbray.

Du Plessis, David, 1970, *The Spirit Bade Me Go: the Astounding Move of God in the Denominational Churches*. Plainfield, NJ: Logos International.

Gee, D., 1932, *Pentecost*. Springfield, MO: Gospel Publishing House.

Gerloff, Roswith I. H., 2010, *A Plea for British Black Theologies*, vol.1, 2nd edn. Eugene, OR: Wipf & Stock.

Hocken, P., 1997, *Streams of Renewal: Origins and Development of the Early Charismatic Movement in Great Britain*. Carlisle: Send the Light.

Irvin, Dale T., 1995, 'Drawing All Together in One Bond of Love: the Ecumenical Vision of William J. Seymour and the Azusa Street Revival', *Journal of Pentecostal Theology* Vol. 6, pp. 25–53. Leiden, Netherlands: Brill.

Kay, W. K., 2002, 'Britain', in Burgess, Stanley M. and Eduard M. van der Maas (eds), 2002, *The New International Dictionary of Pentecostal Charismatic Movements*, revised and expanded edition. Grand Rapids, MI: Zondervan.

Kay, W. K., 2006, *Apostolic Networks: New Ways of Being Church*. Carlisle: Paternoster.

Kay, W. K., 2014, 'Anglican–Pentecostal Dialogue in the UK: an Analysis and Exhortation', *JEPTA* Vol. 24 Issue 2.

Kim, K., 2003, *Mission in the Spirit: The Holy Spirit in Indian Christian Theologies*. London: SPCK.

Kim, K., 2009, *Joining in with the Spirit: Connecting World Church and Local Mission*. London: Epworth Press.

Lim, Timothy T. N., 2016, 'Together Towards Life: a Pentecostal Assessment in Ecumenical Missiology', in Ross, Kenneth R. et al. (eds), *Changing Landscapes and New Conceptions of Mission*. Oxford: Regnum; Geneva: World Council of Churches.

MacLeod, Donald, 1988, *The Spirit of Promise*. Tain, Rosshire: Christian Focus Publications.

Mandryck, J., 2010, *United Kingdom Operation World*, 7th edn. Colorado Springs, CO: WEC/Biblical Publishing.

Osgood, Hugh, 'The Pentecostal and Charismatic Constituency within the British Church: an Internal CTE Explanatory Briefing.' London: 2014 Churches Together in England, www.cte.org.uk/Groups/248695/Home/Resources/Pentecostal_and_Multicultural/The_Pentecostal_and/The_Pentecostal_and.aspx accessed 3 November 2018.

Parr, J. N., 1924, Editorial prime article, *Redemption Tidings*, Vol. 1 No. 2.

Pfister, R., 2014, 'A Pentecostal Journey into Unity', *JEPTA*, Vol. 34 Issue 2.

Sunquist, Scott W., 2013, *Understanding Christian Mission: Participation in Suffering and Glory*. Grand Rapids, MI: Baker Books.

Trotman, Arlington, 1992, 'Black, Black-led or what?' in Edwards, J. (ed.), *Let's Praise Him Again!* Eastbourne: Kingsway Publications.

van der Laan, Cornelis, 1991, *Sectarian against his will: Gerrit Roelof Polman and the Birth of Pentecostalism in the Netherlands*. London/Metuchen, NJ: Scarecrow Press.

van der Laan, Cornelis, 2011, 'Pentecostals in the Netherlands', in Kay, W. K. and A. E. Dyer (eds), *European Pentecostalism*. Leiden: Brill.

Vondey, Wolfgang, 2008, *People of Bread: Rediscovering Ecclesiology*. Mahwah, NJ: Paulist Press.

Wakefield, Gavin, 2007, *Alexander Boddy: Pentecostal Anglican Pioneer*. Milton Keynes: Authentic Media.

Walker, A., 1998, *Restoring the Kingdom; the Radical Christianity of the House Church Movement*. Guildford: Eagle Books.

World Council of Churches, 2013, 'Constitution and Rules', www.oikoumene.
org/en/resources/documents/assembly/2013-busan/adopted-documents-
statements/wcc-constitution-and-rules

Further Reading

Hammaläinen, Arto and Grand McClung (eds), 2012, *Together in One Mission:
Pentecostal Cooperation in World Mission*. Cleveland, TN: Pathway Press.

8

Anglicans, Pentecostals and Ecumenism: Bilateral Dynamics and Broader Resonances

DAVID HILBORN

This chapter sets out a framework for enhanced ecumenical theological dialogue between Anglicans and Pentecostals. In doing so, it builds on key themes identified in a research project undertaken by this author and supported by the Council for Christian Unity of the Church of England in 2011 – a project which led to more formal recognition of the importance of Anglican–Pentecostal relations, and then to an exploratory conference of English Anglicans and representatives of various UK-wide Pentecostal churches and networks at High Leigh Conference Centre in April 2014 (Churches Together in England 2014). The first formal planning meeting to map out this exploratory conference took place at Church House, Westminster on 19 April 2013. That conference involved representatives on both sides from Scotland and Wales as well as England, and also a representative of the Anglican Communion. It in turn spurred further fruitful interaction and discussion, most especially through the formation of a Joint Church of England–Pentecostal Steering Group, through significant Anglican input, to a November 2015 day conference on Pentecostalism and ecumenical relations, hosted by Churches Together in England. There has been also a bilateral consultation featuring representatives of the Church of England and the Redeemed Christian Church of God, held in May 2016 under the banner of the National Leaders Prayer Meeting and took place at the Focolare Centre, Welwyn Garden City.

The CTE consultation focused on mutual responses to the 2013 WCC convergence text *The Church: Towards a Common Vision* (World Council of Churches 2013a). A Joint Church of England–Pentecostal Steering Group has been instrumental in highlighting issues including pneumatology for further consideration. From these more specifically English Anglican and UK-wide Pentecostal interchanges, several themes will be identified here as pertinent for potentially broader development of Anglican–Pentecostal dialogue, both in terms of theological scope and international reach. I will also review existing ecumenical dialogues between other historic churches and Pentecostals, tracing similarities and distinctions between them and the ongoing English/UK Anglican–Pentecostal conversations, and proposing ways in which more concerted Anglican–Pentecostal ecumenical theological endeavour might enrich ecumenism generally.

Since the early 1970s Pentecostals have engaged in either regional or global dialogue with Roman Catholic, Reformed, Lutheran and other major church bodies. By contrast, Anglican–Pentecostal dialogue remains relatively embryonic, despite the encouraging steps taken more recently in the British context, as summarized above. This is somewhat surprising given that it was an Anglican priest who acted as a key conduit for the inflow of Pentecostalism to Britain over a century ago.

At the Lambeth Conference of 1988, a resolution was passed by the bishops resolving to seek dialogue between the Anglican Communion and classical Pentecostal denominations: 'This Conference notes the rapid growth of Pentecostal Churches in many parts of the world, and encourages where possible the initiation of personal contact and theological dialogue with Pentecostal Churches especially at the local level' (Resolution 11). At the next Lambeth Conference in 1998, a further resolution (IV.21) invited the Inter-Anglican Standing Commission on Ecumenical Relations (IASCER) to explore the possibility of conversations 'between the Anglican Communion and the Pentecostal Churches, at an appropriate level'. At the same conference, a complementary resolution (IV.25) was also passed resolving to improve understanding and encounter with 'new churches and Independent Christian Groups' – specifically neo-Charismatic networks such as the Vineyard, which had no 'ecclesial connection with an historic denomination or alliance'. Whereas the resolution on Anglican–Pentecostal dialogue was taken forward on the global Anglican level by IASCER, this second resolution was at first progressed more specifically through the Church of England, in the form of an 'open-textured' group chaired by the then Bishop of Ely, the Rt Revd Prof. Stephen Sykes, at two 'pre-dialogue' meetings of this group held in January and May 1999. Bishop Stephen Sykes' move to become Principal of St John's College, Durham soon after this meant that he was no longer able to chair the Ely group, and it appears from the archive that no suitable or willing replacement for him could be found. Certainly, there were no more meetings of the group after the second one of May 1999. As for IASCER and the Anglican Communion, the subject of Pentecostal and new churches continued to feature as a topic of discussion in meetings and conferences until 2003, as it did in the Inter-Anglican Standing Commission on Mission and Evangelism, but it seems to have faded from focus thereafter until the April 2014 Consultation was attended on behalf of the Anglican Communion by Revd Canon Dr Alyson Barnett-Cowan, its Director of Unity, Faith & Order.

One of the first European Christian leaders affected by the seminal Azusa Street revival of 1906–15, the Norwegian Thomas Ball Barratt (1862–1940), was visited soon after he had made an exploratory trip to America by Alexander Boddy (1854–1930), Rector of the Church of England parish of All Saints, Monkwearmouth, in Sunderland. Boddy was deeply touched by Barratt's ministry, and on his return All Saints became a focus for those pursuing baptism in the Spirit and glossolalia from all over the British Isles (Wakefield 2007a, 2007b), even if Boddy himself stressed that divine love and the exaltation of Christ were more important than speaking in tongues. This so-called Sunderland revival bore significant fruit – both directly in terms of initiatives led by Boddy himself, and indirectly in terms of those touched by his ministry who would go on to pioneer their own more distinctively Pentecostal churches and networks – among them Donald Gee, Howard Carter and Smith Wigglesworth, the last of whom went on to work with George Jeffreys, founder of the Elim Alliance. After World War One, however, Boddy's part in the story began to fade from view, and it would be another four decades, with the rise of the neo-Pentecostal or Charismatic movement in Anglican and other churches, that the two traditions would once again converge in a significant way (Hocken 1997).

Almost a century after the Sunderland revival and half a century after the rise of the Charismatic movement in Anglicanism, in 2013 the Council for Christian Unity identified Anglican–Pentecostal ecumenical relations as a priority for the Church of England, alongside the Anglican–Methodist Covenant and the ongoing Anglican–Roman Catholic conversations in England and worldwide (ARCIC). It should be clear from what follows that this initiative was overdue when announced, and that for all the positive progress made since, it warrants significant further development. It should also become clear that whereas the more classically ecumenical concern with 'faith and order' that has preoccupied so many Anglican theologians has registered far less prominently in Pentecostal theology, there is now a genuine flowering of Pentecostal ecclesiology which promises to make theological dialogue between the two traditions more substantial and more mutually enriching than it might previously have been. Indeed, the various anatomies of Pentecostal ecclesiology offered in recent years by, among others, Simon Chan, Wolfgang Vondey, Frank Macchia, Amos Yong, Veli-Matti Kärkkäinen and Chris Green promise greater ecumenical methodological congruity with Anglicanism than ever before, even if significant differences of focus and emphasis might remain (Chan 2011; Vondey 2010, pp. 141–70; Macchia, pp. 155–256; Yong 2005; Kärkkäinen, pp. 81–146; Green 2016). Indeed, confirmation of this is provided by the fact that among the most sophisticated such Pentecostal ecclesiologies is that produced by the English Anglican priest and scholar Andy Lord.

Pentecostalism and the Changing Shape of Ecumenism

Whether Pentecostals number around 300 or 600 million, their reshaping of the world Christian map has, in Allan Anderson's phrase, 'enormous ecumenical implications' (Anderson, p. 15). Yet as noted above, the Church of England, the Celtic Anglican churches and the Anglican Communion have taken far longer than other major Christian traditions to realize this – or at least, to respond to it in programmatic ecumenical terms. Certainly, despite some promising progress over the past five years or so, Anglicanism still has a good deal of 'catching up' to do on this front. Indeed, there is much that Anglicans can gain by studying past and present dialogues between other historic mainline churches and Pentecostals. In particular, the distinctive history and theological complexion of Anglicanism as a church 'both catholic and Reformed' means that Pentecostal dialogues in recent times with Roman Catholics, Presbyterians and Lutherans are likely to prove the most pertinent.

Pointers from Pentecostal Dialogues With Other Traditions

Roman Catholic–Pentecostal Dialogue

From 1972 onwards the Vatican Secretariat for Promoting Christian Unity sponsored a series of dialogues with 'Leaders of Some Pentecostal Churches' – a process which has continued in one form or another to the present, and which has thus far produced six helpful reports (Roman Catholic Church 1984; Gros, et al. pp. 713–79; Vondey 2013, pp. 95–216; Roman Catholic Church 2015 and links at www. vatican.va/roman_curia/pontifical_councils/chrstuni/sub-index/index_pentecostals.htm). This encounter is significant from an Anglican point of view because many of the topics it has covered over the past 40 years resonate with issues that Anglicans would be likely to highlight in ecumenical discussion with Pentecostals – for example, Christian initiation, charismata in public worship, the relative authority of experience, tradition and scripture, the nature and exercise of healing, orders and functions of ministry, apostolicity and episcopacy, church, koinonia and Christian unity, the communion of saints, the Spirit and the Church, mission, evangelization, proselytism and religious freedom, and conversion and discipleship. Also worth noting here, however, is the fact that this process initially involved Charismatic participants from Protestant churches with whom Rome was in dialogue, as well as Catholics and Pentecostals. Among these additional contributors was Michael Harper (1931–2010), a pioneer of neo-Pentecostal theology and spirituality in the Church of England who had led the influential ecumenical Charismatic network known as the Fountain Trust (Ho Yan Au 2011). However, just as the Pentecostals taking part were doing so as committed individuals rather than as 'delegates' of their denominations or networks, so Harper was invited on the basis of his parachurch role rather than as a spokesman for the Church of England or the Anglican Communion (Sandidge, pp. 79, 98). Nevertheless, Harper's main contributions to the process reflected characteristic 'catholic' Anglican concerns for church and liturgy: in the third round of the first dialogue he contributed a paper entitled 'The Holy Spirit Acts in the Church, its Structure, its Sacramentality, its Worship and Sacraments', and in the fourth round he gave a further paper on 'Principles of Congregational Worship' (Sandidge, p. 90).

As with other ecumenical dialogues in which Pentecostals would be involved, it soon became clear after some preliminary meetings between the Pontifical Council and Pentecostals in 1970–71 that traditional 'faith and order' approaches would need to be modified in this context. As the report on the first quinquennial phase of the dialogue proper notes, 'before it began it was made clear that its immediate scope was not "to concern itself with the problems of imminent structural union" … Its purpose has been that "prayer, spirituality and theological reflection be a shared concern at the international level"' (Gros et al., p. 713). Although by the second Dialogue (1977–82) non-Roman and non-Pentecostal input had been phased out in order to bring 'clearer focus' to the interaction (Gros et al., p. 722), this less formal, more relational ethos has continued down to the present. Furthermore, it established an important template for other bilaterals that would follow – a template that will surely need to be maintained as Anglican–Pentecostal dialogue develops in England, across the UK and beyond.

Pentecostal–Reformed Dialogue

For all its claims to continuity with medieval Catholicism, the Church of England is at least as much if not more defined by its distinctive constitution as a Protestant church in the Reformation period as by its more general pre-existence as a Catholic 'English Church', or by more recent attempts to reassert that Catholic past (MacCulloch, pp. 10–14). Given this Reformation background, any putative Anglican–Pentecostal dialogue would benefit from taking note of the ecumenical exchanges that have happened in the past 20 years or so between Pentecostals, Reformed and Lutheran traditions.

Between 1996 and 2000, the informal tenor of the Roman Catholic–Pentecostal process was echoed in a wide-ranging dialogue between the World Alliance of Reformed Churches (WARC) and 'leaders from some classical Pentecostal Churches' under the heading 'Word and Spirit, Church and World' (World Alliance of Reformed Churches). Once more here, an 'asymmetry' was acknowledged in that Pentecostal representatives were largely participating as respected individuals within their own church contexts, but had no global body such as WARC to mandate them, or to which they were officially accountable. A second phase of dialogue ran from 2001 to 2011 on the subject of 'Experience in Christian Faith and Life', with WARC having changed its name part-way through to the World Communion of Reformed Churches (WCRC) (World Alliance of Reformed Churches 2012). A third phase ensued and is ongoing, with a focus on mission (Tanis 2016, 2017; Hunter 2016). Here, I will focus on the first phase of this process, since that most closely reflects the stage of ecumenical interaction at which Anglicans and Pentecostals currently find themselves.

The 1996–2000 dialogue began by concentrating on spirituality, and this was deliberate – recognition of the fact that Pentecostalism characteristically construes theology through prayer and worship. By contrast the Reformed tradition has typically seen doctrine as framing and defining worship, and on this basis has allowed liturgy to be varied and extemporized within loose, non-prescriptive frameworks as long as it is 'orthodox', and specifically as long as it accords with various dogmatic confessions of faith (Wolterstorff; Old, pp. 1–16; Leith, pp. 174–97). This, in essence, was the aspiration of the Puritan party within the Church of England, but since the reintroduction of the Book of Common Prayer after the Restoration under Charles II, Anglicanism's attachment to authorized liturgical texts has led even its most Calvinistic constituencies to acknowledge liturgy as embodying and delineating the faith of the Church, in accordance with the ancient formula *lex orandi lex credendi* (Harrison and Sansom 1982; Stevenson and Spinks 1991). Likewise, Pentecostals may eschew the prescribed liturgies of Anglicanism, but their characteristic construal of theology as fundamentally doxological should find an echo in Anglicanism which was, perhaps, less apparent in the WARC process.

Under the subsequent heading 'Spirit and Word', both parties in the WARC–Pentecostal dialogue agreed that their respective historic emphases on the ministries of the Spirit (Pentecostal) and the Word (Reformed) should be subjected to more thoroughly Trinitarian examination. While for the Reformed this would mean a reappraisal of the role of charismata in worship, Pentecostals recognized that there would be value in taking account of the generally greater Reformed emphasis on the life of the Trinity in relation to creation – an emphasis which had historically informed a more distinct social and political heritage. To some extent this mutual re-emphasis on the Trinity reflects a broader 'Trinitarian turn' in doctrinal theology, and ecumenical theology in particular, since the 1960s (World Council of Churches 2005, pp. 13–28). Anglican theologians like Rowan Williams, Daniel Hardy, Paul Avis and Tim Bradshaw have made their own valuable contributions to this turn, and with its unique blend of Catholic, Reformed and Lutheran influences, the Anglican contribution to prospective Anglican–Pentecostal dialogue is well set to enhance the good work already done in this area by the WARC/WCRC–Pentecostal process (Williams, pp. 129–80; Hardy 2001; Avis 2010; Bradshaw, pp. 239–301).

In a later section of a WARC–Pentecostal document entitled *The Holy Spirit and the Church*, both parties affirmed that the Church is the creature of the Word and Spirit, that it is the community of the Spirit's leading and of the Spirit's gifts, and that it is in but not of the world. However, whereas the Reformed tradition's characteristic stress on 'covenant' as a key descriptor of God's initiative in forming the Church had led to a strongly corporate and sacramental ecclesiology, Pentecostals had tended toward a pneumatocentric ecclesiology in which the Church is 'formed by the outpouring of the Spirit and shaped by the Spirit's gifts', but in which the role of sacraments or ordinances may not be so obviously linked with the building up of the body. In similar vein, whereas corporately agreed confessions had gone a long way toward defining the faith, life and mission of the Church in the Reformed tradition, Pentecostals were likely to place greater stress on the accumulation of personal testimonies as authenticators of rightness with God (WARC, pp. 21–8). While Anglicanism might not have relied as distinctively on covenant theology, its indebtedness to the

Reformed tradition is reflected in a similarly sacramental ecclesiology which is, if anything, intensified by its simultaneous self-definition as a 'Catholic' church (Williams, pp. 197–221; Bradshaw, pp. 129–95; Hardy, pp. 77–114). This should again complement and extend the insights gained in the WARC/WCRC–Pentecostal exchange.

Under the heading of 'The Holy Spirit and Mission' both parties in the foundational WARC–Pentecostal conversations recognized the centrality of the Missio Dei for their understanding of the Church's witness in the world. While the specific empowerment of the Church for mission is construed more distinctively by Pentecostals in relation to baptism in the Holy Spirit, both parties agreed on the importance of the prevenient work of the Spirit in the missional task – namely that 'the Spirit of Christ goes ahead of the Church to prepare the ground for the reception of the gospel'. While Reformed churches tend to view this prevenient work more positively than Pentecostals in relation to culture and non-Christian religions, both agreed that 'witness to the gospel should be embodied in culture' and that more attention should be paid to how such embodiment might best take place (WARC, pp. 28–31). Pursuing this theme in a final section of the Phase One report headed 'Spirit and Kingdom', characteristic Reformed postmillennialism and Pentecostal premillennialism were frankly acknowledged as tending toward different emphases in social and civic engagement. Whereas Reformed Christians might naturally view themselves as 'stewards of the rich gifts of God' in the whole of creation and might on this basis organize actively to oppose 'social injustices, economic exploitation and ecological destruction', Pentecostals were more likely to view structural and systemic sin in terms of 'spiritual warfare', and to take a more personalised and incremental view of social transformation (WARC, pp. 32–7).

Evangelicals and Charismatics within the Anglican tradition have typically shared Pentecostalism's historic prioritization of evangelism over social concern, but ongoing interaction with more Catholic, liberal and radical streams within their own tradition, as well as more developed hermeneutical understandings of mission on their own account, have seen Anglican evangelicals and Charismatics more recently endorsing and promoting broader definitions such as the 'Five Marks of Mission' developed by the Anglican Consultative Council between 1984 and 1990 ('to proclaim the Good News of the Kingdom; to teach, baptize and nurture new believers; to respond to human need by loving service; to seek to transform unjust structures of society, and to strive to safeguard the integrity of creation and sustain and renew the life of the earth') (Anglican Communion 2018). At the same time, the growth and relative strength of Charismatics within Anglicanism in recent decades has been reflected in denominational reports, such as Mission-Shaped Church (2004), which make traditional 'Pentecostal' concerns with evangelism and church planting central (Church of England Mission and Public Affairs Council 2004; Nelstrop and Percy 2008; Anglican–Methodist Working Party 2012; Lings 2017). Thus as with the WARC/WCRC–Pentecostal process, ecumenical dialogue between Anglicans and Pentecostals has the potential to enrich the nascent Pentecostal political theologies charted in more recent years by Douglas Petersen (1996), Miller and Yamamori (2007) and others (including Marshall 2009), even while reminding Anglicans in a post-Christendom context of their continuing evangelistic obligations.

Lutheran–Pentecostal Dialogues

With the success of the WARC–Pentecostal dialogue in mind, representatives of the Lutheran World Federation embarked in 2004 on an open dialogue with selected Pentecostal leaders. Conscious of the need to allow Pentecostals authentically to 'speak a Pentecostal language', the initial phase of this process focused on the question 'How do we encounter Christ?' A further phase of dialogue commenced in 2016 and is ongoing, but the report on this first round of conversations was published in 2010 (Institute for Ecumenical Research 2010; Lutheran World Federation 2016). This grounding text recognized clear respective emphases in each of the traditions on justification (Lutheran) and sanctification (Pentecostal), on formal and extemporary public worship, on charismata, on orders of ministry and on sacraments.

These themes mirrored several concerns that, as we have seen, had already featured prominently in the Roman Catholic and Reformed–Pentecostal dialogues. However, their reoccurrence in this context bears particular significance for Anglican–Pentecostal interaction. This is because of all those engaged ecumenically by Anglicans, Lutherans are the ones with whom most progress toward unity has been achieved. The Porvoo Common Statement (1992) ensured full visible communion between British and Irish Anglican churches and Baltic and Nordic Lutheran churches, while the Reuilly Common Statement (1999) brought British and Irish Anglicans into closer unity with French Lutheran and Reformed churches. As the Anglican bishops noted at their Lambeth Conference of 1998, 'Anglicans and Lutherans are rediscovering substantial doctrinal agreement and, sometimes with surprise, a similarity in worship, mission and ministry. We have a familial likeness' (Jones, p. 156). On one level this is not surprising: after all,

Luther's retention of bishops and formalized liturgy, together with his relative conservatism compared with other Reformers on questions of Church and state, mean that it is his theology and ecclesiology, more than Calvin's or Zwingli's, which has come more broadly to influence the Church of England (Trueman 1994).

As with the Roman Catholic and WARC dialogues, the problem of Pentecostal representation was acknowledged in this exchange with the Lutheran World Federation, as was the lack of any Pentecostal equivalent to the Lutheran Augsburg Confession (1530) – that is, to a core statement or code of doctrine which might be said to define the movement. Even so, the common Pentecostal formulation of the 'full gospel', in which Christ exercises a five-fold office as Justifier, Sanctifier, Baptizer in the Spirit, Healer and Soon-Coming King, was seen as fertile ground for more convergent understanding of the faith, as was each tradition's commitment to the supremacy of scripture. These touchstones will no doubt also prove helpful should Anglican–Pentecostal discussions develop from their current tentative dynamic into more systematic theological engagement.

World Council of Churches Joint Consultative Group on Pentecostalism (JCGP)

Since 2000, a sustained process of dialogue between the World Council of Churches and Pentecostal representatives has developed in a Joint Consultative Group (JCGP) (World Council of Churches 2005, pp. 169–73). The initial report of the JCGP was published in 2005 and acknowledged the 'fears, stereotypes and apprehensions' which participants carried into the meetings, while constructively addressing key divergences over proselytism, sacraments, discernment of the Spirit and the nature of the Church. A second term of dialogue concentrated on the historic marks of the Church and reported to the Busan Assembly of the WCC in 2013 (World Council of Churches 2013b). The process is currently in its third term, is focused on discipleship and formation, and is due to issue a report on this topic in 2021 (World Council of Churches 2017).

While non-Pentecostals on the JCGP have come from church communities as diverse as Lutheran, Presbyterian, Methodist, Baptist, Russian, Greek and Romanian Orthodox, it is striking that no one has served on the Group as an Anglican representative, despite the fact that Anglican churches have been full members of the WCC since its inception in 1948. Even so, Anglicans have been actively involved in the WCC-sponsored Global Christian Forum (GCF) and the Conference of Secretaries of Christian World Communions (CSCWC). These are loosely constituted relational organizations which provide space for interaction between Pentecostal leaders and representatives of other Christian traditions (Jones, pp. 202–4). The GCF was conceived by the then WCC General Secretary Konrad Reiser in 1999 as a non-affiliated body designed specifically to enfranchise Pentecostals and independent evangelicals, among others. As an Anglican contributor, Sarah Rowland Jones, has described it, the GCF 'aims to bring together the widest possible range of Christians. Rather than focusing on questions of faith and order, its meetings begin with personal encounter through sharing faith journeys and exploring shared challenges faced by Christians ... The Anglican Communion actively supports this "affective" or "spiritual" ecumenism, as a means of complementing and strengthening more traditional ecumenical approaches' (Jones, p. 198). Continuing this more flexible approach, a second Global Gathering of the GCF took place in Manado, Indonesia in September 2011. The Archbishop of Canterbury sent formal greetings to it, and this writer was privileged to represent the Church of England and to read the Archbishop's message there. A third such Gathering of the GCF was convened in Bogota, Colombia, in April 2018 and explored the theme of 'Mutual Love' from Hebrews 13.1, and its role as a witness for peace, unity and discipleship (Global Christian Forum 2018). Both the Archbishop of Canterbury and the Anglican Communion were once again represented.

Although these trends indicate that greater partnership and co-operation is taking place between Pentecostals and a wide range of other church traditions, it remains the case that more distinctive bilateral ecumenical dialogue between Pentecostal and Anglican communities is still significantly underdeveloped – even if it is to move in the more 'affective' or 'spiritual' direction described by Jones. Hence the final section of this chapter proposes a more detailed rationale for theological, and more specifically ecclesiological, understanding between Pentecostals and Anglicans.

Theological and Ecclesiological Considerations

Many of the theological concerns raised in the Roman Catholic–Pentecostal, WARC/WCRC–Pentecostal, Lutheran–Pentecostal and WCC–JCGP bilateral reports are likely to recur in Anglican–Pentecostal dialogue. Pneumatology in general and the understanding and expression of charismata in particular; the process of spiritual discernment and models of biblical authority and hermeneutics; the nature of the

Church and criteria for Christian unity or koinonia; the 'prosperity gospel' and demonology and deliverance ministry – all these issues will surely command attention. However, certain concerns are likely to arise more specifically from the Anglican–Pentecostal dynamic, and not least from the expression of that dynamic in the English Anglican context.

Protestant and Non-Protestant Identities

As we have seen, the Church of England's self-understanding has often been marked by attempts to mediate between its Reformation formularies and its pre-Reformation or 'Catholic' roots. Like Anglicans, Pentecostals differ on the debt they owe to the Reformation, and the extent to which they might claim a 'Protestant' or 'evangelical' identity in addition to their particular claims to 'apostolic' authenticity (Yong 2005, pp. 235–52). A dedicated Anglican–Pentecostal dialogue could helpfully relate these self-understandings to practical ecumenical alignments between Anglicans and Pentecostals, and between Anglicans, Pentecostals and others.

Christian Initiation

Important questions arise at the Anglican–Pentecostal interface with respect to Christian initiation. Since Pentecostal churches are gathered 'believers' churches overwhelmingly practising adult baptism by immersion, Pentecostals can find the Church of England's commitment to infant baptism, and more particularly its undertaking to baptize all parishioners who come or are brought for baptism, challenging. If the issues at stake here are similar to those raised in recent Baptist–Anglican dialogues, a more distinctive question concerns the relationship, if any, between the Anglican practice of confirmation and the key Pentecostal doctrine of 'baptism in the Spirit'. The same New Testament texts (e.g. Acts 8.14–17; 19.1–7) are typically cited in apologetics for each, but for the most part Pentecostalism does not practise or recognize confirmation. Anglican–Pentecostal dialogue could thus usefully explore continuities and discontinuities between Anglican understandings of confirmation and Pentecostal models of conversion and baptism in and/or filling with the Spirit. This in turn would have implications for Anglican Charismatics, who are obliged by canon to hold confirmation and Spirit baptism in creative theological relationship. Possible rapprochement here is suggested by Laurence W. Wood, who construes 'holiness' emphases on Christian perfection in certain forms of Wesleyan and Pentecostal soteriology as a reinterpretation of Roman Catholic and

Anglican rites of confirmation (Wood, pp. 240–57). Hence Anglican and Catholic confirmation, like Wesley's concept of perfection or 'entire sanctification', is 'a second definitive work of grace in the life of the Christian believer', even if the Wesleyan doctrine of entire sanctification 'does not absolutize the concepts of crisis and subsequency' quite in the way that much Pentecostal soteriology tends to do (Wood, p. 242). More practically, the questions posed to Anglicans and Pentecostals by Martin Davie on this subject will be well worth addressing:

[Anglican and other] churches that practise confirmation might want to ask the Pentecostals what prevents them from recognizing the rite of confirmation as providing an occasion for people to receive the power and presence of the Holy Spirit in their lives in a new way ... On the other hand, the Pentecostals might want to ask those churches that practise confirmation for evidence that those who are confirmed really do receive the gift of the Spirit. Where, they might ask, are those supernatural signs of the Spirit's presence that are present in the New Testament accounts of the life of the early church and have been a key part of Pentecostal experience? (Davie, p. 88)

Given the inextricable relationship between pneumatology, initiation and discipleship, and the centrality of this relationship for Pentecostalism and Anglicanism alike (albeit with different emphases and expressions), it bodes well that the Joint Church of England–Pentecostal Steering Group has resolved to make this its first specific, formal area of theological exploration.

The Experience and Legacy of John Wesley

This presentation of Wesley as a 'bridge figure' between Anglican and proto-Pentecostal theologies of confirmation may be extended into other areas of theological dialogue between the two traditions. The rootedness of many Pentecostal churches in Wesleyan Holiness spirituality is significant here, as is the fact that despite his founding of Methodism, Wesley maintained a lifelong commitment to the Church of England (Kay, pp. 25–32). Wesley's development of a theology of experience, and of experience complementing scripture, reason and tradition as sources of theology, has been deeply influential on both Pentecostals and Anglicans. In a 2002 article for *Pneuma*, the journal of the Society for Pentecostal Studies, Edmund Rybarczyk comments on this Wesleyan link, but then makes a suggestive further connection,

via Wesley, between Anglicanism, Pentecostalism and Eastern Orthodoxy:

> Pentecostals built upon and reprocessed Wesley's own experiential
> foundations, foundations that were themselves modifications of the
> implications of Greek patristic theology. Through Wesley, Anglican-
> ism provides some historical connection between Pentecostalism and
> Orthodoxy. Because it severed its ties from Rome but continued to
> maintain the latter's … ecclesial system, Anglicanism understands
> itself to be a via media between Catholicism and Protestantism. [In
> turn] I think Pentecostalism can be viewed as a kind of mystical via
> media between Orthodoxy and more rational branches of Protestant-
> ism. (Rybarczyk, p. 23)

The significance of 'the Anglican Wesley' in this sense should not be
lost amid the fast-growing interest of Pentecostal scholars and leaders
in the 'Methodist', 'Holiness' and 'Perfectionist' Wesley as a precursor
to their own tradition – an interest demonstrated very clearly by the
fact that the 2013 conference of the Society for Pentecostal Studies
took place in conjunction with the Wesleyan Theological Society at the
Methodist-founded Seattle Pacific University, and focused on the theme
of Holiness (programme available at http://storage.cloversites.com/
societyforpentecostalstudies/documents/program_2013.pdf). This is a
subject which bears considerable further exploration at the Anglican–
Pentecostal interface.

Sacraments

Given the emphasis of many classical Pentecostals on believers' baptism, baptism in the Spirit as a 'second blessing' and speaking in
tongues as 'initial evidence' of such Spirit baptism, it might strike more
sacramentally minded Anglicans as strange that the Lord's Supper has
so relatively low a profile in most modern-day Pentecostal churches.
Building on the substantial work done on this area by the Catholic,
Reformed and Lutheran dialogues mentioned above, the more programmatic Anglican–Pentecostal theological dialogue that I am advocating
will need to explore the two traditions' respective understandings of
sacraments and sacramental life, and will need also to offer guidelines
for mutual reception of the Lord's Supper in each tradition. In doing so,
it may well pursue John Christopher Thomas' suggestion that although
many Pentecostals prefer to present sacraments in terms of 'ordinances',
Pentecostal 'sacramentality' might be seen as having been reconfigured

into a five-fold pattern of water baptism, foot washing, glossolalia and anointing with oil, alongside the Lord's Supper understood mainly in terms of Christ the Coming King (Thomas, pp. 18–19).

Ministry, Apostolicity and Episcopacy

Ecumenical dialogues between Anglicans and others have been significantly shaped by Anglicans' insistence on the three-fold order of deacons, priests and bishops as a key mark of their ecclesial identity (Meissen Agreement 1988). Certain Pentecostal churches appoint their leaders as 'bishops', but others do not. Even those who do so, however, typically apply a pragmatic approach related to function rather than any more 'catholic' notion of 'apostolic succession' linked to episcopal orders. As one leader of the New Testament Assembly has put it, 'In the sixties we called them Superintendents; in the seventies we changed the name to Overseers; more recently we have been calling them Bishops' (interview with Nezlin Sterling, 27 January 2011). Most Pentecostal churches term their ministers 'pastors' rather than 'priests', and deacons are rarer. Some ordain women as pastors and bishops; others do not. Some do not ordain church leaders at all, whereas others ordain pastors and non-pastors alike to a wide range of offices and tasks, defined not least in relation to the 'five-fold' pattern of Ephesians 4.11 (apostle, prophet, evangelist, pastor and teacher). Anglican–Pentecostal dialogue would benefit from exploring lines of rapprochement and divergence on such models of ministry and leadership, and could suggest ways in which orders and offices might be mutually recognized across the two traditions.

More specifically, it will be worth noting that the concept of apostolicity has been radically reapplied in certain Pentecostal and Charismatic communities, as a designation merited by those who plant churches, oversee church networks or otherwise lead significant numbers of Christians, regardless of whether or how they might have been ordained (Warrington, pp. 138–42). Terry Virgo, leader of the neo-Charismatic network New Frontiers International, argues for apostleship as a modern-day designation of church planting as well as a description of those directly appointed by Christ or privy to his resurrection (www.terryvirgo.org). Once again this apparently functional, mission-driven approach presents challenges to more institutionalized understandings of apostolicity linked to episcopacy – challenges which have already been recognized and addressed in some depth by the Roman Catholic–Pentecostal dialogue, but which could benefit from fruitful re-examination in the distinct but related context of Anglican–Pentecostal interaction (Gros, pp. 731–3; 747–8).

Mission, Social Action and Proselytism

Dialogues between 'magisterial' Christian traditions and Pentecostals have characteristically revealed differences of theology and practice with respect to mission. Whereas churches shaped by a 'Christendom' paradigm have tended to relate mission to inculturation of the gospel within societies and nation states, and have developed missiologies and public theologies to match, Pentecostals have typically promulgated a 'believers' church' ethos in which mission is understood principally in terms of evangelism, or what the Elim scholar Keith Warrington more precisely calls 'enlargement of the Church' – that is, in terms of personal conversion, immersion baptism and incorporation into the local congregation. Although as noted above some are now developing distinctive Pentecostal theologies and missiologies of social concern, Warrington has nonetheless reported 'limited social involvement' as a trait of Pentecostal mission (Warrington, p. 263), and we have already noted how the WARC/WCRC–Pentecostal dialogue in particular has highlighted the need for Pentecostals to develop a more holistic 'extra-ecclesial' pneumatology in which the gifts of the Spirit are seen to be applied in the service of the common good, and in which the prophetic racial and gender inclusiveness of Azusa Street is recovered and reasserted (WARC, pp. 6ff.). As we have also noted, recent moves by Anglican evangelicals and Charismatics to promote more holistic paradigms such as the 'Five Marks of Mission' mean that creative Anglican–Pentecostal engagement on social action should be possible (Anglican Communion 2018).

Liturgiology and Doxology

As Anne Dyer observes, Pentecostal worship is distinguished by its preference for 'freedom of expression and extempore prayer'. While this might appear to contrast with an Anglican polity defined to a significant degree by its attachment to canonical liturgical texts like the Book of Common Prayer and *Common Worship*, Dyer echoes a number of linguistic and theological studies when she suggests that 'there is often an underlying oral liturgy in Pentecostal services'. The formative work of Bruce A. Rosenberg and subsequent studies by Daniel Albrecht and James Steven bear this out (Dyer, p. 144; Rosenberg; Albrecht). Although Anglican–Pentecostal dialogue will no doubt highlight significant differences of approach in this area, the more general instinct toward 'structuring' and 'ordering' worship, even when it is not codified in writing, will be worth exploring.

Having said this, Anglican Charismatic worship, at least, often sits quite lightly to the canonical liturgies of its own denominational tradition, and typically more resembles the ethos of Pentecostal worship. By the same token, fieldwork undertaken on ten core services in eight Pentecostal and Charismatic congregations by this author as part of the research that helped persuade the Council for Christian Unity to designate Anglican–Pentecostal relations as an ecumenical priority in 2013 revealed the emergence of a more generic version of 'free worship', distinct in certain respects from the ethos of classical Pentecostalism. For example, whereas the open exercise of charismata is typically taken to be a defining mark of Pentecostalism, not one of the services studied featured a prophecy, word of knowledge, tongue or interpretation from within the congregation. Nor was 'ministry' to individuals conducted within the service itself; rather, it was offered as a separate event after the service proper had concluded with a blessing or dismissal. Likewise, whereas regular celebration of the Lord's Supper has been identified as a mark of earlier classical Pentecostal worship (Hollenweger, pp. 385–90), communion was celebrated in only one of these ten services (survey of public worship services conducted between January and March 2011).

This apparent shift of approach to public worship resonates with a key trend highlighted by Dyer – namely the rise of the 'music leader' and 'the music group', whose playing of extended 'praise songs' has become a common feature of worship in these contexts. Such songs, indeed, seem now to offer the main opportunity for ecstatic congregational expression in these settings, with the exercise of charismata by 'the people' becoming relatively less prominent. Calvin Johansson has also noted these trends, and has critiqued them as seemingly spontaneous but in fact 'highly scripted' and 'carefully orchestrated', on the basis that 'orders of songs, numbers of repetitions, keys and decibel levels require pre-planning and rehearsal' (Johansson, pp. 370–1). Indeed, for Johansson, Pentecostal worship has 'maintained its subjective and emotional approach but ... to a considerable extent it has dropped true congregational spontaneity and a good share of congregational participation for the appearance of spontaneity which is highly planned and dominated by worship leaders' (Johansson, p. 371).

Perhaps this pattern was reinforced in the generally larger congregations featured in the survey for the Council for Christian Unity, where the ability of all to hear a prophecy, word of knowledge or tongue was limited, and where the imperatives of starting, finishing and even broadcasting successive services on time made for a more programmatic and controlled style, driven 'from the front'. Anglican–

Pentecostal dialogue could helpfully explore the development of this new 'common order' and assess what has been lost and gained by it in relation to more established approaches in each tradition, and in relation to the implicit pneumatology being mediated in each case.

Continuing the 'Harper Legacy'

As the dialogue outlined above is developed, it will owe much to Michael Harper. Although he later left the Church of England to become a priest and then archpriest in the Antiochian Orthodox Church, there can be little doubt that apart, perhaps, from Boddy, he was the most influential ecumenical partner to Pentecostals that Anglicanism has yet produced.

Shortly before he died in 2010, Harper gave an address at an event held to mark the centenary of the Sunderland Revival (Harper). Among other things, the address was a passionate call to Pentecostals and Charismatics to engage with Eastern Orthodox theology and spirituality, and Harper would be glad to know of recent attempts by Harold Hunter and others to take forward the interaction between these traditions that he fostered toward the end of his life (Hunter 2017). Warming to his theme, Harper rejoiced in the increased openness of Pentecostals to historic ecumenical concerns with 'the Church itself, her sacraments, liturgy and authority'. Yet he also rejoiced in the successive 'waves of the Spirit' that had refreshed and energized that same church in revival, Pentecostal outpouring and Charismatic Renewal. 'Let us weigh all things carefully, let us test the spirits', he concluded, 'but let us then welcome the new waves as they come in, and bathe ourselves in them' (Harper, p. 21). It is sincerely to be hoped that this judicious blend of discernment, openness and enthusiasm will mark the future development of Anglican–Pentecostal dialogue that has been mapped out here, and that with its distinctive features and themes, that dialogue will make a major contribution to the wider ecumenical understanding of Pentecostalism, and to Pentecostalism's appreciation of the world-wide church.

References

Albrecht, Daniel E., 1999, *Rites in the Spirit: A Ritual Approach to Pentecostal/Charismatic Spirituality.* Sheffield: Sheffield Academic Press.
Anderson, Allan, 2004, *An Introduction to Pentecostalism: Global Charismatic Christianity.* Cambridge: Cambridge University Press.

Anglican Communion, 2018, 'Marks of Mission', www.anglicancommunion. org/mission/marks-of-mission.aspx accessed 6 November 2018.

Anglican–Methodist Working Party, 2012, *Fresh Expressions in the Mission of the Church*. London: Church House Publishing.

Avis, Paul, 2010, *Reshaping Ecumenical Theology: The Church Made Whole?* London: T&T Clark.

Bradshaw, Tim, 1992, *The Olive Branch: An Evangelical Anglican Doctrine of the Church*. Carlisle: Paternoster.

Chan, Simon, 2011, 'Pentecostal Ecclesiology: An Essay on the Development of Doctrine' *Journal of Pentecostal Theology Supplement series*, 38. Blandford Forum: Deo Publishing.

Church of England Mission and Public Affairs Council, 2004, *Mission-Shaped Church: Church Planting and Fresh Expressions of Church in a Changing Context*. London: Church House Publishing.

Churches Together in England, 2014, 'Anglican-Pentecostal Consultation', www.cte.org.uk/Groups/238045/Home/Resources/Ecumenical_Dialogues/ Anglican_Pentecostal_Consultation/Anglican_Pentecostal_Consultation.aspx accessed 4 November 2018.

Davie, Martin, 2011, 'Confirmation and Christian Unity', in Avis, Paul (ed.), *The Journey of Christian Initiation: Theological and Pastoral Perspectives*. London: Church House Publishing.

Dyer, Anne, 2004, 'Worship: Introduction', in Kay, William K. and Anne E. Dyer (eds), *Pentecostal and Charismatic Studies: A Reader*. London: SCM Press.

Global Christian Forum, 2018, 'Take up the Challenge of "Mutual Love" as Witness for Peace, Unity and Discipleship urged Global Christian Forum Message', https://gcforum.worldsecuresystems.com/news accessed 6 November 2018.

Green, Chris E. W. (ed.), 2016, *Pentecostal Ecclesiology: A Reader*. Leiden/ Boston: Brill.

Gritsch, Eric W., 'Was Luther Anti-Semitic?' *Christianity Today*, Issue 39, www. christianitytoday.com/history/issues/issue-39/was-luther-anti-semitic.html

Gros, Jeffrey FSC, Harding, Meyer and Rusch, William G. (eds), 2000, *Growth in Agreement II: Reports and Agreed Statements of Ecumenical Conversations on a World Level, 1982–1998*. Faith and Order Paper, no 187. Geneva: WCC Publications; Grand Rapids, MI: Eerdmans.

Hardy, Daniel W., 2001, *Finding the Church: The Dynamic Truth of Anglicanism*. London: SCM Press.

Harper, Michael, 2008, *The Waves Keep Coming In: The Evangelical, Charismatic*, Orthodox Axis, Cambridge: Target.

Harrison, D. E. W. and Michael C. Sansom, 1982, *Worship in the Church of England*. London: SPCK.

Ho Yan Au, Connie, 2011, *Grassroots Unity in the Charismatic Renewal*. Eugene, OR: Wipf & Stock.

Hocken, Peter, 1997, *Streams of Renewal: The Origins and Early Development of the Charismatic Movement in Great Britain*, 2nd edn. Carlisle: Paternoster.

Hollenweger, Walter, 1972, *The Pentecostals*. London: SCM Press.

Hunter, Harold, 2016, 'International Dialogue between the WCRC and Classical Pentecostals.' IPHC, https://iphc.org/gso/2016/12/23/international- dialogue-wcrc-classical-pentecostals/ accessed 5 November 2018.

Hunter, Harold, 2017, 'Orthodox–Pentecostal Conversations', https://iphc.org/gso/2017/03/16/orthodox-pentecostal-conversations/ accessed 6 November 2018.

Institute for Ecumenical Research et al., Lutherans and Pentecostals in Dialogue, World Council of Churches, 2005, Joint Consultative Group WCC-Pentecostals (JCPG) 2000–2005: Excerpts from the Report to the Ninth Assembly, in *Programme Book: Ninth Assembly*, Porto Allegre, WCC: Geneva

Institute for Ecumenical Research, David Du Plessis Center for Christian Spirituality & European Pentecostal Charismatic Research Association, 2010, *Lutherans and Pentecostals in Dialogue*. Strasbourg; Pasadena; Zurich: Institute for Ecumenical Research, www.strasbourginstitute.org/en/dialogues/lutheran-pentecostal-dialogue/

Johansson, Calvin, 2002, 'Pentecostal Worship', in Bradshaw, Paul (ed.), *New SCM Dictionary of Liturgy and Worship*. London: SCM Press.

Jones, Sarah Rowland (ed.), 2009, *The Vision Before Us: The Kyoto Report of the Inter-Anglican Standing Commission on Ecumenical Relations, 2000–2008*. London: Anglican Communion Office.

Kärkkäinen, Veli-Matti, 2002, *Toward a Pneumatological Theology: Pentecostal and Ecumenical Perspectives on Ecclesiology, Soteriology and Theology of Mission*. Lanham, MD: University Press of America.

Kay, William K., 2009, *Pentecostalism*. SCM Core Text. London: SCM Press.

Leith, John H., 1981, *Introduction to the Reformed Tradition*, revised edn. Atlanta: John Knox.

Lings, George, 2017, *Reproducing Churches*. Abingdon: BRF.

Lord, Andy, 2012, *Network Church: A Pentecostal Ecclesiology Shaped by Mission*. Leiden/Boston: Brill.

Lord, Andy, 2016, 'Mission Eschatology: A Framework for Mission in the Spirit', in Green, C. (ed.), *Pentecostal Ecclesiology*, pp. 113–23. Leiden/Boston: Brill.

Lutheran World Federation, 2016, 'Lutheran-Pentecostal Dialogue Aims to Create Better Understanding and Witness.' Baguio, Philippines; Geneva: LWF, www.lutheranworld.org/news/lutheran-pentecostal-dialogue-aims-create-better-understanding-and-witness accessed 6 November 2018.

Macchia, Frank, D., 2006, *Baptized in the Spirit: A Global Pentecostal Theology*. Grand Rapids, MI: Zondervan.

MacCulloch, Diarmaid, 1991, 'The Myth of the English Reformation', *Journal of British Studies*, Vol. 30 Issue 1.

Marshall, Ruth, 2009, *Political Spiritualities: The Pentecostal Revolution in Nigeria*. Chicago: University of Chicago Press.

Meissen Agreement, 1988, text available at www.churchofengland.org/sites/default/files/2017-11/meissen_english.pdf accessed 6 November 2018.

Miller, Donald E. and Tetsuanao Yamamori, 2007, *Global Pentecostalism: The New Face of Christian Social Engagement*. Berkeley, CA: University of California Press.

Nelstrop, Louise and Martyn Percy (eds), 2008, *Evaluating Fresh Expressions*. Norwich: Canterbury Press.

Old, Hughes Oliphant, 1992, *Themes and Variations for a Christian Doxology: Some Thoughts on the Theology of Worship*. Grand Rapids, MI: Eerdmans.

Petersen, Douglas, 1996, *Not by Might nor by Power: Pentecostal Theology of Social Concern in Latin America*. Carlisle: Paternoster.

Roman Catholic Church, 1984, *Final Report of the Dialogue between the Secretariat for Promoting Christian Unity of the Roman Catholic Church and some Classical Pentecostals,* www.vatican.va/roman_curia/pontifical_councils/chrstuni/pentecostals/rc_pc_chrstuni_doc_19840509_final-report-pentecostals_en.html accessed 5 November 2018.

Roman Catholic Church, 2015, *'Do Not Quench the Spirit': Charisms in the Life and Mission of the Church: Report of the Sixth Phase of the International Catholic–Pentecostal Dialogue(2011–2015),* www.vatican.va/roman_curia/pontifical_councils/chrstuni/pentecostals/rc_pc_chrstuni_doc_2011-2015_do-not-quench-the-spirit_en.html accessed 5 November 2018.

Rosenberg, Bruce A., 1970, *The Art of the American Folk Preacher.* Cambridge: Cambridge University Press.

Rybarczyk, Edmund, 2002, 'Spiritualities Old and New: Similarities between Eastern Orthodoxy and Classical Pentecostalism', *Pnuema*, Vol. 24 Issue 1.

Sandidge, Jerry L., 1987, *Roman Catholic/Pentecostal Dialogue (1977–1982): A Study in Developing Ecumenism.* Frankfurt am Main: Peter Lang.

Steven, James H. S., 2003, *Worship in the Spirit: Charismatic Worship in the Church of England,* Carlisle: Paternoster

Stevenson, Kenneth and Spinks, Bryan (eds), 1991, *The Identity of Anglican Worship.* London: Mowbray.

Tanis, Phil, 2016, 'Reformed–Pentecostal Dialogue Focuses on Mission and Salvation.' World Communion of Reformed Churches, http://wcrc.ch/news/reformed-pentecostal-dialogue-focuses-on-mission-and-salvation accessed 5 November 2018.

Tanis, Phil, 2017, 'Reformed–Pentecostal Dialogue Focuses on Mission and Ecclesiology.' World Communion of Reformed Churches, http://wcrc.ch/news/reformed-pentecostal-dialogue-focses-on-mission-and-ecclesiology accessed 5 November 2018.

Thomas, John Christopher, 1998, 'Pentecostal Theology in the Twenty-First Century', *Pneuma*, Vol. 20.

Trueman, C. R., 1994, *Luther's Legacy: Salvation and the English Reformers 1525–1556*, Oxford: Clarendon Press.

Vondey, Wolfgang, 2010, *Beyond Pentecostalism: The Crisis of Global Christianity and the Renewal of the Theological Agenda.* Grand Rapids, MI: Eerdmans.

Vondey, Wolfgang (ed.), 2010, *Pentecostalism and Christian Unity: Ecumenical Documents and Critical Assessments.* Eugene, OR: Pickwick.

Vondey, Wolfgang (ed.), 2013, *Pentecostalism and Christian Unity (Vol Two): Continuing and Building Relationships.* Eugene, OR: Pickwick.

Wakefield, Gavin, 2007a, *The First Pentecostal Anglican: The Life and Legacy of Alexander Boddy.* Cambridge: Grove Books.

Wakefield, Gavin, 2007b, *Alexander Boddy: Pentecostal Anglican Pioneer.* Milton Keynes: Paternoster.

Warrington, Keith, 2008, *Pentecostal Theology: A Theology of Encounter.* London: Continuum.

Williams, Rowan, 2000, *On Christian Theology.* Oxford: Blackwell.

Wolterstorff, Nicholas, 1992, 'The Reformed Liturgy', in McKim, Donald K. (ed.), *Major Themes in the Reformed Tradition*, pp. 273–304. Grand Rapids, MI: Eerdmans.

Wood, Laurence W., 1980, *Pentecostal Grace*. Grand Rapids, MI: Francis Asbury.

World Alliance of Reformed Churches, 2000, 'Word and Spirit, Church & World', https://ecumenism.net/archive/docu/2000_pent_warc_word_spirit_church_world.pdf

World Alliance of Reformed Churches, 2012, 'Experience in Christian Faith and Life: Worship, Discipleship, Discernment, Community, and Justice: the Report of the International Dialogue between Representatives of the World Alliance of Reformed Churches and some Classical Pentecostal Churches, 2001–2011', *Cyberjournal for Pentecostal–Charismatic Research*, #21, www.pctii.org/cyberj/cyberj21/WARC_2011d.html accessed 5 November 2018.

World Council of Churches, 2005, *The Nature and Mission of the Church*. Faith and Order Paper 198. Geneva: WCC.

World Council of Churches, 2013a, *The Church: Towards a Common Vision*. Faith and Order Paper No. 214. Geneva: World Council of Churches.

World Council of Churches, 2013b, 'Report of the Joint Consultative Group between Pentecostals and the World Council of Churches.' Document 14. Bossey, Switzerland: WCC, downloaded from www.oikoumene.org/en/resources/documents/executive-committee/2013-03/jcg-report accessed 6 November 2018.

World Council of Churches, 2017, 'WCC and Pentecostals Discuss Discipleship and Formation in California', www.oikoumene.org/en/press-centre/news/wcc-and-pentecostals-discuss-discipleship-and-formation-in-california accessed 6 November 2018.

Yong, Amos, 2002, 'The Word and the Spirit or the Spirit and the Word: Exploring the Boundaries of Evangelicalism in Relationship to Modern Pentecostalism', *Trinity Journal* Vol. 3 Issue 2.

Yong, Amos, 2005, *The Spirit Poured Out on All Flesh: Pentecostalism and the Possibility of Global Theology*. Grand Rapids, MI: Baker Academic.

9

The European Protestant Reformation and Global Pentecostalism

ALLAN H. ANDERSON

One of the most famous Christian women in the world in the early twentieth century was the Indian scholar and philanthropist Pandita Ramabai, a remarkable Christian leader, social reformer and Bible translator, who penned these words in 1905:

> Let the revival come to Indians so as to suit their nature and feelings, [as] God has made them. He knows their nature, and He will work out His purpose in them in a way which may not conform with the ways of Western people and their lifelong training. Let the English and other Western missionaries begin to study the Indian nature, I mean the religious inclinations, the emotional side of the Indian mind. Let them not try to conduct revival meetings and devotional exercises altogether in Western ways and conform with Western etiquette. If our Western teachers and foreignised Indian leaders want the work of God to be carried on among us in their own way, they are sure to stop or spoil it. (*Bombay Guardian and Banner of Asia*, 7 November 1905, p. 9)

This quotation has implications for discussion on the legacy of what was a very Western European dispute, the Reformation. She reminds us not to rely on Western forms of Christianity to try and satisfy 'nature and feelings' that are found in very different cultures worldwide.

Those churches in the Western world that were a direct outcome of the Reformation are mostly denominations in serious decline. It is an open question whether they have much relevance in the contemporary world, especially in their countries of origin. The future of Christianity seems to lie elsewhere, perhaps in Charismatic Catholicism and evangelicalism, especially of the Pentecostal and Charismatic varieties. It can be argued that the transformation in world Christianity during the past century has been more profound than the Reformation ever was

(Anderson 2013). On the other hand, we live in a very different world today, where Christianity no longer dominates the political, economic and social landscape as it did in sixteenth-century Europe. As William Kay points out, for this reason Pentecostalism 'is closer to a renewal movement than a movement of broad reformation' (Kay, p. 3). However, the majority of Christians now live outside the Western world, and a significant proportion are Pentecostals and Charismatics. This alone makes the European Reformation rather a distant influence.

In this chapter, I will first address the historical and theological context of global Pentecostalism. Although it is historically and theologically linked to the European Reformation through its origins in radical forms of evangelicalism, the transformations that have occurred in recent years have taken it far beyond the Reformation principles. It will be seen nevertheless that these principles continue to characterize all evangelical forms of Christianity. Second, I focus on evangelical missions, their role in the emergence of Pentecostalism throughout the world, and in what ways they are a part of the legacy of the Protestant Reformation. Finally, I consider what relevance if any, this legacy has for global Pentecostalism today.

The Historical and Theological Context

October 2017 was the 500th anniversary of Luther's posting his 95 theses on the church door in Wittenberg, heralded as the beginning of the Protestant Reformation. There was much in this event that meant a new era for all forms of Christianity. Luther's principles railing against organized and ritualistic religion, and his insistence on 'faith alone, grace alone, scripture alone' continue to be founding principles of both contemporary evangelicalism and its offspring Pentecostalism. One could even say, as many scholars have, that evangelicalism is the contemporary result of the Reformation. Luther's Protestantism was a 'protest' against the prevailing practices of the Catholic Church in German states, and he affirmed the priesthood of all believers, salvation by grace through faith (without the need for clergy or sacraments) and a reliance on the Bible (*sola scriptura*) as the basis of final religious authority (Balmer, p. 13). The Reformation remains a 'defining point of reference' in evangelical consciousness for these reasons, but there were also differences. As McGrath points out, evangelism (in the sense of converting 'unbelievers') was not a priority for either Luther or Calvin, except when it meant the conversion of Catholics to Protestantism (McGrath, p. 15). It would be almost two centuries before any Protestant missionaries were sent out. Evangelism has been a priority of evangelicalism and Pentecostalism that has set them apart from most of the historic Reformation churches.

The Reformation also created a new plurality within Christianity. The individualistic ideas of the Reformation quickly created a splintering within Protestantism in Luther's lifetime that he was later to regret, but which has now come to characterize Pentecostalism ever since its beginnings in the early twentieth century. As one of my friends once put it, Pentecostalism has succeeded in creating more schisms in a century than it took the rest of Christianity in two thousand years. Each split considers itself to have discovered the true meaning of the Bible. The sad fact is that the Reformation set off a chain of schisms within Western Christianity that continue to the present day in Pentecostal and Charismatic churches.

It is an almost impossible task to define what we mean by 'Pentecostalism' with any precision, for it is an incredibly diverse movement that has gone through a constant process of division, recombination and re-formation. I consider most Pentecostal denominations today to be a subset of evangelicalism, although with certain distinctions. Defining these movements is particularly an acute task when even 'evangelical' has become a dirty word in the media, particularly through the so-called 'Religious Right'. White American 'evangelicals', including most Pentecostals, have been notorious in their support of Donald Trump, even though the vast majority of black-led evangelical and Pentecostal churches, and Hispanic ones, did not. So we need to be clear that 'evangelical' is a theological position rather than a socio-political one.

Historically, the radical, or Anabaptist, Reformation is often seen as the only really 'evangelical' Reformation, more so than either the Lutheran and Reformed Reformations were, for the latter were still wedded to the idea of a Church–state union. The Anabaptist movement represents a type of proto-evangelicalism. The term 'Anabaptist' means 'rebaptizer' and at first signified a heretic, and therefore someone subject to condemnation and execution. The Augsburg confession of 1530 condemned the Anabaptists in three articles: because (1) they denied the validity of the office of the bishop; (2) they denied the authority of the established Church (whether Catholic or Protestant); and (3) they repudiated infant baptism because they believed that an infant was not ready to receive baptism on New Testament terms. They called for baptism only on confession of faith and commitment to discipleship by the candidate. For them, infant baptism was not biblical baptism, and so they denied that they were 'rebaptizers'. But their real objection to the name 'Anabaptist' was that they refused to be classed as heretics and to be reckoned as not being the true Church. On the contrary, they had a deep conviction that they were the true Church and that the Roman Catholic and Protestant churches were the false churches.

We should also not romanticize the Lutheran Reformation. Luther himself tolerated no dissent in the German lands he influenced, and he led a fierce persecution of Anabaptists, condemning them to death. His criticism of them was that because 'we have heard or learned a few things about Holy scripture, we think we are already doctors and have swallowed the Holy Ghost, feathers and all' (Zrimec 2010). This searing criticism was extended: 'No yokel is so rude but when he has dreams and fancies, he thinks himself inspired by the Holy Ghost and must be a prophet.' Luther supported a violent suppression of the peasants' uprising to demand their human rights in 1525. Luther was also a virulent anti-Semite who advocated the burning of Jewish houses and synagogues and the plundering of their goods, which undoubtedly paved the way for Hitler's Holocaust (Gritsch; Kay, p. 9). In short, Luther would not take kindly to the majority of Pentecostals today.

Most Anabaptist groups emigrated to South Russia, the Netherlands and North America to escape the severe persecution. The seventeenth-century English Baptists, who had met Anabaptist Mennonites in the Netherlands during their exile there, took part of the 'Anabaptist' name and passed it down to their millions of spiritual descendants, one of the largest evangelical denominations today. Not all Anabaptists and Baptists are evangelical, but the majority are. The importance of this movement to Pentecostalism is their emphases on the priesthood of all believers, the separation of the true Church from the state, a personal experience of Christ through new birth before a person could be called a Christian, and a high standard of morality in communities separated from the world. These remain defining characteristics of most Pentecostal churches today.

In the English-speaking world, the word 'evangelical' now has a narrower meaning to include those groups of different denominations that were associated with the 'evangelical revivals' that started in the eighteenth and nineteenth centuries. Their roots are found in John Wesley's Methodism and the Reformed revivalism of Jonathan Edwards and George Whitefield, and continued through such well-known figures as Charles Finney and Dwight Moody. These revivals could also be identified as 'proto-Pentecostal' as they were characterized by long, emotional services and ecstatic manifestations of the moving of the Spirit. They resulted in a surge in evangelical missionaries heading all over the world. Historically, these included the early Methodists in the late eighteenth and early nineteenth centuries, and those revivalists associated with the Great Evangelical Awakening of the eighteenth century and the Second Evangelical Awakening of the mid-nineteenth century. Significantly for this subject, the evangelical revivals resulted in a rapid increase in numbers of 'evangelical' missionaries coming to India, China, Africa and other parts of the world in the nineteenth century and beyond.

Today there are many thousands of different groups and denominations worldwide who call themselves 'evangelical'. They share many things in common with Pentecostals, but especially these two: a high view of the Bible as having supreme authority in matters of life and doctrine, and the need for evangelism or sharing the faith with those who are not Christians – according to evangelical definitions of what a 'Christian' is. The aim is that the 'unconverted' might be converted, 'born again' or 'saved' through the atoning work of Christ. There have been various attempts to define evangelicalism by reference to its theological emphases. Most of these attempts say the same things in different ways. Although general theological principles may be said to characterize evangelicalism as a whole (and indeed, they also characterize the early Protestant Reformation), they do not all have the same emphasis in different movements or at different times in history. Evangelicalism has remained stubbornly diverse.

Evangelical Revivalism and Missions

The statement that the Protestant Reformation and the Evangelical Revivals had consequences for evangelicalism and, by proxy, Pentecostalism today needs qualification, especially when referring to the majority world. As Diarmaid MacCulloch points out, 'It is always unpredictable as to which beliefs from the Reformation past will suddenly re-emerge' (MacCulloch, p. 700). For a start, the Reformation could be said to have had only an indirect effect on global Pentecostalism. In seventeenth-century Western Europe a spiritual renewal movement within Protestant churches known as Pietism began, where the importance of individual holiness or 'piety' through Bible study and prayer was the focus. The Pietists saw themselves as the true heirs of the Reformation principles. In the next century a similar renewal movement began in Britain, Ireland and the American colonies marked by revivalist meetings and evangelistic fervour. The revivals associated with the early Methodists and the Congregationalist Jonathan Edwards in North America, known in Britain as the 'Evangelical Revival' and in America as the 'Great Awakening', were the ancestors of the evangelicalism and Pentecostalism that was to spread throughout the world in the twentieth century.

Evangelicalism as we know it today has a long past, but the term only acquired its present meaning in the mid-nineteenth century. Most of the evangelical revival movements in the last three centuries were accompanied by various ecstatic manifestations and spiritual gifts. There was always a measure of 'Pentecostalism' in evangelical history. Most historians agree that the most enduring influence on evangelicalism, and consequently on Pentecostalism, came through eighteenth-century Methodism, which in turn was heavily influenced by the Moravian movement led by Count Nikolaus Ludwig von Zinzendorf, himself a graduate of the Pietist-inspired Martin Luther Halle University in Germany. He was also a disciple of its famed professor August Hermann Francke, the leading Pietist of the time. At first Pietism was a movement within the Lutheran churches in German states seeking a return to the Reformation ideals of personal piety and evangelical devotion. The Danish-Halle Mission was the first Protestant mission, initiated by the Pietist Danish King Frederick IV to send missionaries to the Danish colony (1620–1845) of Tranquebar, in south-east India – part of present-day Tamil Nadu. The first Protestant missionaries were German Pietists: Bartholomeus Ziegenbalg and Henry Plütschau went there in 1706 from Halle.

The legacy of the Protestant Reformation is seen in its effect on Christian missions, that quickly began the expansion of Christianity into a global movement. The 'Great Century' of missions was the period after the French Revolution until the beginning of World War One, when Europe imposed its will and ideas on the whole world. Christianity was seen as inseparably connected with European civilization. By 1800, Asia and Africa had hardly been touched by Christianity in proportion to the overall populations, and Indian Christianity was restricted to the south-west of the subcontinent, almost entirely Syrian Orthodox or Roman Catholic. The nineteenth century was relatively peaceful in Europe and the Industrial Revolution gave Europe the advantage in speed and power. There was a new passion for exploration and expansion into unknown lands. Captain James Cook led the way to Australia and the Pacific in the eighteenth century, and the missionary David Livingstone brought home stories of the exotic interior of Africa a century later. European countries, but especially Britain and France, began their conquest of Asian and African lands. A religious awakening in Europe accompanied the colonization that occurred throughout the world.

Despite the rather bad press given the foreign missionaries' links with colonization, there can be little doubt that they contributed much to

Christianity throughout the world. As a direct result of the Protestant Reformation's emphasis on *sola scriptura*, one of the biggest contributions made by Protestant missionaries was to translate the Bible into the vernacular. They saw this as their first and perhaps most important task. During the nineteenth century the number of Bible translations rose from 70 in 1800 to 520 by 1900, consisting of 100 whole Bibles and 120 New Testaments. In addition, missionaries established many schools for training leaders for the church and teaching people to read the Bible. These schools were often the foundation for democratic nationalistic movements, and especially pioneered the education of women. They promoted improvements through hospitals and agriculture, trained doctors and nurses, and established universities and colleges that exist to this day. Single women missionaries began to be sent to Asia in the mid-1800s, and by 1900 women missionaries greatly outnumbered men.

The training of the future indigenous leaders of the Church was another legacy of Protestant missions. At first, missionaries also made use of what was called 'Native agency'. By 1900, in many missions, numbers of ordained nationals exceeded foreigners but they were often subordinate. This was stark in the case of the Roman Catholics and the Anglicans. By 1900 neither Church had a bishop of non-European origin, and Protestant missions were no better. Although Protestant mission leaders Henry Venn, Secretary of the Church Missionary Society, and Rufus Anderson of the American Board of Commissioners for Foreign Missions called for self-governing, self-supporting and self-propagating churches in 1854, this policy was not fully implemented for another century.

It is clear that missions and colonialism were in a complex relationship. Missionaries almost always preceded colonizers, because wherever British missions were, British rule often followed. There was often conflict between the colonial powers and their respective missionaries, who were often banned and expelled. Missions had to negotiate with colonizers, who could restrict them. Colonial governments kept Christian missionaries out of Muslim areas, thereby indirectly promoting the advance of Islam. The British East India Company (EIC) financed Hindu and Muslim religious festivals, but banned Indian Christians from military or government jobs and refused Christian missionaries permission to work in British India. However, in 1813 the EIC was forced by Parliament to allow them, through pressure by evangelical elites in the Clapham Sect, famous for their efforts to abolish slavery. Their belief in the need for the evangelization of India was their second most important cause.

In 1813, when the EIC's charter came due for renewal, the Clapham Sect mobilized public opinion in Britain and secured half a million signatures on petitions. They eventually succeeded in overturning the vested interests of the company and gained a 'Missionary Clause' in the new charter. Thus the precedent was set for missionaries to go not only to India and China but to any place where Britain had a presence – much of the world in those days. The new British evangelical missionaries after this were not as sensitive as the earlier ones had been. As Mallampalli described the situation in India, they 'employed a style of preaching that fomented tensions' and 'attacked Indian cultural and religious traditions' (p. 539).

So, sometimes missionaries acted like colonial agents, especially when financed by the state, as in the case of Spain and Portugal. But white colonialists also often silenced and punished troublesome missionaries, and distrusted missionaries on the whole as promoters of dangerous egalitarian doctrines. British missionaries sometimes used their influence to attempt to change colonial policies, but they did not always want an end to colonialism. Some missionaries opposed slavery and forced labour in Kenya and South Africa, and the opium trade in China; they supported indigenous land rights in Africa, and called for the punishment of abuse by settlers and colonial officials in Africa and India. Most missionaries were not activists, but saw that their primary role was to convert people to Christianity. But they also tried to reform societies in such practices as polygamy, child marriage, widow-burning, female infanticide, female circumcision, foot-binding and indigenous slavery. Of course, these reform attempts also had hostile reactions from local people.

The Reformation Legacy for Global Pentecostalism

This was the situation when early Pentecostal missionaries began going all over the world at the beginning of the twentieth century. At this time there was a sharp increase in missionary activities. Societies of the 'faith mission' type were increasing and non-denominational independent missionaries abounded. Places like India and China were regarded as lands of unparalleled opportunities. As far as they were concerned, these were countries whose people were receptive to the gospel as never before. Pentecostal missionaries were inspired by their evangelical forebears. One missionary report quoted in the British Pentecostal Missionary Union magazine in 1913 put it:

> The removal of long standing obstacles, the eagerness of the people to hear, the growing friendliness of all classes, the deepening sense of the inadequacy of the old religions to meet their spiritual needs, and the, as yet dim, but sure, convictions that in Christ their soul hunger can find satisfaction – all these constitute an opportunity the like of which has never been witnessed before. The splendid spiritual harvests of past years are harbingers of still greater to come.

We must remember that evangelical missionaries were products of revival movements. Many of them retained their revivalist instincts and as a result, when news of the new Pentecostal revival reached them, some of them joined the new movement.

Pentecostalism itself was still in its formative stage in the first two decades of the twentieth century, but it was born in revivals, not only in North America, but in other places as far-flung as India, Korea, China, Chile, Nigeria and Madagascar. It was the work of the so-called 'native workers' that spread Pentecostalism globally in the early years, and much of the recent growth has had nothing to do with foreign missionaries. Some years ago while researching early Pentecostal missions (Anderson 2007), I was unable to find much detail of the lives of the indigenous pioneers who spread Pentecostalism in villages and cities all over the world, because of the emphasis in the newsletter sources on 'their' foreign missionaries. But here and there we get a glimpse – even in these rather chaotic beginnings – from scattered reports.

Foreign missionaries depended almost entirely on indigenous evangelists and the so-called 'Bible women' for communicating effectively and for the growth of their work. These workers are sometimes referred to in their reports. Will Norton, born in India and son of a former Methodist missionary, believed that Pentecostals had no time to lose. They had the solution for the salvation of the lost millions of India, whose 'awful need of help' could be met through the power of the Spirit. Preparing themselves in prayer for 'Pentecostal power' was 'right now needed for world witnessing'. He said that there were 'millions of people now in India' who had 'never once heard the Name of Jesus, a heaven to go to or a hell to be warned of'. Thousands of these people were 'dying daily without Christ' (*Triumphs of Faith*, Vol. 36 Issue 9, September 1916, p. 202).

The problem was not receptivity, but the great shortage of missionary volunteers, according to these circles. Pentecostals were urged to join an 'aggressive campaign' to reach the 'depressed classes'. The Indian caste system was one of the greatest challenges for Western missionaries. Pentecostals joined in its general condemnation by Christian missionaries, pointing to the benefits of the message that proclaims unity and equality of all in Christ (*Latter Rain Evangel*, Vol. 5 Issue 7, April 1913, p. 17). The 'Pariah' (Dalit) caste was considered the most open to Christian advances and missionaries were urged to penetrate into their villages (*Flames of Fire* 9, January 1913, p. 3).

There were also specific social benefits brought about by missionary activities, including providing education for the masses, including women, producing vernacular textbooks and teacher training, founding universities and teaching languages, medicine, public health and agriculture. Protestant missions in particular encouraged mass printing, producing vernacular Bibles and newspapers. Missionaries were important transmitters of Western medical ideas, providing doctors and nurses, promoting female literacy, public health training and medical schools; this also had an impact on life expectancy and infant mortality, among other things. Missionaries also transmitted ideas about Western democracy. Christian missions brought about a religious transformation worldwide. Not only was Christianity fast becoming a world faith, but all major world faiths themselves were affected by the encounter with Christian missions. As a result they became more text-based, they created their own social reform movements and vernacular education systems, and their doctrines were sometimes reformulated in reaction to missionary critique.

The early Pentecostal missionaries were not as involved in the philanthropic activities of other Protestant missions; indeed, their resources were meagre. The spread of Pentecostalism throughout the majority world came about primarily through local agency rather than through foreign missionaries, even when the latter sometimes initiated and facilitated the process. Multiple Pentecostal missions resulted in multiple new churches, and encouraged independent churches, especially when schism resulted from the patronizing attitudes of foreign missionaries.

One of the questions hotly debated by scholars is: if Christianity makes exclusive and absolute demands on other people's religious allegiance, is this a form of religious or cultural imperialism? So-called 'postcolonial' Christianity has had a great impact on the changing religious demographics. Some of the salient points are that Christianity has become increasingly non-Western, despite the increasing twentieth-century American involvement in mission. In the late twentieth century we have also witnessed the phenomenon of 'reverse mission' to Europe and North America from those who have brought their particular brand of usually Pentecostal Christianity from Asia, Africa and Latin America. Increasing numbers of leaders and members of European-based denominations are non-European in origin and theologically conservative.

We cannot discuss the legacy of the Reformation without also looking at the schisms that continued into the twentieth and twenty-first centuries. To take one example from India, according to one estimate more than half of India's Christians (the author writes of 62 million) were 'Independents' in 2002 (Barrie-Anthony, p. 627). Many of these churches founded in the twentieth century are Pentecostal or Charismatic churches, and several significant churches had their origins in the state of Kerala, where India's Thomas Christians are found. The history of Indian Independency is a complicated one, with so many complex relationships and historical connections between its main protagonists. There were important influences encouraging Indian independency in the early twentieth century, including that of Pandita Ramabai and the Christian mystic Sadhu Sundar Singh. Both these leaders promoted a truly Indian Christianity, in distinction to Western Christianity. Sundar Singh was the inspiration for a focus on the experiential and the ecstatic through his adopting elements of the Hindu bhakti (devotion) tradition, and Ramabai's Mukti Church is still active today (Hedlund, pp. 157–67).

Independent Pentecostal and Charismatic churches have developed rapidly throughout the world. There are thought to be over ten thousand independent churches in Africa alone. The emergence of the phenomenon of these independent churches raises several issues. First, there is the question of relevancy in a culture that is used to 'powerful' phenomena in religious life. One of the main reasons for the popularity of Pentecostal and Charismatic forms of Christianity is that they appear to provide a more 'powerful' religion than either the Catholic, mainline Protestant, or other older churches had done, and they address issues relevant to the popular worldview and religious consciousness. Western theologies tend to ignore or minimize the awareness of the spirit world with its destructive, evil and powerful forces that underlie the religious consciousness of many peoples worldwide. Particularly in their practices of healing and deliverance from evil spirits, independent Pentecostal churches demonstrate that Christianity has this power, and they appeal to people oppressed by sickness, misfortune and affliction. Independent churches represent valuable case studies of a theology that may begin to examine hitherto unexplored questions. Many of these independent churches are evangelical in theology and have much in common with Western-founded denominations, but have also taken a stand against all that is seen as foreign forms of Christianity.

Roger Hedlund has outlined some of the doctrinal distinctives of Indian independent churches, but warns us against generalizing about such diverse movements. Many of these distinctives are particularly appropriate in India's Hindu context, including 'mysteries' explained from the Bible, meditation as a method of understanding the Bible, and an emphasis on the experiential dimension of 'knowing God' through intense and prolonged prayer. Sometimes the leaders occupy a similar function to the Hindu gurus (and are sometimes called 'Christian gurus'), highly respected by their disciples as authoritative guides and examples who provide daily guidance for living. Hedlund says that there are also a number of 'deviant' ideas among a few Indian churches, such as tritheism and an emphasis on extrabiblical prophecies and 'new revelations' (Hedlund, pp. 233–53).

But the independent churches demonstrate what Maggay in the Philippines context has described as the reason for their growth: 'it connects receptivity to a religion oriented towards power'. She says that 'to incarnate Christianity more genuinely within the context of Filipino culture is to become, not only perhaps more Christian, but also more Filipino' (Maggay, pp. 363, 372). This is what independent Pentecostal churches worldwide are also concerned with, or as Ramabai had put it, 'to suit [Indian] nature and feelings'.

There can be no doubt that in many parts of the majority world, Pentecostalism has made an enormous impact. In countries like the United States, Guatemala, Brazil, Nigeria, India, the Philippines, China and South Korea, if we include the Pentecostals and independent churches, evangelicals form the majority of Protestants and have shown remarkable growth during the last century. The Pentecostal and Charismatic movements might be the future of evangelical Christianity because they attract young people in particular, in contrast to the older churches originating in Western Europe with an increasingly ageing membership in the lands of their origin.

Most Pentecostals and Charismatics are 'evangelical' in beliefs. This chapter has attempted to show that the Protestant Reformation has set off a spiral of events and ideas that have had a profound, if indirect, influence on global Pentecostalism. This in turn is the result of the rapid increase in missionary activity that followed in the wake of the attempts to revitalize Protestant Christianity through the revivals in the Western world. But most contemporary Christians will find their own legacy in the work of those indigenous pioneers who have blazed the way toward a type of Christianity that fits their own context, one that is very, very different from that of sixteenth-century Europe. More could be said about the need for contextualization, but it is hoped that this chapter will provoke some thought into the legacy of these pioneers.

References

Anderson, Allan, 2007, *Spreading Fires: The Missionary Nature of Early Pentecostalism*. London: SCM Press.

Anderson, Allan H., 2013, *To the Ends of the Earth: Pentecostalism and the Transformation of World Christianity*. Oxford: Oxford University Press.

Balmer, Randall, 1999, *Blessed Assurance: A History of Evangelicalism in America*. Boston, MA: Beacon Press.

Balmer, Randall, 2010, *The Making of Evangelicalism: From Revivalism to Politics and Beyond*. Waco, TX: Baylor University Press.

Barrie-Anthony, Steven, 2003, 'Religion in Contemporary India', in Melton, J. Gordon and Martin Baumann (eds), *Religions of the World: A Comprehensive Encyclopaedia of Beliefs and Practices*, 4 Vols, pp. 627–35. ABC-Clio.

Hedlund, Roger E., 2000, *Quest for Identity: India's Churches of Indigenous Origin*. London: SPCK.

Kay, William K., 2017, 'Luther and Pentecostalism', *Journal of the European Pentecostal Theological Association*. London: EPTA.

Latourette, Kenneth S., 1976, *A History of Christianity, Vol. II*. London: Harper & Row.

MacCulloch, Diarmaid, 2004, *Reformation: Europe's House Divided 1490–1700*. London: Penguin.

McGrath, Alister, 1995, *Evangelicalism and the Future of Christianity*. London: Hodder & Stoughton.

Maggay, Melba P., 1998, 'Towards Sensitive Engagement with Filipino Indigenous Consciousness', *International Review of Mission* 87, pp. 361–73. Geneva: WCC.

Mallampalli, Chandra, 2016, 'South Asia', in Sanneh, Lamin and McClymond, Michael J. (eds), *The Wiley Blackwell Companion to World Christianity*. London: Wiley Blackwell.

Noll, Mark A., 2003, *The Rise of Evangelicalism: The Age of Edwards, Whitefield and the Wesleys*. Westmont, IL: IVP.

Zrimec, Steve, 2010, 'Choking on Feathers: A battle on two fronts', https://confessionalouthouse.wordpress.com/2010/06/01/choking-on-feathers-a-battle-on-two-fronts-2/

www.christianitytoday.com/history/issues/issue-39/was-luther-anti-semitic.html

Post Pentecostal and Charismatic Expressions

EMMANUEL KAPOFU

Pentecostalism as a phenomenon in Britain began from a campaign in Sunderland by Thomas Ball Barratt in 1907 (Cartwright 2015). Among the 17 people who were baptized in the Holy Spirit was a black man, a Ghanaian businessman by the name of T. Brem-Wilson. The new church moved several times under the pastoral leadership of Brem-Wilson, who died on Good Friday in 1929.

Pentecostalism, as the worldwide phenomenon it is known today, is traced ordinarily to Azusa Street in Los Angeles, USA. However, Anderson (pp. 13–27) shows how these outpourings of the Holy Spirit were to a great degree simultaneous in a number of places. For example, in addition to Sunderland and Los Angeles, in India what is now known as the Mukti Revival started in 1901, as a result of united and continuous prayer at a mission station among Christian women workers at Mukti. Anderson adds that, between December 1901 and July 1902, 1,200 people were baptized, continuously and consistently crying out to God. In July of that year the revival was refuelled and the people had daily meetings which continued to grow until nearly 600 were influenced by the Pentecostal phenomenon. The news of this revival reached Australia in 1903.

The Welsh revival (1904–05) was a Holy Spirit church renewal with the evidence of speaking in tongues (otherwise known as glossolalia), which fed thousands of Christians into the Welsh churches. Wilkinson (p. 11, citing McGee, a Christian historian) gives a figure of 100,000 converts to Christianity between September 1904 and June 1905 as a direct result of the Welsh revival. In the years that followed, the Welsh and UK churches lived on the momentum of that revival. The Welsh revival, at its peak, and with it the advent of Pentecostalism, altered the fabric of the Christian faith in the British Isles. This revival was led by Evan Roberts (1878–1951), a 26-year-old collier and trainee minister. Wherever Pentecostalism spontaneously arose it sought by the power of the Spirit to bring the sinner to the Saviour who promised to fill them with power to be witnesses to the saving grace of God in Jesus Christ.

Klaus points to a chasm between what Pentecostalism was and what it is today. A substantial pedigree of the historic Pentecostal movement is comprehensively intertwined with an eschatology imperative that began in the twentieth century and went on to sustain a worldwide missionary outreach. Now, in the twenty-first century, the authoritative imminent eschatological view, which was prominent at the inception of the phenomenon, is on the wane. The missionary identity inherent in the Pentecostal movements from the twentieth century to date may need re-examination, especially as the eschatological element is no longer as apparent as before.

The time is therefore ripe to revisit the context of Pentecostalism and fully objectify its continuing development and nature nationally and globally. Furthermore, and critical to the topic here, the telling of contemporary Pentecostal narrative includes what has occasioned expressions of neo-Pentecostal/neo-Charismatic faith expressions such as Hillsong, Chemin Neuf, and other newer churches/expressions that do not quite fit the Pentecostal/Charismatic historic mould. Are these latest expressions of Pentecostalism the Holy Spirit's latest response to a renewal that needs another boost, especially a renewing of the eschatological imperative of evangelism in these last days? I will now examine how the neo-Pentecostals/neo-Charismatics have or are coming into being, and even expanding as a global brand.

A self-evident characteristic of these churches is a tendency to grow into megachurches. How do they become 'mega'? The megachurches according to Turner and Salemink (p. 402) are akin to business corporations. They have targets of membership to reach – SMART goals (specific, measurable, agreed upon, realistic, time-based), clear to the leadership and the membership. The congregation are encouraged to explore their God-given gifts (whether people, skills or creativity) and use them. Most of the time the senior pastor is unreachable by the ordinary member, so the cell group becomes the place where vision is expounded, discipling administered and embryos multiplied; the cell leader becomes like the line manager. The cell group is the place where the members get affirmations from the cell leader. The megachurch (Anderson 1979) has made a positional move taking adherents from social discontent and protest to social consciousness. Neo-Pentecostals or progressive Pentecostals are headed beyond internal purity toward action for social transformation.

Unlike the traditional Pentecostal church, where doctrine and accurate exegesis are critical, these neo-Pentecostals provide a space to experience the divine in what has been defined as secularization of the sacred, using their size, social media and market logic to create an atmosphere of worship. Therefore, doctrine does not bind their large, youngish congregations together, but their collective aesthetic systems that can encourage spiritual practices and felt manifestations of God (Klaver 2015). 'Promotion of religion is not a metaphor' but akin to present-day reality (Usunier, p. 37). Usunier (2016, p. 1) reads Mara Einstein's findings that, whereas decades ago there was debate on the role of social media and church (how the former secularized the latter,) now it is evidently clear that the traditional Pentecostals who stuck to programmes and a worship-oriented approach declined in weekly attendance and overall structure is wilting. The neo-Pentecostals who have been progressive and 'promoted religion' have, at the risk of being labelled as propagators of merchandized religion, remained on the rise.

The distinguishing characteristic of neo-Pentecostals, according to Grey (2016) is like a mirror image, which is familiar and alien at the same time: familiar in that it is the reflection of the real, but alien in that it is a reverse image. The modern globalized world is not a religious wasteland, but just as religious as ever, only looking different because of pluralism. The recognizable but alien argued for by Grey is the change in the adherents from being predominantly Western communities to non-Western communities, with the rise of migrant churches particularly of the Pentecostal variety. This, according to Grey, has birthed a re-evangelization of Europe (at times called reverse mission), by people from former colonies, thereby creating a new dynamic of post-colonialism that may need addressing. Therefore, one can identify typical Pentecostal characteristics, but the make-up of the congregants is not characteristically Western. Twentieth-century Pentecostalism thrived among the underclass throughout the world, but now has become predominantly middle class. At its inception, Pentecostalism's missiology centred on its urgent eschatology; however, the praxis in the twenty-first century is now balancing social action and spirituality.

Usunier and Stolz (p. 6) note that traditional church denominations were mostly institutional, as opposed to the not-for-profit organizations they have become. The fundamental difference is that in the twentieth century and before, churches were institutions where individuals and families belonged, often for generations; the church would be linked to schools and hospitals and various other power structures in the societal framework of a given community. The new church expressions, on the other hand, have transformed themselves into voluntary associations, like gym clubs or other charitable societies. Of necessity, due to the nature of non-profit organizations, new church expressions must now compete for membership, for financial support, for commitment – all these require some form of marketization and brand construction. Many of these neo-Pentecostal and neo-Charismatic church expressions belong to what are also known as megachurches. Megachurches, according to Goh (pp. 284–304), are churches that have an array of distinguishable features like an average weekly attendance of a thousand people plus, an up-to-date worship style complete with all modern electronics and media devices and vibrant and charming pastors. The worship service in this type of church is generally textured to appeal to seekers as opposed to mature believers; the dress code is less formal and the atmosphere well set, but functional.

Beyond these few distinguishing characteristics will be many other variables commensurate with culture, geography, doctrine, brand building and imaging, peculiar to each individual church. Because these neo-Pentecostal churches are often personality-centred, that personality or character can often permeate to the church's values. Such a leader is best described as a 'pastorpreneur' who blends entrepreneurial business skills together with the traditional Christian message, developing a neo-Pentecostal style of spirituality (Jackson, p. 242). This mix of market logic and spirituality is usually reflected in the membership.

Hillsong

A case in point, that fits this category of neo-Pentecostal church expressions, would be the Hillsong Church originating in Australia. The exponential growth of Hillsong Church may be called Houston-centric, featuring Frank Houston and his son Brian. Its origins lie in a revival that was going on across Australia. The Assemblies of God Australia, from which Hillsong Church came, recorded exponential growth from 15,000 in 1979, to 250,000 Pentecostals in 1999, a growth rate unprecedented worldwide.

Riches and Wagner (p. 21) trace the founding of the Hillsong Church to July 1977, as a denominational affiliate of Australian Christian Churches (formerly known as Assemblies of God Australia) into a local congregation that became known as Sydney Christian Life Centre. The inaugural service was attended by 14 people and in six months 150 people were in attendance, and 1,000 by 1982. Frank and Hazel Houston's son Brian, and his wife Roberta (Bobbie) arrived from New Zealand in 1978 to join a ministry team which was already producing extraordinary results. The Sydney Christian Life Centre was already in two locations and outgrowing them (Riches and Wagner, p. 26). In the early 1980s, renowned figures like David Yongi Cho and Don Tek of the Haggai Institute were invited to teach at seminars and conferences. In the midst of the growth and expansion culture, Brian and Bobbie Houston were 'released' from Sydney CLC, although not supported financially to pioneer Hills Christian Life Centre (Hills CLC) in 1983 (p. 28).

By 2017, the local church had metamorphosed into 100,000 global adherents in 15 countries on five continents. Globalization – the movement of people, practices, ideas and materials – has been adapted into church culture, to maximum effect, by Hillsong Church. This neo-Pentecostal expression has captured the 'imagination of migrating cosmopolitan and diaspora cultures and transmitted religious ideas within its cultural products and multimedia and drawn constituents into particular practices of the body that build solidarity among its members, promoting the materials of its faith, including, of course, the Bible' (Wagner 2016, p. 28). The Hillsong brand of music appears to have been the spearhead in the internationalizing of the local church.

Hillsong Church has played a significant role, according to Riches and Wagner (p. 15) in global Christian renewal through their production of congregational music. 'On 10 June 2015, *Christianity Today* magazine reported that one of Hillsong's hit songs, "Oceans (Where feet may fail)", had remained on the Billboard Hot Christian Songs list for a record 50 consecutive weeks – longer than any other Christian single' (2017, p. 2). On YouTube, the song had hit 35 million views, and by 2016 the song had 73.5 million plays.

The unique selling point (USP) for Hillsong has been the music. From the formative stage under Frank Houston the goal was a church of thousands, with capacity to attract the best of musicians. Brian Houston, his son, has perpetuated this trajectory to today, where contemporary Christian rock created by world-class musicians has ever been the draw point, attracting everyone from global celebrities to just students from around the world. In the creative process of song-writing, two criteria are critical; first, the song-writer must be recognizable and second the lyrics of the song must be accurate and consistent with the Hillsong Church's teachings (Wagner, p. 65). Before an album is put together, prominent songwriters like Joel Houston and Reuben Morgan must be on it. A couple of songs from the congregation may be included, but not just out of tokenism since every song will have to go through a rigorous analytical process, which includes being used in everyday worship in their Australian Hillsong churches. The congregants' reaction to the song is observed to see if the consistency of meaningful worship is there. Only when the Australian churches can engage with a song, does it pass the test of being included on a Hillsong album. Since every song is 'field tested' in Australia, the Australian church members have a dual role in the album creative process: first they are the umpires of the Hillsong brand of music, and second they determine the sense of taste and flavour of this music, on behalf of the worldwide church network (Wagner 2016, p. 2).

The making, mastering, production and marketing are all done in Australia, making Australia the centre for Hillsong. While a lot of 'Australianness' is used in the manufacturing of the Hillsong brand, it must be stated that a standardization is effectively put into place to make the songs be at home in the many live arenas and congregations worlds away from Australia. That standardization is systematically replicated in the Hillsong churches, through both the instruments and vocals, so that the song sounds the same as when it was recorded. When the Hillsong Church members in Australia have engaged with a song, then that song is ready to be included on the next album. This process of 'field testing' is run by Robert Fergusson, a Baulkham Hills Campus senior pastor. While Hillsong Church is outward-looking – evidenced by the crowds drawn to their meetings and conferences, with millions of viewers and followers online via YouTube and Facebook – the central ethos is not eschatological. The song lyrics and central message do not have a futurist redemption doctrine, but a contemporary spiritual and social relevance.

Hillsong's use of worldwide advertising mechanisms (Riches and Wagner p. 3) sets it at a distance from its mother, the Assemblies of God Australia (later renamed Australia Christian Churches), who are largely still a traditional Pentecostal church eschatologically. Hillsong Church is therefore both renewal and reformist because it has carved for itself a unique and distinct character/brand, known the world over, without being known as a part of Assemblies of God Australia, yet still within the denomination, with Brian Houston its leader having had his turn to lead as National President of AOGA from 1997. On a global scale, Hillsong Church would have been reformist, judging by the influence they have had on the Sunday song lists across the world, using the globalization tools (Berger, p. 311), people, practices, ideas and materials, influencing churches wittingly across the world.

Singapore

Chong (2015, p. 218) cites three outstanding characteristics of Singapore's megachurches. The first is that they emanated from the Pentecostal variety, appeal to the emergent socially mobile middle class, this class springing from either working or lower middle classes. These class-transcending professionals, who are upwardly mobile, converge into the contemporary Pentecostal Church where they find they fit in. Second, the leaders of these churches bring spirituality and market logic together, thereby significantly altering this classes social construct, enabling the congregants to better engage with the world while still being spiritual. Third, because they are broadly appealing to international evangelical movements, and their membership is drawn from what might be called transnationals (people working and living in a country not of their birth, but still linked to the country of their birth), they are able engage in social action programmes for the local needy where the church is, without conflicting with government; at the same time, their global connectivity and ministry does not compromise their local relevance.

It may be worth noting that whereas in traditional Pentecostalism families remained loyal to a denomination (Chin, p. 244), in the independent neo-Pentecostal churches 'many members are first generation converts from a variety of social, educational and religious backgrounds' (Chin, p. 106). This exponential growth in the neo-Pentecostals is the reason for the growth of Protestantism in Singapore. In Chin's survey, the choice of which church to attend by new converts was decided by where there was lively music in church worship, and the role of small groups in the new convert's life. The new converts, typically young and socially mobile, were shown in the survey to have a real interest in social action, whereas the traditional church preferred to confine social-political discourse to private conversation and individual life. The relationship between the new church expressions and the religious other is rather markedly different to the traditional churches in Singapore. Chin found that the traditional church member generally aimed to proselytize those of other religions while the neo-Pentecostals were more likely to hang out and holiday easily and more regularly with the religious other. This was attributed to the latter being new in the faith and so still connected to parents and friends who were still of Buddhist or Taoist faith.

The survey reported by Chin saw a tendency for church growth to be linked with upward mobility. Money and finance in the neo-Pentecostal Church is therefore intimately connected to spirituality. This may be partly to do with market strategizing being intertwined with theological discourse in the neo-Pentecostal narrative.

Chemin Neuf

An example of neo-Charismatic expression is the Chemin Neuf (which means 'new road'). According to Oliver (1999) it developed as a Catholic post-Charismatic expression in 1973 in Lyon, France, where a seven-member prayer group of Catholic Charismatics, after Holy Spirit baptism, chose a more dedicated way of practising their faith and chose to live in community. It manifests itself in three different forms: the Community, the Religious Institute and the Communion. The Community incorporates the membership of the Chemin Neuf from Catholic and non-Catholic backgrounds. The Religious Institute at the core of the association was established by the Archdiocese of Lyon for the purpose of respecting the various denominations which make up the Chemin Neuf while endeavouring to not lose its Catholic character. The Communion consists of persons who have specific apostolates, with authority in various facets of the Chemin Neuf. Non-Catholics and Catholic members of the Chemin Neuf have full membership, but the Catholic members enjoy more rights in the Community than the non-Catholic counterparts. Oliver explains this using the analogy of United States citizenship status. A naturalized American and a person born in the United States of America are both full American citizens. To run for the office of President, however, the citizen has to have been born in the United States of America. The Chemin Neuf enjoins a structured life in what they call fraternities. There are two types of fraternities: neighbourhood fraternities where the Community members live within the same area, and the household fraternities where the members of the Community live in the same house. Members have set daily times and weekly times to pray communally and personally. During the week the members have a communal meal several times. Every member of the Chemin Neuf is expected to work for the Community itself, or for Christian charitable organizations outside the Chemin Neuf Community. While a simple life is the general goal, those who live in the household fraternity have their needs met by the Community, while those in the neighbourhood fraternities generally look after themselves.

Oliver (p. 21) reports a doctrine of unity in Christ between the Communities and the Catholic Church that enables non-Catholics to be in fellowship with Catholicism within the Chemin Neuf. There are non-Catholics who agree with what the Chemin Neuf stand for – prayer and Charismatic influence. Therefore, to underpin that teaching, there is a system of mentors or 'spiritual guides' for every Community member. Once a year the whole community gathers to share a meal and celebrate. The Chemin Neuf enjoys a canonical affiliation with the

Archdiocese of Lyon, and a rapport with the Holy See in Rome. The Chemin Neuf's website claims a following of 2,000 people in some 30 countries. These statistics disqualify the community from 'megachurch' status. A megachurch (Thumma and Bird, p. 18) is a Protestant church that sees on average 2,000 people in weekly worship meetings. Chemin Neuf's umbilical cord remains attached to the Archbishop of Lyon, the Catholic Church and the Holy See, and is therefore best understood as renewal, not a reformist movement within Catholicism.

International Life Centre

Speaking as a critical insider, the ILC church in Wolverhampton and its networks across the United Kingdom, while not a megachurch, fits in as a post-Charismatic or neo-Pentecostal type of church. The emphasis of being all things Pentecostal remains embedded in both worship and doctrine at ILC, but eschatology is not prominent. The church culture, based on their website (www.ilcchurch.com/), membership, demography and actual practice, reflects globalization – the number of African and Asian nationalities represented, the song list choice, social action and experiential worship depict ILC as a newcomer among neo-Pentecostals. The ILC is not structured denominationally with a top-down leadership but a rather inclusive broad type of leadership. While this broad approach is contemporary and popular, it inhibits imposition of doctrinal ideology, as consensus must always be sought. Missionally, since the inception of the ILC in the UK in 2001, they have only once been involved in a city-wide intentional evangelistic outreach, when they joined churches across the city in July 2018 on a mission called Ablaze18 (www.ablazewolverhampton.co.uk/). Growth at ILC has tended to largely be based on word of mouth invitations and 'friendship evangelism'. The words 'mission' and 'evangelism' pop in here and there, but this is done by, for example, students inviting other students, colleagues inviting workmates – like invites like. Mission, together with eschatology, appears to be sacrificed for social action, upward mobility and 'fitting in' with modern forms of doing church.

Conclusion

Emerging expressions of a neo-Pentecostal/Charismatic nature are springing up around the world. Although not looked at in this chapter, Fresh Expressions in the Church of England and the aforementioned Chemin Neuf in the Roman Catholic Church appear as intradenominational renewal movements. Expressions like Hillsong appear to be on an evolutionary reformist path, mapping new identities while remaining within a denominational brand name. Independent churches are emerging, loosening the culturally conservative Pentecostal preoccupation with dogmatic theological and doctrinal positions. Singapore is not unique but provides an example of the genealogy of the megachurch that appears to be a trend among new expressions of Pentecostal and Charismatic churches. Whether these are internal renewal movements like Chemin Neuf or more reformist ones like Hillsong, the new trend leans toward renewal more than reformist movements. The Chemin Neuf community have largely remained a part of the Catholic Church, and are recognized as such. Hillsong, the megachurches of Singapore, and the International Life Centre in the UK would be more reformist in that they have all but severed ties with their parent denomination. In some cases there remains only an honorary relationship and mutual respect, because the new church expressions have a whole new DNA.

The traditional Pentecostal denomination focused on eschatology and mission. The neo-Pentecostals'/Charismatics' main selling point is globalization, social mobility and social action. The leaders of the neo-Pentecostal/Charismatic churches are developing new social and spiritual constructs, showing how to converge metaphysical and market logic, thereby metamorphosing Christians on their way to heaven into congregants that better engage with the world while still (purporting to be) unworldly.

References

Anderson, Allan (ed.), 2010, *Studying Global Pentecostalism Theories and Methods.* London: University of California Press.

Berger, Teresa (ed.), 2012, *Liturgy in Migration: From the Upper Room to Cyberspace.* Collegeville, MN: Liturgical Press.

Cartwright, Desmond, 2015, 'Black Pentecostal Churches in Britain', *Journal of the European Pentecostal Theological Association*, Vol. 27 Issue 2, pp. 128–37.

Chin, Clive S., 2017, *The Perception of Christianity as a Rational Religion in Singapore: A Missiological Analysis of Christian Conversion.* Eugene, OR: Pickwick Publications.

Chong, Terrence, 2015, 'Mega churches in Singapore: The Faith of an Emergent Middle Class', *Pacific Affairs, a division of the University of British Columbia,* Vol. 88 No. 2, pp. 215–35.

Goh, Robbie, 2015, 'Hillsong and "Megachurch" Practice: Semiotics, Spatial Logic and the Embodiment of Contemporary Evangelical Protestantism', *The Journal of Objects, Art and Belief,* Vol. 4 Issue 3, pp. 284–304.

Grey, Jacqueline, 2016, 'Through the Looking Glass: Reflections on the Re-evangelization of Europe through a Post-colonial Reading of Isaiah 2:1–5', *Journal of the European Pentecostal Theological Association,* Vol. 37 Issue 1, pp. 28–39.

Jackson, John, 2003, 'Pastorpreneur', *Leadership Journal,* retrieved from www.christianitytoday.com/le/2003/fall/7.59.html and quoted by Mark Alan Charles Jennings, 'Great Risk for the Kingdom: Pentecostal–Charismatic Growth Churches, Pastorpreneurs, and Neoliberalism', in Pascal, Ana-Maria (ed.), *Multiculturalism and the Convergence of Faith and Practical Wisdom in Modern Society.* Advances in Religious and Cultural Studies series. Hershey, PA: IGI-Global.

Klaus, Byron, 2015, 'Growing Edges Have Shifted: Pentecostal Mission in the 21st Century', *Journal of the European Pentecostal Theological Association,* Vol. 30 Issue 2, pp. 65–81.

Klaver, Miranda, 2015, 'Pentecostal Pastorpreneurs and the Global Circulation of Authoritative Aesthetic Styles', *Culture and Religion: An Interdisciplinary Journal,* Vol. 16 Issue 2, pp. 146–59.

Oliver, James, 1999, *Ecumenical Associations: Their Canonical Status with Particular Reference to the United States of America.* Rome: Gregorian University Press.

Riches, Tanya and Tom Wagner (eds), 2017, *The Hillsong Movement Examined: You Call Me out upon the Waters.* London: Palgrave Macmillan.

Thumma, Scott and Warren Bird, 2015, 'Megafaith for the Megacity: The Global Megachurch Phenomenon', in S. Brunn (ed.), *The Changing World Religion Map.* Dordrecht: Springer.

Turner, Bryan and Oscar Salemink (eds), 2014, *Routledge Handbook of Religions in Asia.* London: Routledge.

Usunier, Jean-Claude, 2016, '"9591": The Global Commoditization of Religions through GATS, WTO, and Marketing Practices', in Usunier, Jean-Claude and Jörg Stolz (eds), 2016, *Religion as Brands: New Perspectives on the Marketization of Religion and Spirituality.* London: Routledge, pp. 27–44.

Wagner, Thomas, 2016, 'Branding, Music, and Religion: Standardization and Adaptation in the Experience of the "Hillsong Sound"', in Usunier and Stolz, pp. 59–74.

Wilkinson, Michael, 2006, *The Spirit Said Go: Pentecostal Immigrants In Canada.* New York: Peter Lang Publishing.

Part Four

Pentecostal and Charismatic and Socio-Political Issues

Theological Education and Training among British Pentecostals and Charismatics

R. DAVID MUIR

Early Pentecostals were not very interested in 'theological education'. Seized by an 'eschatological urgency' to preach the 'Word of God' they were more concerned to proclaim their new message of baptism in the Holy Spirit, divine healing and the imminent return of Christ. Contemporary Pentecostal leaders are not less concerned about these things, but they are equally preoccupied with the need for proper theological education and ministerial training to equip leaders for effective mission in postmodern society. This chapter looks at the changing attitudes of Pentecostals and Charismatics to formal theological training, as well as some of the broader questions in the current political economy of higher education with its institutional competition, the quality assurance framework and the 'intellectual skills and competencies' students are expected to have after completing a theology or religious studies degree. The chapter concludes by raising questions about the type and desired level of theological education needed by Pentecostals and Charismatics, wedded as they are to a tradition of 'orality', 'experience' and the 'guidance of the Holy Spirit'.

Contemporary Christian mission and witness brings its own challenges and opportunities, not least because of the multiplicity of moral visions and ideological narratives competing for hegemony privately and publicly. Narratives of religious certainty and transcendence, like all other 'grand narratives', no longer hold positions of hegemony in our postmodern and post-Christian culture. The view popularized by Jean-François Lyotard, characterizing 'postmodern' as 'incredulity towards metanarratives', poses a number of challenges – and dare I say opportunities – to how we do Christian theology and missions today (Lyotard 1984). At the turn of the century, the theologian Colin Gunton was bemoaning the fact that 'relatively fewer students than was the case even a quarter of a century ago will be studying theology as a way into ordained ministry' (Gunton, p. 442). Today, of course, most denominations are struggling to recruit sufficient numbers for the ministry. For Pentecostals and Charismatics, these challenges are no less acute; and in many respects they can benefit from the experience and expertise of the more established churches and their institutional resources.

In this chapter, I make no real distinction between Pentecostals and Charismatics: I make the assumption that all Pentecostals are Charismatics, though not all Charismatics are Pentecostals. And I further recognize that Pentecostals are not just located in black majority churches, as many of them belong to the older white Pentecostal denominations, 'classical' Pentecostals. Having stated that, what I have to say applies equally to black and white Pentecostals and Charismatics outside the mainline denominations, as they often share many of the same reservations about theological education. I draw attention to three areas. First, to indicate in a very general sense something of the current need for theological education for Pentecostals and Charismatics; second, highlight aspects of the nature and diversity of current provision; and last offer some provisional thoughts about the way forward to stimulate further discussion and research.

Pentecostal and Charismatic churches, like any other church and congregation, engage in some kind of teaching programme, ministerial training and education. There is a sense in which all didactic activities – Sunday school teaching, Bible studies, sermons, 'exhortations', testimonies and 'biblical literacy' teaching – can be thought of as exercises in 'theological education'. And all Christians are 'theologians' of one sort or another in that they all try to articulate, contemplate, and live in and with the Trinitarian mystery, reality and economy of God's plan of redemption. In this broad sense, theologians like Paul Tillich would affirm that all Christians are 'theologians' not only because they are able 'to receive spiritual knowledge', but also because they have been grasped within the Church 'by the Divine Spirit' and 'affirm that Jesus is the Christ' (Tillich 1962, pp. 123–4).

And this is more so when we consider that all Christians are called to bear witness and to be ready 'to give an answer' for their hope in Christ (1 Peter 3.15), as well as to exercise what Macquarrie refers to as the 'universal and quite fundamental ministry of all Christians' to participate in 'the ministry of reconciliation' (2 Cor. 5.18) (Macquarrie, pp. 375–6). Contemporary Pentecostals and Charismatics would certainly agree with the two views above, even though they would recognize the need for formal theological education and ministerial training with appropriate qualifications from reputable higher education universities and institutions. However, when we consider the early decades of the Pentecostal movement we see that this was not always the case.

Given what we have now come to view as emblematic of the Charismatic Renewal and its Pentecostal antecedents – glossolalia, faith healing, prophecy, the working of miracles and other Charismatic manifestations – it is not surprising that a perennial tension continues to the present day when it comes to Pentecostal/Charismatic piety and practice and its study and exploration in universities and higher education institutions. In an introduction O'Connor recognizes that the Pentecostal movement is 'perhaps the most vigorous religious movement of this century', but views these emblematic features as 'bizarre phenomena' (O'Connor 1978). If education, especially higher education in liberal arts settings, is fundamentally about freedom of thought and enquiry, or the intellectual aim of 'the seeking of truth by disagreement and discussion' (Gunton 2001), then a number of methodological and epistemological conflicts are bound to arise between a Pentecostal/Charismatic self-understanding (experience) and the secular and so-called 'scientific' (explanation) approach to reality. Indeed in his concluding essay in 'Doing Theology in the University Today', Gunton refers to the 'two ends' the university is dedicated to: the 'intellectual' and the 'practical', the latter being the demands of modern governments 'to train personnel for the complex social and economic structures of the modern world'.

Pentecostals and Charismatics believe that Acts 1.8 – 'But you will receive power when the Holy Spirit has come upon you' – has particular resonance for their understanding of Charismatic gifts and power for ministry and evangelism. Commenting upon the theology of the nineteenth century and the approach of the preceding century to the subject matter of theology, Karl Barth argued that God became 'humanized'; and that this process of 'humanization' meant 'if not the abolition, at least the incorporation of God into the sphere of sovereign human self-awareness', making Christianity and the subject matter of its 'final' claims relative and provisional (Barth 2001, pp. 69–70).

In the formative decades of the Pentecostal movement, there was a reluctance to privilege theological education. Indeed, in many quarters there was outright antipathy and animosity toward what was perceived to be the fruit of 'theological education', namely, a liberal theological mood emerging from the nineteenth century questioning the inerrancy of scripture, the God of miracles and the dynamic power for mission evidenced in Spirit baptism. For Pentecostals, this resulted in a 'dead church', powerless to reach the 'unsaved' and spiritually ill-equipped for the 'end time' mission to usher in the Kingdom. Gripped by an eschatological urgency, Pentecostals had little time, or desire, for the kind of theological education emerging from what they saw as 'liberal' academies and seminaries. What they wanted and prized above all, however, was a thorough knowledge of the Bible. According to Kay, this was primarily to ensure doctrinal conformity to the 'fundamental truths espoused by their denomination' (Kay 2009, p. 202).

Historically, this has left something of a 'hermeneutics of suspicion' among many Pentecostals when it comes to formal theological education. Ironically, we see early Pentecostal pioneers like William J. Seymour attending Charles Parham's Bible School – albeit sitting outside the classroom, with the door ajar to conform to 'Jim Crow' legal and cultural dictates of the day – to acquire a basic biblical education, on the one hand, while the British Pentecostalist Alexander A. Boddy, on the other hand, has the privilege of a theology degree from the prestigious Durham University (UK) and is ordained by the renowned New Testament scholar Bishop J. B. Lightfoot (Hollenweger, p. 343). Here, of course, education is a function of both race and class: Boddy was an English aristocrat; Seymour, the son of former slaves, whose life and theology is excellently portrayed in Nelson's PhD thesis (Nelson 1981). In Pentecostal historiography the theme of race, and to lesser extent class – notwithstanding Anderson's characterization of Pentecostalism as 'a movement of "the disinherited"' (Anderson 1969) – was recognized by the Memphis gathering of Pentecostals in 1994 as a critical factor informing their organizational development and institutional relationships. In October 1994, leading Pentecostals gathered in Memphis, Tennessee, to reflect on their shared history and racial tension. It was an inter- and intra-Pentecostal attempt at 'truth' and 'reconciliation' about racism in Pentecostalism, leading to the production of a Racial Reconciliation Manifesto.

Although there was an ambiguous and ambivalent relationship in early Pentecostalism to 'formal education' and theological training, that is not to say that Pentecostals were not interested in 'ministerial education'. Indeed, centres for training and ministry formation were established quite early among the leading denominations like the Church of God in America, the Assemblies of God and Elim Pentecostal Church. According to Kay, these centres which have blossomed into liberal arts colleges have been 'generated by a sequence of historical factors: first, the protection of doctrine, then the formation of denominations with accredited ministers, and then the training of such ministers in line with the denominational norms, and finally the flourishing of genuine higher education' (Kay 2009, p. 300). It could be argued that this sequence of historical factors corresponds to the three stages of development in 'Pentecostal biblical hermeneutics'. According to Archer, the trajectory is as follows: first, there is the 'pre-critical period' from 1900 to the 1940s; this is followed by the 'modern period' 1940s–1980s; and finally, the 'contemporary period' 1980s through the present (Archer, pp. 112–13). Needless to say, the reality of Pentecostal biblical hermeneutics did not always follow this linear periodization.

Over the last three decades we have witnessed something of a proliferation of Bible schools, colleges, and ministerial training institutions. This proliferation signals both the personal and denominational need for education and training for ministry and mission, especially to address some of the challenges of urban ministry identified as long ago as in the *Faith in the City* report and the requisite balance needed in ministry formation between candidates 'whose gifts are other than academic' and those 'who received the conventional academic training' (*Faith in the City*, p. 67). Generally, it also says something about the importance and significance of theology and related subjects as a way of introducing students to traditions of scholarship and intellectual discourse. For some, this may be seen as a false dichotomy in ministry formation. However, it does highlight the importance and necessity of appropriate and contextual ministerial training, recognizing that 'ministerial gifts' are diverse (Rom. 12.3–8; 1 Cor. 12.4–11) and need not lead to 'a flight from theology'.

Given that theology is a 'function of the Christian Church' (Tillich 1962, p. 3), and that God has throughout the centuries equipped his Church richly in this regard, *Faith in the City* adopted a judicious, quintessentially Anglican 'middle' way worthy of note for all institutions engaging in theological education and ministerial training:

> The Church requires competent theologians, as much as it ever did, and must continue to make provision for their recruitment and training. The question being asked here is about the importance given to academic criteria in church life generally and in ministerial training in particular. If we are now being able to see not just the possibility but the necessity of presenting and receiving the Christian faith in forms other than that of a doctrinal package, we may be able to begin to take seriously schemes for accrediting ordained ministers on other than academic criteria. (*Faith in the City*, p. 67)

Today, there is an attempt to bring most of the main higher education institutions up to the same standards as a typical secular liberal arts university. Looking at what is provided in the main denominational institutions we see a greater uniformity in the curriculum offered, the method of study and the entry qualifications. The table provides a sample of the wide variability of provision and costs among key Pentecostal churches in 2015.

Institution	Church/ Denominational Affiliation	Partners/ Validating Body	Typical Qualifications	Fees: £ per year
School of the Prophets Academy of Learning	Ruach	No higher education partners	Certificate in Practical Theology (Unvalidated)	300
Believers' College	New Wine Church, Woolwich	No higher education partners	Certificate (Unvalidated)	80
Institute of Theology & Counselling	New Testament Assembly (NTA)	Roehampton University	Certificate in Applied Theology	300 per module
London School of Theology	Interdenominational	Middlesex University	BA, MA, PhD	7,696
Cliff College	Interdenominational	University of Manchester	Cert Th., BA, MA	6,725
Mattersey Hall	Assemblies of God	University of Chester	BA, Grad.Dip, MA	6,400
Leadership Centre	New Testament Church of God (NTCG)	Lee College (USA), Pentecostal Theological Seminary (USA)	NTCG Ministerial qualifications for ministerial/ leadership office	600– 700
Regents Theological College	Elim Pentecostal Church	University of Chester	BA, MA, PhD	6,930
Spurgeon's College	Baptist	Manchester University, University of Chester	BA, MA	7,570
Redcliffe	Methodist	University of Gloucestershire	BA	6,000
Queen's Foundation	Interdenominational	Durham University, Newman University	BA, MA	4,980
Canterbury Christ Church University	Anglican	Validating body with numerous national and international partners	BA, MA, PhD	9,000
Roehampton University	Interdenominational	Validating body with numerous national and international partners	FdA, BA/BTh, MA PhD	9,000
Christ Redeemer College	Redeemed Christian Church of God (RCCG)	Middlesex University	Diploma, BA	6,000

The political economy of higher education now means that colleges offering theological education for ministry formation are becoming highly competitive. Students who want to study Religious Studies and Theology have a wide choice from a number of old and new universities. At Leeds, Durham and King's College London, students can opt for a range of modules covering the full menu of subjects covered in systematic theology; many of these students will come to these courses with no faith or confessional interest, but merely want to deepen their study of the humanities with their religious and philosophical underpinnings. At Leeds University, for example, students study theology within the broader humanities framework (particularly with philosophy and classics). In trying to promote Leeds as the place to study, the prospectus informs students that the department of Theology and Religious Studies is 'principally interested in asking whether, why and how religion matters to public life', as well as the fact that students will benefit from being taught by 'people who have an international reputation in their field' and are 'recipients of prizes and awards in both teaching and research'. Institutions like Christ Redeemer College and Christ College (a London-based independent higher education institution recently validated by Canterbury Christ Church University) started off by offering pathways to degree qualifications through a combination of business, leadership/counselling, and theology modules.

With the recent growth and development of African and Caribbean Pentecostal and Charismatic churches, as well as 'Charismatic expressions' in the established churches, there are new demands for a range of theological education provision. In London alone, which accounts for the largest concentration of congregations and ministers from the denominations affiliated to the theological institutions listed in the Table, we see significant numbers of students from Pentecostal and Charismatic backgrounds doing undergraduate and post-graduate theology/ministerial theology courses at places like the London School of Theology, Spurgeon's College, Christ Redeemer College and Roehampton University. In a press release of autumn 2014, Roehampton University advertised itself as 'the largest UK university provider of theological education for students from African and Caribbean majority churches'. With a total of six academics actively researching issues related to Pentecostal and Charismatic churches, along with global Christianity and Public Theology and Community Engagement, and more than 120 students from these churches, Roehampton appears to be the university of choice for a significant number of students doing courses in Theology and Religious Studies/Ministerial Theology in an ecumenical learning environment.

Earlier in the discussion, I hinted at what I referred to as the political economy of higher education, that is, the regime of charges and tuition fees, internal and external competition, 'value for money', module and credits transfer, and the research and public profile of the university. It could be argued that the new political economy in education in general, and in theological education/ministerial training in particular, amounts to what can be termed the 'commodification of education' where it is determined and conditioned by market forces. In this regard, we see the Resourcing Ministerial Education Task Group of the Church of England Archbishops' Council getting to grips with the sort of resource management issues that medium-to-large size businesses and corporations have to wrestle with; issues like reviewing the effectiveness and value for money of the Church's investment in ministerial education, and defining precisely what 'effectiveness of investment' looks like, along with so-called 'objective evidential means' to measure effectiveness. While this mirrors the language one typically encounters in shorter MBA courses, this is the reality of the current education environment; and theological colleges and higher education institutions that don't take cognisance of this are doomed to failure, and closure. yup again

Survival now means business rationalization and making 'the business case' for certain types of programmes of study and ministerial education to equip people to serve the Church in the modern world of pluralism, mixed economies of educational provision and declining numbers of individuals training for the ministry. In this political economy of higher education provision understanding your 'market share' and doing your 'market research' are critical success factors. It is certainly true, as M. J. Jackson mooted decades ago, that 'Market research will not reveal the kingdom of God, which does not come by observation' (Jackson, p. 27). But it is becoming equally true that without some attention being paid to such management and sociological tools, ministerial education and effective mission are put at risk.

In the final part of this chapter I want to raise a number of issues around theological expectations, the teaching and learning experience, qualifications and the way forward. Given the diversity in provision and variability in academic standards and accreditation, one is forced to raise questions about the future of theological education for Pentecostal and Charismatic churches and those concerned with ministerial training. The proliferation of institutions involved in theological education and ministerial training is, undoubtedly, a cause for both celebration and concern: celebration in that there is a growing desire among lay people and those in a variety of Christian ministry and leadership positions for forms of formal theological education and ministerial development; a concern in that the proliferation brings with it inherent quality assurance challenges.

The new Common Awards in Theology, Ministry and Mission bring a degree of efficiency, rationality, economies of scale and standardization to theological education and ministerial training. Developed primarily for the Church of England and its partners under the auspices of Durham University, the Common Awards bring under one umbrella educational programmes of over 20 theological and ministerial educational institutions that were previously validated by 19 universities, as stated in the Preface to the Common Awards in Theology, Ministry and Mission, October 2012.

What can we expect from a person at the end of a BA Honours programme of study in Theology and Religious Studies? I suspect that one would assume that they understand the importance of religion and theology, and its place among other intellectual disciplines. For those undertaking ministerial training they will be engaged in incarnational theology – attempting a judicious balance between theory and practice, or what Laurie Green referred to as an 'inextricable unity of action and reflection' (Green 2012). In short, ministerial theology students are expected to be reflective practitioners, using theory/theology and experience to engage with the problems and challenges of Christian ministry and mission. To a large extent, the Quality Assurance Agency for Higher Education (QAA) guidance goes a long way in reflecting this, along with many of the generic skills and qualities expected of ministerial theology students and those studying humanities subjects.

The QAA subject benchmark statement for Theology and Religious Studies gives an indication of what can be reasonably expected of a graduate in the subject in terms of their knowledge, understanding and skills at the end of their studies. The subject should provide students with the opportunity to engage in the two-fold exercises of exploration and analysis according to the QAA Subject Benchmark Statement: Theology and Religious Studies, October 2014 (UK Quality Code for Higher Education, Part A: Setting and maintaining academic standards), section 2.4:

- exploring the religious thought of one or more traditions so as to understand each in its integrity and diversity, and grasp its integrative role in relation to life styles, practices and ethics;
- analysing the historical, social, philosophical, cultural and artistic role of religion or belief systems in diverse contexts.

In addition to the above, there are particular 'qualities of mind' that students are expected to acquire and display. There are nine in all. The following is a summary of three of them:

- The ability to understand how people have thought and acted – and continue to think and act – in contexts other than the student's own; how beliefs, doctrines, traditions and practices have developed within particular social and cultural contexts; and how religious traditions have changed over time and continue to evolve in the contemporary world.
- Sensitivity to the problems of religious language and experience, and to the issues of multiple and conflicting interpretations of language and symbols, texts and traditions. Simplistic, literalizing or doctrinaire explanations are less likely to be advanced by a student of theology and religious studies.
- The ability to employ a variety of methods of study in analysing material, to think independently, identifying tasks, set goals and solve problems.

These qualities, regarded as 'intellectual skills and competencies', not only signal to the student what is expected of them, they also inform potential employers about the academic and personal qualities of a theology and religious studies graduate. Additionally, it signals to educational institutions and providers the level and quality of teaching and learning they have to provide to produce the intended outcome.

With these kinds of quality assurance demands – and the rigour inherent in the inspection framework for monitoring compliance especially for those institutions seeking validation from established universities – there is bound to be something of a 'survival of the fittest' in operation, as institutions compete for students. The reality is that some institutions just won't crack it; they will go under not just because they cannot provide the teaching and learning to produce the intellectual skills and competencies students need in the modern world, but because, like other 'goods' and 'services' in the economy, students will seek out alternatives that will enable them to compete and progress effectively into teaching or research for higher degrees.

In respect of black majority churches (BMCs), this poses a number of issues. Because many of the leaders in these churches are theologically 'untrained', the existence of a plethora of Bible schools and training taking place in them 'gives churches the impression that they are preparing their leaders for ministry'. However, according to Sturge, most of what is on offer is nothing more than 'fool's gold'; that is, people 'engaged in costly study for certificates or qualifications that go unrecognized elsewhere, or be granted doctorates or degrees after only one year of study' (Sturge, p. 167). As a former General Director of the African and Caribbean Evangelical Alliance (ACEA) Sturge was in a good position to see the benefits, or a lack of it, of theological education and ministerial training in Pentecostal and Charismatic churches first hand. One gets the impression that he was disappointed with what he saw in some of these churches and the way the theological institutions were failing to produce the kind of leaders suitable for the BMCs in the future. There is the suggestion of 'setting up our own' institutions to address this 'deficit' and what is often characterized as 'a dogmatic approach' to ministry in many of these churches and organizations.

Today, Pentecostals and Charismatics are receiving theological education and ministerial training in a variety of educational environments, including confessional and ecumenical ones, as seen from the sample of providers in the Table above. Before its sad demise in 2002, a number of Pentecostal leaders benefitted from the 'intercultural theological education' provided by the Centre for Black and White Christian Partnership (CBWCP) in Birmingham. Under the leadership of people like Walter Hollenweger, Roswith Gerloff, Patrick Kalolombie and Joe Aldred, the Centre provided a safe space for Pentecostals and Charismatics to do and develop aspects of their theology and spirituality.

At CBWCP, Pentecostals and Charismatics rubbed shoulders with Anglicans, Catholics, Methodists and others in an environment of mutual trust, respect and shared ministry experience and challenges. Pentecostals were able to study their history and traditions, articulate and reflect upon their 'Charismatic experiences', while at the same time learning about the function of higher criticism and other hermeneutical tools and approaches to 'the Word of God'. Pentecostal leaders like Bishop Martin Simmonds of the First United Church of Jesus Christ (Apostolic) and Prophetess F. N. Onyuku-Opukiri of the Born Again Christ Healing Church were among the first graduates of the Centre. The same can be said for the work and mission of Queen's Foundation. Queen's is known as the interdenominational institution where 'Black Theology' was developed and sustained as a serious theological discipline. It appointed Robert Beckford in the early 1990s as the first black lecturer in Black Theology in the UK. Out of the work at Queen's and CBWCP came the UK's first Black Theology journal in 1998, *Black Theology in Britain: A Journal of Contextual Praxis*, which has since been renamed *Black Theology – an international journal*. There are the numerous publications of Anthony Reddie on Black Theology and related themes. Queen's is still one of the few places in the UK where there is a tradition of ministerial training and development in Black

Theology, and where students are encouraged to critically engage in this theological discourse and to pursue it at post-graduate level. Its recent appointment of Dulcie McKenzie as tutor in Black Theology, Ministries and Leadership continues to build upon the work started by John Wilkinson in the 1980s.

Experiencing ministerial training and theological education in an ecumenical setting has a number of benefits, not least the opportunity to study with, and learn from, Christian brothers and sisters who are equally concerned with serving 'the people of God' where they are called and from the ecclesial tribe in which they find themselves. This experience can be both enriching and humbling as pastoral and ministerial joys and challenges are shared (and problems often solved), as people bring their collective insights, wisdom and experience to bear on common pastoral problems and encounters. Places like the London School of Theology, Roehampton University and Spurgeon's College do this extremely well.

As one of the main institutions catering for the largest group of leaders from the African and Caribbean churches, Roehampton University has uniquely pioneered a two-year foundation degree in Ministerial Theology. This foundation degree in the arts (FdA) is designed for people engaged in 'any form of Christian ministry (paid or unpaid)'. As a workplace-based practical degree, the FdA is designed to help students become more theologically reflective about their ministry. Students who successfully complete the FdA can decide to convert this into an honours degree in Ministerial Theology, earning them the Bachelor of Theology (BTh). The flexibility of the programme, along with the academic and pastoral support provided, is proving very attractive to large numbers of Pentecostal pastors and leaders. With historic connections with the Anglican, Methodist and Catholic churches, and a teaching staff representing a wide cross-section of Christian life and experience, Roehampton University offers what is probably one of the best models for the future of theological education and ministerial training. An integral part of the course is the training and development of mentors; ministerial theology students are assigned a mentor for the duration of their training.

With the establishment of the Common Awards and the academic rigour stipulated in the QAA subject benchmark statement, theological education and ministerial training can only improve. There will be raised expectations all round, providing quality assurance in teaching and learning to make a qualitative difference in the student experience. I believe this will serve Pentecostals and Charismatics well, enhancing their ministry and, hopefully, transforming the communities they serve.

Of course, appropriate qualifications are needed in all professions and vocations. While many Pentecostal and Charismatic ministers and leaders are qualified in other fields and professions, I believe theological education is imperative if they are to effectively fulfil the 'Great Commission' in contemporary society in partnership with other Christians. Indeed, one would struggle to engage in a meaningful way with the ethical, political and cultural challenges we face today without some formal training in theology and religious studies. Theological training allows us to speak to, and participate in, our 'common culture' in ways not too dissimilar to what we witness of Paul in Acts 17.

Recognizing that Christian theology is a vast ocean, entering via the small streams of our own traditions and ecclesiology is not a bad place to start, so long as we don't stop there. Pentecostals and Charismatics certainly have a lot to offer in ministerial theology and ministry formation, but they can also derive great benefit from other Christian traditions. According to Hollenweger, mainline churches can learn from Pentecostals without trying to become Pentecostals; they can find their own 'charismata' because 'charismata of oral cultures' are present in all churches even though they are mostly 'suppressed' (Hollenweger, p. 339). I often come across Pentecostals who tend to think that the Spirit of God only started to 'move' again in 1906 with the Azusa Street phenomenon. Tell that to the ante-Nicene and the post-Nicene fathers, the Desert Fathers and Mothers, or to Calvin and Luther and other servants and faithful witnesses down the ages. One would like to think that encountering live Christian traditions and preparing for ministry in an interdenominational environment would disavow us of some of our prejudices and ecclesiological blind spots.

Charismatics? What should they do and encourage? I want to suggest three things briefly by way of an observation, a question and some recommendations.

First, there is definitely a new enthusiasm among Pentecostals and Charismatics for leaders to be better trained and 'equipped for the ministry'. This is both desirable and necessary if these congregations are to grow and continue to be 'salt and light' in their communities.

There was the notion, slightly overstated in my view in respect of Pentecostals, that Pentecostals and Baptists are 'frustrated' by national churches' 'partnership with the political state' and that the 'ecumenical vision is hard to envision' for these groups (Haymes, p. 129).

But things are changing. And the number of Pentecostals, especially those from African and Caribbean churches, opting for interdenominational institutions of higher education is bound to inform and influence how they 'do ministry'.

Second, there is the controversial question as to the appropriate level of formal qualifications needed for 'ministry'. I suspect this will largely depend on what we mean by 'ministry', as well as the level and scope envisaged. In his most recent work, Robert Beckford argues for greater political engagement and theological training for leaders in Pentecostal churches. He argues for a minimum qualification of a BA (in theology, religious studies/ministerial education) for ordination; he also wants the larger denominations to introduce 'mandatory educational development' for new and existing clergy, as well as a clear demarcation line between 'earned' and 'honorary' degrees to reflect theological competence (Beckford, p. 194). To a large extent the anecdotal trend among Pentecostal leaders is moving in that direction. And if there is to be the development of what Adedibu calls the 'repository of scholars and writers to espouse and articulate the theological underpinnings of BMCs while avoiding the potential drift from the Pentecostal ideal', then the question of qualifications and training becomes more critical (Adedibu, p. 249).

Finally, a few recommendations. One of the things that the former Archbishop of Canterbury (Dr Rowan Williams) and the Archbishop of York (Dr John Sentamu) set in motion was a Memorandum of Understanding (MOU) between black-led (Pentecostal) churches and the Church of England. I had the privilege of drafting this document with Revd Sonia Barron and Bishop Dr Joe Aldred. Although as yet not officially adopted, the MOU can be seen as a good model of ecumenical partnership; it recognizes the areas of shared mission, partnerships, and unity that already exist between the two denominations and wants to develop and strengthen these. In giving substance to the desire for greater unity and partnership, the MOU outlined a commitment to theological education and leadership development thus:

- To develop partnership agreements and protocols for the Church of England to share its experience and expertise in theological training and ministry formation with black-led churches and training institutions;
- To work together by way of mutual learning to discover effective strategies for leadership development.

It is hoped that the recently formed Anglican Pentecostal Theological Steering Group will build upon the work done concerning the MOU. One would like to hope that in the field of theological education and ministry formation that Pentecostal and Charismatic churches and denominations would tap into the resources and experience of the Church of England, especially with the new curriculum and ministerial training available in the Common Awards validated by Durham University.

Younger Pentecostal and Charismatic leaders and pastors want, and are seeking, the kind of theological education and ministerial training that will enable them to be effective communicators of the Christian faith today. In the black church manifesto there is a specific recommendation to address this issue; it calls for black majority churches to 'collaborate with each other and partner with higher education institutions to provide theological education for its leaders' (Muir and Omooba, p. 6). In the past, some Pentecostal students wasted a lot of time and money going to institutions and graduating with qualifications that had little or no transferable value in the wider academic world. The theological challenge Aldred spoke of facing the black church is one that still affects Pentecostals and Charismatics in general: there is still a fear of 'academic theological studies' (Aldred and Ogbo, p. 225). Pentecostal leaders, especially denominational leaders, need to encourage bridge-building, as Aldred recommends, between the church and the academy. In some circles, this is being done through Black Theology and Contextual Theology.

Although there is a seductive tendency to privilege certain types of theological education and ministry formation, there can be no doubt that in our pluralist and postmodern world all Christian leaders and those who 'feel the call of ministry' would benefit from a theological education producing the 'intellectual skills and competencies' stipulated in the QAA subject benchmark statement noted above. With its emphasis on such 'generic skills' as 'empathy and imaginative insight', 'commitment to lifelong learning', the 'ability to attend to others and have respect for others' views' and the 'ability to engage critically with the meaning of documents and recognize that meanings may be multiple', one cannot help but see how critical theological education and proper ministerial training are to the effectiveness of those in Pentecostal and Charismatic churches called to ministry and for the health and efficacy of the Church in carrying out God's mission in the modern world.

References

Adedibu, Babatunde, 2012, *Coat of Many Colours: The Origins, Growth, Distinctiveness and Contributions of Black Majority Churches to British Christianity*. Blackpool: Wisdom Summit.

Aldred, Joe, 2010, 'The Challenges Facing Black Church Leadership', in Aldred, Joe and Keno Ogbo (eds), *The Black Church in the Twenty-first Century*. London: Darton, Longman & Todd.

Anderson, Robert Mapes, 1969, *Vision of the Disinherited: The Making of American Pentecostalism*. New York: Oxford University Press.

Archer, Kenneth J., 2012, 'Hermeneutics', in Stewart, Adam, *Handbook of Pentecostal Christianity*. Illinois: Northern Illinois University Press.

Barth, Karl, 2001, *Protestant Theology in the Nineteenth Century: Its Background & History*. New edn. London: SCM Press.

Beckford, Robert, 2014, *Documentary as Exorcism: Resisting the Bewitchment of Colonial Christianity*. London and New York: Bloomsbury.

Faith in the City: A Call for Action by Church and Nation – The Report of the Archbishop of Canterbury's Commission on Urban Priority Areas, 1985. London: Church House Publishing.

Green, Laurie, 2012, *Let's Do Theology: Resources for Contextual Theology*. London and New York: Bloomsbury.

Gunton, Colin, 2001, 'Doing Theology in the University Today', in Gunton, Colin, Stephen R. Holmes and Murray A. Rae (eds), *The Practice of Theology: A Reader*. London: SCM Press.

Haymes, Brian, 2002, 'The Baptist and Pentecostal Churches', in Avis, P. (ed.), *The Christian Church: An Introduction to the Major Traditions*. London: SPCK.

Hollenweger, Walter, 1997, *Pentecostalism: Origins and Developments Worldwide*. Peabody, MA: Hendrickson Publishers.

Jackson, M. J., 1974, *The Sociology of Religion: Theory and Practice*. London & Sydney: Batsford.

Kay, William K., 2000, *Pentecostals in Britain*. Glasgow: Paternoster Press.

Kay, William K., 2009, *Pentecostalism*. London: SCM Press.

Lyotard, Jean-François, 1984, *The Postmodern Condition: A Report on Knowledge*, translated by Geoff Bennington and Brian Massumi. Manchester: Manchester University Press.

Macquarrie, John, 1966, *Principles of Christian Theology*. London: SCM Press.

Memorandum of Understanding Between the Church of England and British Black (African and Caribbean) Led Churches, 2011 (unpublished).

Muir, R. David and Ade Omooba, 2015, *Black Church Political Mobilisation – a manifesto for action*. London: National Church Leaders Forum Publications.

Nelson, Douglas J., 1981, *For Such a Time as This: The Story of Bishop William J. Seymour and the Azusa Street Revival: a Search for Pentecostal/Charismatic Roots*. PhD Thesis, University of Birmingham, England.

O'Connor, Edward D., CSC (ed.), 1978, *Charismatic Renewal*. London: SPCK.

Sturge, Mark, 2005, *Look what the Lord has Done! An Exploration of Black Christian Faith in Britain*. Bletchley: Scripture Union.

Tillich, Paul, 1953, *Systematic Theology*, Vol. 1. Welwyn, Herts: James Nisbet.

Tillich, Paul, 1962, *The Shaking of the Foundations*. Harmondsworth: Pelican Books.

12

Pentecostalism and Prosperity Theology: A Call for Reappraisal of Acceptance and Rejection

MARK STURGE

Prosperity theology has proven to be an issue that provides significant challenge to Christians of all denominations and theological persuasions. A significant contributor to disparities and hostilities is the lack of appropriate stewardship and scholarship in handling the subject. There seems to be a dearth of scholarship on the subject from those who believe that 'prosperity is the birthright' of believers. And it is often left to theology students to address the subject, sometimes by indulging in the defamation of proponents. Christian belief on the subject is therefore guided by personal conscience, impressions and the teachings they have been exposed to. This background provides an unsound and unsatisfactory basis for the level of confidence expressed by proponents and opponents alike, with entrenched views showing no sign of abating.

The irreverently labelled 'name it and claim it', 'blab it and grab it', or even 'prosperity gospel' make it difficult to conduct a reasoned examination without instinctively reinforcing the disdain in which it is sometimes held by opponents, or siding with enthusiasts. Even more polarization occurs because there is rarely any personal, congregational or leadership relationship between the camps. I started a conversation on prosperity theology in my book *Look What the Lord Has Done! An Exploration of Black Christian Faith in Britain* (Sturge, pp. 138–41). There, my intention was to be an honest broker; to take a step back and examine the argument from both sides. The temptation here is to do the same. However, to do so would be worse than cowardice; it would be a betrayal of the witness of scripture and deny my own conscience. It would also mean that my thinking has stagnated and imply I have made little or no development in my understanding of the issues. My approach to this conversation is therefore firmly on the side of 'contend[ing] for the faith' (Jude 3).

Whatever our perspective, each of us must consider how we over-come the level of abject poverty and disenfranchisement in our com-munities and world. We must also wrestle with the fundamental question, 'Could it ever be morally right and acceptable that one per cent of the world's population own and control 75 per cent of the world's resources?' (Savage 2018). Equally, we must ask, 'What is our ambition for justice, fair economic trade and practices, as well as equal opportunities of participation, influence and dissent in the decisions that affect poor people's lives?' While the general understanding is that prosperity is about financial, monetary and material acquisition, and personal success, prosperity gospel proponents are most likely to see it as the flourishing and well-being of the spirit, soul and body. While I agree with this tripartite approach to prosperity I will, however, limit my discussion to material wealth as this is the festering sore.

The Premise of Faith

One of the hallmarks of Pentecostalism is the belief that God, through the work of the Holy Spirit, has not ceased in giving gifts, and inter-vening to transform people's lives. This being so, and with no statute of limitation, the door is always open for a God who is forensically concerned about every area of our lives to respond to our individual and communal needs and circumstances. The assurances and warnings pronounced by Jesus in Luke 12.1–7 encouraged his hearers, and now its readers, to believe that everything they have done, and everything that has been done to them, is transparent before God. Moreover, God is committed to continually protecting and seeking their justice. For Pentecostals, these characteristics form the very nature of God, who does not change (Mal. 3.6; Matt. 24.35; Heb. 13.8). Therefore, it would be unthinkable, first, to assume that God is uninterested in the adverse plight of the poor and, second, that God is so mean-spirited, classist or even xenophobic that he has confined large geographies, ethnicities and people groups, in perpetuity, to experience the worst excesses of deprivation and a diminished image of himself.

At the heart of the conversation on prosperity is the 'Word of Faith Movement' (WoFM), which responds to the importance of faith in the life of the believer. Alongside the Charismatic movement, which redis-covered and promoted the gifts of the Holy Spirit in the Church, they revisited 1 Corinthians 12 and took seriously the notion that faith was a special and distinct gift of the Holy Spirit. The WoFM recognized that this gift was different from 'sola fide', the faith by which we are justified before God (Rom. 5.9, 18). Instead, as one of the special gifts from God, it needed to be manifested in the life of the recipient and be used for the benefit of the church and the world.

The exercise of the 'gift of faith' therefore challenges notions of human limitation, common sense and the natural order. Instead, it wholly trusts in the omnipotence of God and the working of the Holy Spirit to provide. The recipient of the gift of faith becomes a conduit or fully yielding servant, in whom and through whom God has chosen to exercise his sovereignty and abundant love for his creation. This belief also leads us to expect that believers must break free from the limitations and the confines of natural law and order. It requires the redeeming of our thinking too. Any notion of 'facts' that conflict with the ambitions of God, as evidenced in scripture or as declared to his servants for a specific circumstance, should be challenged and channelled through the lens of faith. Such an application of faith is necessary to embrace and benefit from the supernatural order, which is the kingdom and realm of God (Heb. 11.6).

Those who possess the 'gift of faith' have a higher degree of confidence that God will defy or use the natural order of things to achieve his purposes. This faith is a believing faith that turns impossibility into possibility because 'faith is the assurance of things hoped for, the conviction of things not seen' (Heb. 11.1); and we serve 'the God ... who gives life to the dead and calls into existence the things that do not exist' (Rom. 4.17).

The Gift of Giving

Alongside the gift of faith, the 'gift of giving' looms large for Pentecostals. The primary purpose of this spiritual gift is for 'the common good' – blessed to be a blessing (1 Cor. 12.7). Giving should exhibit a spirit of generosity (Rom. 12.3), cheerfulness, willingness and humility, not grudging, arrogant and boastful (2 Cor. 9.1–8). The Old and New Testaments present us with believers and heathens using their wealth to support those who lacked – relatives (Lev. 25.35), tithes for the benefit of the priests, strangers, widows and orphans (Deut. 1.28–29); Cornelius (Acts 10.1–2), Dorcas (Acts 9.36–39) and Zacchaeus (Luke 19.8). The temptation is to reduce the 'gift of giving' to time, a smile, empathy, practical help and the like. However, the Bible offers its own clarity by referencing the 'gift of mercy or compassion', and elsewhere the gift of 'helps' (1 Cor. 12.28 KJV) and hospitality (1 Peter 4.9; Rom. 12.13).

The adage 'you can't give what you don't have' helps our thinking. The poor contributes as a collective in what the apostle Paul calls the 'ministry of the saints'. This means that the Church is also endowed with the 'gift of giving'. For his evidence he uses the churches in Macedonia who were under significant oppression and lived in poverty. Yet, they received the grace of giving and were able to give out of and beyond their ability. The apostle Paul wanted the Corinthians to experience the same joy as the Macedonians by participating in this grace of giving (2 Cor. 8.1–9; 9.1–5). A reappraisal of prosperity theology can make a case for differentiating as well as outworking the role of wealthy individuals and the collective contributions of the Church.

Bad Cases Making Poor Laws

The old adage 'Hard cases make bad laws' stands to remind us that it is a dangerous precedent to establish or validate the legitimacy and efficacy of a principled position by starting with extremes, especially since each of us will have numerous examples to prove our position. Much of the practice of prosperity theology emanates from the United States of America and is prevalent in developing nations such as the continent of Africa, South and Latin America and Asia. Its early adopters are now considered the founders or fathers of the movement and they have one thing in common – they started life in financial lack, as poor, ill or from difficult family lives. Their personal experiences led to a desperate reliance on God and the exercise of faith, after encountering God. This is understandable as poor individuals and communities, wholly reliant on God for the supply and provision for their daily needs, are often perceived as being more earnest in profession, prayer and faith.

The way 'the gift of faith' is applied is often challenged and ultimately discredited based on outcomes from utterances, professions or manifestations. The case for the rediscovery, acceptance and embrace of the 'gift of faith' becomes even more difficult when prominent leaders compound the issue by poor stewardship, selfish ambition and misuse of financial resources for their own benefit. The ultimate test of the application of faith is the fruit that it produces. Testimonies and evidence of outcomes are often presented with confidence, but received, often rightly, as arrogance or boasting. The impression given is that it is the gifted who are responsible for triggering the blessing, which is inconsistent with the wisdom of scripture (Prov. 16.18; 21.4; 27.2).

Jesse Duplantis hit mainstream headlines in the media by asking his supporters to believe with him for a $54 million Dassault Falcon 7X private Jet (30 May 2018), and before him Creflo Dollar requested $65 million (13 March 2015). Kenneth Copeland and Mike Murdock have asked for and boasted of similar blessings. The media interest in these stories stems from the belief that such behaviour is inconsistent with good stewardship, an abuse of a position of influence and power, and preying on the vulnerable. Critically, all the social media platforms were alight with commentary and opinion pieces.

In response, Duplantis argues that he did not ask his followers for money, just to believe with him for the blessing, debt free. This seems disingenuous and he should be courageous enough to defend his conviction. However, John Burton challenges us to consider the question, 'Why are you threatened by his (Jesse's) faith?' He continues, 'We need more people to believe for absolutely shocking, magnificent, world-shaking things. Celebrate when men and women of God are not only dreaming big but actually putting action to their faith. Visionaries have always threatened those with no vision for their lives' (Burton 2018). Burton further cements his argument in scripture: 'And without faith it is impossible to please God, for whoever would approach him must believe that he exists and that he rewards those who seek him' (Heb. 11.6).

In response, international Gospel artist Kirk Franklyn took to Instagram:

> I'm posting this because now that we see popular culture stand up to the injustices in mainstream society, I believe the church should do the same for its own as well. We should take the lead when there is an abuse of power that affects our message to the masses; our silence can be as loud as the bigotry and racism we see in the public square. Many of these 'ministries' built their wealth on the backs of poor rural minorities that put their trust in the hands of 'God's shepherds' only to see the prosperity benefit those doing the preaching. Again, there are GREAT Christian leaders, and there is NOTHING wrong with having a plane ... but if the burden falls on the less fortunate and GREED is the check written by those drowning in socio-economic rivers of systemic disparities, GOD is not flying that plane. (Franklyn, Instagram, May 2018)

While it is right to hold the church and its leaders to a higher moral standard than the rest of society, we must also look to ourselves. We are complicit and readily accept, without criticism, a number of exploitative relationships. For example, the poor are exploited daily, through exorbitant prices, by those who provide essential services (gas, electricity, water, mobile). Their and our moral conscience must be challenged.

To analyse prosperity teachings appropriately it is necessary, as a starting point, that we examine the source and the purpose of wealth, how it is used, and its associated benefits and risks. We also need to go a step further to understand its compatibility with scripture and what, if any, is relevant to our worldview and everyday personal and communal lives.

The Purpose of Wealth: An Economic View

To ensure that we are standing on the same platform and speaking with the same understanding, let us take a moment to remind ourselves of the differences between wealth, money and cash. Economically speaking, wealth is the assets one accumulates that contribute to, or provide an income for our overall well-being and/or our satisfaction. Material wealth therefore will include property: homes, artistic works, jewellery, antiques, etc.; stocks, shares, cryptocurrencies, education, networks and circles of influence, unique or in-demand expertise and any other income generators.

Money on the other hand is the agreed method used in exchange for goods and services. The range of available monies over centuries and in different communities became very evident to me some years ago while serving on the British Museum's Wealth of Africa Advisory Group. The displays of salt, shells, cloth, silver and copper all demonstrated that money could be any agreed commodity used as a settlement, between the supplier (seller) and recipient (buyer), for goods and services. Some communities use livestock, agricultural goods and whatever they can trade with. The main challenge is establishing what is a fair exchange between a wide variety of goods and services. For most of us, the offer of our knowledge, time and labour (work) is given in exchange for money, unless we are volunteering or being exploited. Alternatively, if one neighbour has need of bread and the other needed sugar they could agree that for a loaf of bread the other would offer a cup of sugar. At that moment the money is sugar and bread. The problem is, new technology aside, it is not always easy, convenient or time-efficient to match what you offer with what your neighbour needs. It is for this reason that cash is the most convenient way to settle a transaction. Cash is therefore the available resources one can access on demand and when needed, whether it is deposited in a bank, stored under a mattress or kept in a plastic bag. We often hear of liquid assets, which is considered equivalent to cash as it can be converted to cash without losing its value. Liquid assets are the investments that can be cashed in within 60–90 days.

Almost every aspect of our world is geared toward the generation and acquisition of wealth. The primary purpose of every business is to create wealth for its owner. Our education system is designed to provide a pipeline of wealth managers and the supporting cast. We need to look no further than the founders of hugely influential companies such as Bill Gates of Microsoft, Warren Buffet, CEO and Chairman of Berkshire Hathaway, Mark Zuckerberg of Facebook and Jeff Bezos of Amazon to understand the leverage and influence they exert over other businesses, governments and a significant part of our daily lives. Yet, these wealthy magnates are also some of the world's best-known philanthropists. Leaving aside any moral justification or repudiations – monopoly, oligopoly and predatorial behaviours, tax avoidance, unfair advantage that deprive other companies, individuals and countries from participating in and benefitting from development and generating alternatives – wealth plays a significant role in influencing the priorities of communities, civil society and decision makers. It can be used for social good, and provide direct lifestyle and societal benefits for its owners. It offers privileges and opportunities not usually available to other citizens – access to other influencers, the political classes and the best professional support and advice, which sometimes undermines 'everyday' justice. The privileges significant wealth affords go way beyond belonging and identity, or ensuring its owners never lack or want for the essentials in their lives or lifestyles.

By the same token, one's circle of influence, clubs and societies, and who you know also forms part of your wealth. Herein lies the adage, 'it is not what you know but who you know'. It has been well established that if you attend a certain private school or prestigious university then your future trajectory may include opportunities in politics, broadcasting and other large companies waiting with open arms. By this and other means many have secured wealth through social, economic and political capital.

Those who understand wealth and provide wealth management services also claim that lasting wealth has to be intergenerational and wealth in a single generation is not guaranteed to last beyond that. This means that another function of wealth is to secure a legacy and the place of future generations in their families, communities, business and society as a whole.

Material wealth, as a vehicle for progress and opportunity, is very attractive and it is no wonder those who possess it do not openly acknowledge the many privileges it affords.

Poverty and the Poor

The contrast to wealth, money, cash, privilege and choice is poverty, disenfranchisement, injustice and lack of choice. As someone who works with a large international development organization, through my day-to-day work I am confronted and challenged daily by the stark impact of poverty on the poor. The poor lack power and often the means to create and sustain wealth. For good reasons, there is resistance within the charity sector to defining poverty merely in terms of income and accessible finance. Nevertheless, the notions of poverty such as losing a child to illness – brought about by unclean water; being sick and not able to see a doctor; not having access to school and not knowing how to read; powerlessness, lack of representation and freedom; structural, gender, class and ethnic inequalities; not having a job; fear for the future; living one day at a time; point consistently to the primary source of most of these causes – the lack or misuse of wealth, money and cash. This does not negate the many other factors that contribute to poverty, including catastrophic personal circumstances such as natural disasters, conflict, climate and inclement weather patterns and the like; even poor and irresponsible governance. Significantly, even these are more harshly felt in underdeveloped environments and communities. Basically, the flimsier your economic infrastructure, the greater your vulnerability to adversity.

On 25 September 2015, 193 countries signed up and agreed to deliver the United Nations Sustainable Development Goals, a commitment to implement 17 goals to transform our world. These included: no poverty, zero hunger, good health and well-being, gender equality, good education, clean water and sanitation and decent work and economic growth. All of these goals aimed to ensure that the citizens of our world have the prospect of a fruitful and fulfilled life. The call to action is for each of us to play a part in ensuring that no one is left behind and to bring an end to abject poverty in a generation. On the face of it, world leaders are very clear where they want to take people from and everyone agrees that we must. However, what is not so apparent is where they want them to be. If the Church is to play its full part, then she too needs to have a theological framing that draws attention to the issues of poverty and wealth and, at the very least, propose a solution for what the end goal should look like. This theology needs to move from the keyboards and pages of the intellectual elite to the pews and lives of congregations.

We should also take seriously the public conversations of the former British Chancellor of the Exchequer, George Osborne, 'Well look, no one takes pleasure from people making money out of the misery of others, but that is a function of capitalist markets' (Osborne, on BBC Television's *Newsnight* programme, 17 September 2008). And even further, 'Just as we should never balance the budget on the backs of the poor, so it is an economic delusion to think you can balance it only on the wallets of the rich' (quoted in Wintour and Watt 2012).

The big question is, are we interested in the poor living fulfilled and sustainable lives to achieve their ambitions and that of God (John 10.10)? Alternatively, do we simply want to change their status from being dependants into that of being first-class consumers? Any conversation about prosperity theology that does not consider the plight of the poor is at best grandstanding, unchristian and at its worst merely copying the rhetoric of others.

Prosperity Theology's Response to the Poor

Properly considered, 'prosperity theology', as its name suggests, is concerned with the fundamental human problem: what does a God – who owns all things, knows all things and controls all things – have to say to the poor, the disenfranchised, the downtrodden and the socially excluded, those who find themselves in a rut and feel that only a miracle, wherever it comes from, can make a difference? Is the 'divine exchange' at the cross, where Christ took our place, of no consequence to our lives apart from the salvation of the soul? Are we not marginalizing and misrepresenting the Christian faith if we close off salvation from the cares of this life?

It might be helpful to think of prosperity theology as having the same ambitions as liberation theology, in understanding what scripture has to say about the plight of the poor. While liberation theology starts from the point of the individual's experience and then explores what scripture has to say about that experience, prosperity theology has its origin in scripture and seeks to ensure that the individual's experience matches what God has already declared it should be in his word. Both theologies seek the same basic objectives:

- to highlight, from scripture, God's deep concern for the poor, the marginalized, the rejected, the suffering and the outsider;
- to renounce poverty as a quasi-blessing or a curse deserved by people from particular ethnic groups or geographical locations, or a specific tribe, caste or class;
- to dispel the myth that humanity's hope for the future rests only in our eschatology – when Jesus returns, and we experience a new life in heaven. Instead, both theologies proclaim that we can and must

experience God's fullness and blessings now, in this life, as well as in the future;

- to challenge people's negative perceptions of themselves, their circumstances and their future, and to offer hope in place of despair.

Where the two theologies part company is in their response to social, economic and political structures. Proponents of prosperity theology seem to favour the idea that capitalist ideology, infrastructure and methodology can be used as vehicles for change. They are committed to missions of mercy. It would be highly unusual for churches and organizations not to have long- and short-term commitments to building schools, hospitals, managing orphanages or providing for the daily needs of communities. However, unlike liberation theologians, they do not see identifying with the poor and disenfranchised as becoming one with them; rather, the emphasis is on transformation and transportation – that is, a change in circumstances and change in location, if that is what is needed. Proponents themselves become the exemplars: it is their success, testimonies and lifestyles that demonstrate what is possible. 'Follow me as I follow Christ' seems to be the clarion call (1 Cor. 11:1). The contentions this evokes is whether this is the way of a justice-seeking Christ who resisted and violently confronted the abusers of the poor (Matt. 21.12–13) and was himself intimidated by death threats when he confronted the exploiters and the powerful (Luke 4.29; Matt. 12.14).

Another area of difference is that prosperity theology focuses on the individual's ability to respond positively to his or her own plight. Not much is made of capitalism's discriminating structures, economic policies and political bias in favour of the rich and wealthy. The desire is to share in the prevailing economic prosperity in spite of how it is generated. Participation in the social and economic norm is advocated and therefore their interest lies in the prosperity of the existing order without rocking the boat (Jer. 29.7).

Key Doctrines in Prosperity Theology

Prosperity theology also takes and forms its reference point from core themes in scripture (Sturge, pp. 139–40):

- Covenant: The believer is the seed of Abraham and therefore an inheritor with him of the promise. Although we have a better covenant in Christ, God did not cancel the old covenant; rather, he made it available to the whole world through the death of Christ (Rom. 4.11–12; Gal. 3.16–17, 29).

- Sowing and reaping: The Old Testament agricultural enterprises provided the backdrop for demonstrating God's blessings, favour and providence. As types and equivalents, the New Testament understanding of the measure you sow is the measure you will reap (Luke 6.38; 2 Cor. 9.6; compare with 1 Cor. 9.14) remains intact. Therefore, giving with a willing heart is a prerequisite for blessing, as God loves a cheerful giver (2 Cor. 9.7). This also includes the promise of a hundredfold blessing (Matt. 19.29; Mark 10.30).
- Being the head and not the tail: The believer is encouraged to see him or herself as the leader of the pack, victorious and successful. This theme is amplified in areas such as being overcomers rather than the overcome (2 Peter 2.19) and being 'more than conquerors' (Rom. 8.37). It would be a travesty for the people of God to constantly lack and evoke the ridicule, 'Where is your God?' (Ps. 42.3, 10; 79.10).
- Blessing and cursing: An attribute of God is to confer blessings on the obedient and curses for those who violate and disregard his laws as depicted in Deuteronomy (11.26–27; 30.1, 9; 27.12–13) and through the prophets (Mal. 2.2). Therefore, there is a blessing available to the righteous and a curse for those who reject God's way (Prov. 10.6, 22, 29).
- Divine wealth transfer: There is a belief that a just God will not ultimately allow the wicked to prosper and their ultimate end will be the demise of their temporary prosperity (Prov. 28.2). The eventual beneficiaries will be the righteous. The wealth of the wicked is therefore being stored up for the righteous (Prov. 13.22; Eccles. 2.26).

To live out these principles, believers need the anointing of the Holy Spirit (Acts 2), the revelation of the Holy Spirit (Eph. 1.17), the power of the Holy Spirit (Acts 3.1–8), and the divine favour and provision of the Lord in their lives (Acts 2.44–47). God's favour is the basis for blessing, success in every area of life and the courage to pursue, against the odds, your purpose and destiny until you overcome and are victorious. God's blessing can extend from individuals (Ps. 1.1) to whole nations (Ps. 33.12).

The Purpose of Wealth: A Biblical View

The evidence of scripture, particularly the Old Testament, suggests that God uses wealth, or the lack of it, to establish his order, secure devotion and sovereignty above all creation and other gods (1 Sam. 2.27–36; Zech. 14). The stripping away of personal, family and communal wealth (Gen. 11.5–9) serves as a stark reminder that 'it is a fearful thing to fall in the hands of the living God' (Heb. 10.31).

The disruptive and punitive nature of captivity, exile and slavery all conjure the idea of removal and banishment from an ideal and perfect will of God. The earliest and most notable stripping away of wealth and opportunity are recorded in the beginning of the biblical record of human existence. Adam and Eve (Gen. 2.24) and subsequently Cain (Gen. 4.16) are banished from the presence of God. Those who experience exile found hope when there was some opportunity to put down roots or hear encouraging news of restoration (Jer. 25.4–6; Isa. 65.17–25). God's people are left in no doubt that wealth comes from the Lord (Prov. 10.22; Deut. 8.17–18).

Most of the patriarchs emerged as wealthy clansmen – from Abraham to Lot, Isaac to Jacob and Joseph. King David and Solomon his son also possessed unparalleled wealth. The call of Abram ushered in the Abrahamic Covenant, and came with a huge price tag and compensation for any inconvenience leaving his relatives would incur (Gen. 12.1–3). From an economic perspective, this offer could not be refused. Job's wealth became a bargaining tool to establish whether his love for God was conditional on the blessings, good fortunes and protections he had received (Job 1.8–12).

In the New Testament, wealth is presented as a barrier to entering into the kingdom of God (Matt. 9.24; cf. John 3.3). A stark choice was often demanded: 'Jesus, looking at him, loved him and said, "You lack one thing; go, sell what you own, and give the money to the poor, and you will have treasure in heaven; then come, follow me"' (Mark 10.21). Moreover, the rich and powerful are often encountered as abusers of their privileged position and office (Luke 19.1–10). Even when persuaded to enter God's kingdom, wealth stifles, chokes and prevents the opportunity from flourishing (Matt. 13.22).

An unhealthy attitude to riches is often despised and the love of money is presented as the gateway to evil (1 Tim. 6.10); and for Jesus it is a polarizing force, therefore one 'cannot love God and money' (Luke 16.13). Money is also in mind when considering not loving 'the things of the world' (1 John 2.15–16). Moreover, wealth is fleeting, and it is better to place one's hope in God (1 Tim. 6.17). Ultimately, it will testify in judgement against its owners when it is gained by exploitative practices (James 5.1–6). Jesus also often presented the tension of wealth as a means to generate social transformation and personal preservation (Luke 19.1–5; Mark 12.43–4). His parables often sought to alter the marred and warped perspectives of the rich and the poor toward each other (Luke 16.14–15). Yet he considered being faithful in the generation of wealth as a qualifying criterion to handle 'true' wealth (Luke 16.10–12), that is, things that have eternal value – things pertaining to the kingdom of God.

A Theology of Providence and Promise

It cannot be justifiable to ignore one of the central themes of scripture in the debate over prosperity – soteriology, the doctrine of salvation. For it is here we find God using covenants, promises and providence to achieve his purpose of rescue, redemption and the reconciliation of humanity with himself. This is the story of the Bible and in the outworking of the drama we are presented with numerous actors – patriarchs, prophets, priests, judges and kings, as well as Jesus and his apostles – who bring to life the providence of God.

A reformist view of providence readily accepts that God provides for his creation, cooperates with it and governs over it (Grudem, p. 315). We are introduced to *Jehovah Jireh*, i.e. the Lord who provides, when God asked Abraham to sacrifice Isaac, his long promised teenage son (Gen. 22). Trust in God's provision was vindicated when a ram materialized as a substitute (verses 9–14). Through a basket and guile, Moses' life was saved and nurtured in Pharaoh's palace (Ex. 2.1–10). In Joseph, a promise in a dream was preserved through slavery (Gen. 37.18–36). Stories of women like Esther and Ruth also contribute to this narrative. In Jesus, and subsequently his apostles, these themes follow through in the feeding of thousands, the commissioning of the disciples, and the restoration to usefulness of lives blighted by infirmity or demonic control (Matt. 9.20–22; John 5.1–15; Mark 5.1–17; Acts 16.16–21).

To reject the narrative of providence is to reject also the testimonies and songs of the psalmist, the songs of Miriam and the Israelite women and men (Ex. 15.1–21). It is to overlook the life and times of Caleb, Joshua, Elijah and Elisha. The bald truth is that while scripture holds out these now iconic characters, it was the ordinary people, in everyday and unusual circumstances, that were the ultimate beneficiaries in these episodes. These are also reminders of whose we are (Heb. 13.8) and the confidence we can have in God (Num. 23.19).

An Incomplete Framework

If prosperity theology was to be accorded a holistic dimension: given that true prosperity emerges from faithfulness, obedience, selflessness, the renewing of the mind, holiness, righteousness and doing God's will, it would fall short of encompassing the full biblical witness, due to its omission of the pursuit of justice. It would lack the communal dimension as it focuses on the individual's ability to exercise faith or release the favour of God for themselves. It falls short by not prioritizing the pursuit of justice and dignity as ends in themselves. Therefore, the charge of Jesus in Matthew 23.23 stands as a stern rebuke: 'Woe to you, scribes and Pharisees, hypocrites! For you tithe mint, dill, and cummin, and have neglected the weightier matters of the law: justice mercy and faith. It is these you ought to have practised without neglecting others.'

I am persuaded that poverty and lack, in the main, are undesirable political and societal realities – not possible to explore here. Nonetheless, Jesus' identity with the poor (Matt. 25.25ff.), and his demand for justice (Matt. 23.23) clearly admonishes us that he desires an alternative experience of his love and fullness – an abundance of life (John 10.10). Through parallel scriptures, both the prophet Micah (6.8) and in Jesus' teachings recorded by Matthew (23.23) we are admonished of the importance of God's 'triple lock' – justice, mercy and faithfulness to God. Seeking favours, privileges and opportunities from people in power, whether local politicians, civic leaders and business owners are not acts of justice. Justice takes us to the source of the 'mercy problem' and demands change of oppressive practices and structure; unjust customs and practices; exploitative, discriminative and unfair laws; and exclusion from participation, whether they emerge from intentional designs or are mere unintentional consequences.

The question however remains, should prosperity theology be judged by a different standard to other forms of evangelical or orthodox theologies and practices from which justice is often marginalized? I think not. The existence of prosperity theology, as with liberation theology, demands a more robust discourse of how the kingdom of God is presented, represented and experienced in our day. Only then will we be able to offer and demonstrate a credible relationship with God and acknowledge his providential abundance. We must also measure our contribution by James' standard: 'Religion that is pure and undefiled before God, the Father, is this: to care for orphans and widows in their distress, and to keep oneself unstained by the world' (James 1.27).

For some unexplained reason the priorities of the Church have been skewed, in favour of busyness in mercy, at the expense of the full gospel of justice, mercy and love for God. Good news to the poor (Luke 4.18–19) and the gospel of peace (Acts 10.36; Eph. 6.15) seem not to be fully understood as essential gateways to the Kingdom. Instead, we now have to rely on civic society to be the conscience of the nation – highlighting the injustices that prevail. This should be the hallmark of the Church.

There is justification for some of the criticisms that have been meted out to aspects of prosperity teaching:

- Making every issue a spiritual battle between good and evil on the one hand generates an 'opposition mentality' and removes personal responsibility to the point where the believer becomes fatalistic. If something happens then it must have been God's will, which goes against the core teachings in prosperity theology.
- Prosperity theology can generate an irresponsible approach to ministry. Often leaders and their ministries are direct beneficiaries, and this raises huge issues around motives and conflict of interest. It also means that less care and attention is given to prudence, as the body of Christ is there to underwrite every adventure and misadventure.
- There is often little generosity of spirit toward those who do not measure up to 'the measure of faith' so as to bring about transformation in their own circumstances (Eph. 4.13).
- There is little critique within the movement itself when adherents are either proven to be deceptive, exploitative, lacking in integrity or are known to have misappropriated resources.
- Finally, it is not enough to ignore biblical scholarship or hermeneutics because it suits the movement's purposes. Consistency must be maintained in the understanding and application of scripture.

Fundamentally, prosperity theology has highlighted an area of scripture that the Church has neglected; unfortunately, in so doing, it has become reactionary and dogmatic. Even so, it has a significant spiritual, sociological and physiological part to play in the life of poor Christians. It generates what is often referred to as 'redemptive lift' which changes the socio-economic standing of an individual or family because they have made different life choices.

Reappraising Our Position

At the heart of rejecting prosperity theology as biblically normative is the belief that it is as abusive as it is exploitative and vulnerable people need protecting. Furthermore, it is presented as a betrayal of truth that undermines trust in the faith. The rallying call is an obligation to embrace the truth of scripture and repudiate its misrepresentation. 'Although everyone is a liar, let God be proved true, as it is written, "So that you may be justified in your words, and prevail in your judging."' (Rom 3.4).

Of course it is not sufficient to decry prosperity theology unless we have an answer to a creation that once 'groaned' but now is 'hollering' and 'bawling' for justice (Rom. 8.19–22). Noting that it is in this context that God responds to the cry of his people (Ex. 3.7; 1 Sam. 8; Isa. 13.19). At the very least we should adopt the posture of the apostle Paul in Ephesians (3.1, 14–19) on behalf of the outsiders and less privileged Gentiles – falling on our knees before God and asking that from God's riches they 'may have the power to comprehend, with all saints, what is the breadth and length and height and depth and to know the love of Christ that surpasses knowledge, so that you may be filled with all the fullness of God'.

In other words, the Jewish community had full knowledge of a God who liberates, provides for their nation and was more powerful than all other gods. They understood that he appoints kings and they govern at his command (Prov. 8.15–16). Such an understanding needed to be burned into their hearts if they were to remain unshakeable in their faith. Therefore, if we continue to spiritualize the various dimensions (breadth, length, height and depth) and the 'fullness' of God, we are then no longer talking about the God of the Bible because he 'is able to do far more abundantly than all that we ask or think, according to the power at work within us' (Eph. 3.20).

To contend for the faith, and as an act of renewal, we too can ask God for the 'strength to comprehend'.

In a global context, we must also wrestle with questions of how we refine or redefine long held theological positions that condemn large swathes of humanity below the bottom rung of Maslow's hierarchy of need, whether they be on our doorstep or part of our global community. Dare I ask, what should replace the Protestant work ethic theology in situations where walking miles for a pail of water is not a sign of grace? As we move toward a world driven by artificial intelligence, and virtual and augmented reality environments, where computers, automations and robots are commissioned to deliver from the mundane to high human dependency work – specifically designed to remove labour from production – a variant theology of human participation in society is required.

Notions of predestination by which God foreordains whatsoever comes to pass and that God, from eternity, has already chosen a body of people for himself, require challenging when they lead to mere acceptance – confining people's economic status or regretfully the lottery of birth to being part of God's plan. We cannot endorse theologies that readily accept that the world is simply divided into the haves and have nots, haves and soon to have, those who have made it and those who are soon to make it. False optimism needs tempering and despair needs hope emanating from sound and robust theology fit for the emerging world.

John Wesley wrestled with one of the hazards of 'redemptive lift' when he observed:

> I fear wherever riches have increased, the essence of religion has decreased in the same proportion. Therefore, I do not see it possible, in the nature of things, for any revival of true religion to continue long. For religion must necessarily produce both industry and frugality and these cannot but produce riches. But as riches increase, so will pride, anger and love for the world and all its branches. (Wesley; Isaacs, pp. 113–14).

He continues:

> Is there no way to prevent this continual decay of pure religion? We ought not to prevent people from being diligent and frugal; we must encourage all Christians to gain all they can, and to save all they can that is, in effect, to grow rich.

This is a noble objective as it is not credible to believe that the poor should look after the poor. For this reason, Jesus calls us to pay attention to the issue now, in our productive lifetime, because he will pay close attention on the Day of the Lord (Matt. 25.25–34). He reminds us that 'those who give to the poor lend to the Lord'. And working with the poor is working with Christ.

How then can we assure ourselves that our actions do not bring the gospel into disrepute? Is there a litmus test or some key principles that leaders could use to outwork their conviction and calling? And, before we point the finger, we must keep the whole counsel of scripture (1 Cor. 6.9–10). I propose six litmus tests to avoid exploitation and abuse in the area of prosperity theology:

1 Beneficial Ownership test – Are leaders receiving the benefit of goods, services, property, that legally belong fully and exclusively to the organization and are therefore outside their 'reasonable' contractual terms and conditions?
2 Public Benefit test – Are the activities being pursued designed for the benefit of the general public, causing no harm to individuals or to the organization? Are they accessible to members and adherents on the same terms as the decision makers and is any leadership benefit merely incidental?

3 Governance Covenant test – Is remuneration reasonable and proportionate to the size of the organization's revenue? Are there double dipping benefits, where wages are enhanced through extracurricular actives at the expense of the organization and other opportunity costs? Are resources and benefits generated during the 'paid-for time' treated as private and copyright property?

4 Impact test – Are activities pursued providing evidence of achieving desired outcomes and are lessons learned integrated into future practice?

5 Reputational Risk test – Does a particular action compromise the individual, the organization or the wider body of Christ?

6 Theological Soundness test – Do teachings have a basis in scripture? Can it be said that they do not undermine inerrancy of scripture?

These criteria are designed for debate and reflection, not for dismantling organizations. They should be carefully considered as an alternative or accompaniment to the journey to better engage with the 'fullness of God' in our world.

> Do you not know that God entrusted you with that money (all above what buys necessities for your families) to feed the hungry, to clothe the naked, to help the stranger, the widow, the fatherless; and, indeed, as far as it will go, to relieve the wants of all mankind? How can you, how dare you, defraud the Lord, by applying it to any other purpose? (Wesley)

References

Burton, John, 2018, '10 Things to Consider Before You Judge Jesse Duplantis for Believing for a $54M Jet', *Charisma Magazine,* www.charismamag.com/life/culture/37242-10-things-to-consider-before-you-judge-jesse-duplantis-for-believing-for-a-54m-jet accessed 9 November 2018.

Grudem, Wayne, 2016, *Systematic Theology: An Introduction to Biblical Doctrine.* Leicester: IVP.

Isaacs, Mark D., 2006, *Centennial Rumination on Max Weber's The Protestant Ethic and the Spirit of Capitalism.* Boca Raton, FL: Dissertation.com.

Savage, Michael, 2018, 'Richest 1% on Target to Own Two-thirds of All Wealth by 2030', *Guardian,* 7 April.

Sturge, Mark, 2005, *Look what the Lord has done! An Exploration of Black Christian Faith in Britain.* Bletchley: Scripture Union.

Wesley, John, 1820, *The Works of the Rev. John Wesley, Sermons: Vol. 1.*

Wintour, Patrick and Nicholas Watt, 2012, 'George Osborne Unveils Employee "Shares for Rights" Scheme', *Guardian,* www.theguardian.com/politics/2012/oct/08/george-osborne-shares-rights-scheme accessed 9 November 2018.

13

Pentecostalism and Political Engagement

R. DAVID MUIR

Pentecostals are traditionally seen as apolitical. Since the world of politics is seen as corrupt, some find partial justification for this stance in the narrative of 1 John 2.15 to 'not love the world or the things in the world'. This chapter explores the relationship between Pentecostalism and political engagement. It outlines the case for political engagement from a biblical perspective, as well as championing the Aristotelian and Crickian view of politics as the 'master science' capable of humanizing social relations. In arguing for active Christian citizenship, it invokes Jeremiah's 'Letter to the Exiles' as a foundational document and a prolegomenon for negotiating questions of Christian leadership and participation in the cultural politics of contemporary society. The fundamental argument is that Christians cannot be indifferent to the political institutions, ideas and culture where they live, for the degree to which society's politics and economy prospers is the degree to which all people, including Christians, prosper. The chapter looks at how Pentecostal organizations are evolving a theology of political engagement for the common good.

I want to attempt three things briefly. First, to say something about the nature of politics. Second, to outline some possible sources for a biblical theology of political engagement and make some comments upon two Resolutions in a classical Pentecostal tradition explicitly encouraging socio-political engagement. Third, reflect upon the political document that came out of the African and Caribbean Christian community in 2015, namely, its manifesto for political mobilization produced by the National Church Leaders Forum (NCLF) and its implications for Pentecostals.

On the Nature of Politics

Generally speaking, we have two definitions of politics: a broad definition and a much narrower one (Stott, p. 34). The broad definition, according to John Stott, denotes the life of the polis, city and the responsibilities of the citizens. The narrow definition sees politics as the science of government, often associated with directing and administrating states or other political units (McLean, p. 147). One recognizes the contested nature of defining politics and political activity in modern societies and contemporary discourse. What is clear is that politics are concerned with our common life together in communities, however defined. The creed reminds us of the political impact of the Roman Empire on the life and ministry of Jesus: he was crucified under Pontius Pilate (Barth, pp. 108–13).

At a time when many have become disillusioned with politics and politicians, the so-called political elites, you can adopt a number of views about politics and the political process, including the one that it is all a mess – a bit of a dog's dinner (without being too unkind to dogs). Equally, you can adopt the general Hobbesian view and say that political life is not too dissimilar to the state of nature which is characteristically 'poor, nasty, brutish, and short' (Hobbes, p. 186). But in the face of the current cynicism you can also take the view celebrated by the late Professor Bernard Crick in his classic book *In Defence of Politics* (1962). This Crickian view is that politics is, in the Aristotelian sense, the master science; it is that great humanizing activity, that process of discussion demanding a dialect of opposites and competing interests to sustain itself; it is that principled acknowledgement that some tolerance of different truths and some recognition that government is possible, indeed best conducted, amid the open canvassing of rival interests. Sir Bernard goes on to say:

> Politics, then, can be simply defined as the activity by which differing interests within a given unit of rule are conciliated by giving them a share of power in proportion to their importance to the welfare and survival of the whole community. And to complete the formal definition, a political system is that type of government where politics proves successful in ensuring reasonable stability and order. (Crick, p. 21)

This high view of politics thus described is, of course, intimated in Sophocles' *Antigone* and has particular resonances with Karl Popper's 'open society' thesis in which he critiques those he calls enemies of democracy and the open society, including Plato, Hegel and Marx (Popper 1966).

In the *Antigone* we hear something of the importance of plural and competing voices in the polis, as well as the dangers and implications of autocratic rule in the dialogue between Creon the King of Thebes and his son Haemon:

> Creon: The people of Thebes! Since when do I take my orders from the people of Thebes?
> Haemon: Isn't that rather a childish thing to say?
> Creon: No, I am King, and responsible only to myself.
> Haemon: A one-man state? What sort of state is that?
> Creon: Why, does not every state belong to its ruler?
> Haemon: You'd be an excellent king – on a desert island.

For the Christian, in such a contested arena, there is still a lot to play for if we believe in, or we get a glimpse of, the Imago Dei in the other, then we have a moral responsibility to fight for and struggle to create institutions and social conditions conducive to that dignity. Of course, as we will see later, the basis on which we frame the socio-economic and political discourse for Christian activism can be purely pragmatic, instrumental and rooted in self-enlightened interest (Jer. 29.7).

Citizenship and the 'Two Kingdoms'

As a constituent part of Protestantism, Pentecostals share the evangelical characteristics, or the quadrilateral of priorities, outlined by David Bebbington: this means that they are concerned with conversionism, activism, biblicism and crucicentrism (Bebbington, p. 17). In focusing on activism in this quadrilateral it is important to point out the rich theological and historical pedigree of Christian concern for socio-economic and political engagement. The metaphor of salt and light in the Gospel (Matt. 5–7) provides clues as to our redemptive and transformatory role in society. But we also have examples of the kind of engagement with the world and its structures of power by Old Testament prophets, New Testament writers, as well as Christian thinkers and church leaders down the centuries. Sometimes this is done at a great cost; and at times when the Church is under severe attack and criticism there arises an apologetic for the Church which clarifies the relationship between Church and state, the 'kingdom of God' and the 'kingdom of Caesar' (the doctrine of the 'two kingdoms') and the 'two cities' identified by Augustine.

In the case of Augustine's monumental work, it was an apologetic against those who attributed the fall of Rome to its abandonment of the city's traditional pagan gods for the Christian God; or as Augustine says: 'enemies against whom the City of God has to be defended'. In 20 books, Augustine writes about the origin, the development, and the destined ends of the two cities. One of these is the City of God, the other the city of this world; and God's City lives in this world's city, as far as its human element is concerned, but it lives there as an alien sojourner. At other times it discloses the nature of Christian commitment to active citizenship and the transformation of communities, as can be seen in the second-century CE *Letter to Diognetus*.

The Bible is a political document, therefore rediscovery of Christian socio-political engagement as the norm is essential. When we speak of biblical and theological roots of socio-economic and political engagement, we are generally referring to those critical norms and sources that inform the way we think about and reflect upon society and a particular Christian vision of its transformation and reimagining. The Old and New Testament, along with Christian tradition, offer a rich repository for the way we approach key social ideas and political institutions. The demarcation between religion and politics is often blurred; and some would like to delineate the two categories in rigid parallel so as to keep them apart – a kind of 'non-overlapping magisterial' (NOMA) advocated by the evolutionary biologist Stephen Jay Gould in the way we speak of religion and science. This is typically expressed by those who say that 'religion and politics shouldn't mix'. That those who express such views are misreading Christian tradition is clear from the new forms of Christian activism we are seeing among Pentecostals in the UK (an example of which is expressed in the 2015 Black Church Manifesto) and elsewhere, along with the rediscovery of this rich and vibrant Christian norm and legacy. Of course, here in the UK, we only have to think of the Christian Socialists and the formation of the Labour Party (Bryant 1993). And the quip is that the Labour Party owes more to Methodism than to Marxism. Richard Bauckham aptly sums it up in the rediscovery of the Christian 'norm' of political engagement:

> Many Christians have recently been discovering the political dimension of the message of the Bible. This is really a return to normality, since the notion that biblical Christianity has nothing to do with politics is little more than a modern Western Christian aberration. (Bauckham, p. 1)

In respect of the Bible, which Pentecostals take very seriously, and what we can glean from it to guide our political actions and inform our political philosophy, Michael Walzer in his book on politics in the Hebrew Bible is right to remind us that the Bible is above all a religious book and that there is no political theory in it, for political theory is a Greek invention (Walzer 2012). Having said that, he is keen to argue that the Bible's content makes it also a political book. From the history of Israel, a number of important political observations are made by Walzer which resonates with our own time and political lexicon: we witness regime change as the tyranny of Pharaoh gives way to the leadership of Moses and Joshua; followed by the rule of God under the judges, who are rejected by the elders and the people who demand a king. Later the kings are overthrown by conquering armies of the Assyrians and Babylonians, Greeks and Romans and replaced by foreign emperors and their priestly collaborators (Walzer, p. xii).

According to Walzer, most of the biblical writers are monarchists; republics and democracies make no appearance in the biblical texts (Walzer, p. xiv). There are, of course, elements of 'antipolitics', as Walzer terms it, in the Old Testament; the 'biblical writers are obviously interested, and explicitly so, in law and justice – which are for us, if not for them, highly politicized subjects' (Walzer, p. xiii). And when we think of the prophets and their role in biblical history, they are seen by Walzer as poets of social justice, utopian visionaries (Walzer, p. 72). Walter Brueggeman describes them as 'passionate poets who will not be silenced, speaking ... words grounded in Yahweh's own disclosure' (Brueggemann, p. 632).

Two things are clear from the preceding discussion: first, the Bible can be seen as a political document (Barr 1980); and second, while there is not a single version of the good political life or a preferred regime, there is little doubt that one can find in the Bible 'all the material necessary for a comparative politics' (Walzer, p. xii). Therefore, ideas of justice, social solidarity, equality before the law, constitutional monarchy and separation of powers can all be gleaned from biblical theology. It is clear from Exodus that God is not indifferent to injustice when we read: The Lord said, 'I have observed the misery of my people who are in Egypt; I have heard their cry on account of their taskmasters. Indeed, I know their sufferings' (Ex. 3.7); or when the prophet Micah (6.8) reminds his fellow Israelites: 'and what does the Lord require of you but to do justice, and to love kindness, and to walk humbly with your God?'

'Saints' in the Political Economy – Prolegomenon for a Pentecostal Biblical Theology of Socio-political Engagement

What I want to suggest at this juncture is that Jeremiah's 'Letter to the Exiles' constitutes a veritable prolegomenon for a Pentecostal biblical theology for socio-political engagement and new forms of Christian activism. Jeremiah 29.11 is a favourite verse for many Christians. In it God says: 'For surely I know the plans I have for you ... plans for your welfare and not for harm, to give you a future with hope.' However, there is a socio-political and economic imperative in the injunction of Jeremiah 29.7 that establishes a dialectical relationship and a civic duty between the 'saints' and society. The relationship is one of mutuality and interdependence in the political economy of the society in which we find ourselves: 'seek the welfare of the city where I have sent you into exile, and pray to the Lord on its behalf, for in its welfare you will find your welfare'.

The message of the text implies that Christians, including Pentecostals, cannot be indifferent to society's social, political and economic structures and operations; for the degree to which we prosper correlates to and is dependent upon these factors. Their success or failure directly impacts our well-being. To put it another way: we have a vested interest in our society's political economy and its socio-political and institutional development.

The foregoing poses a number of problems and hermeneutical challenges around our understanding and critique of the Christ-culture (Niebuhr, p. 45) problematic and the ensuing culture wars especially in light of 1 John 2.15 ('love not the world') and Romans 12.18 ('live at peace with all people, if possible'). In this classic study of the Christ-culture problematic, Niebuhr highlights the gospel's uncompromising affirmation of the sole authority of Christ over the Christian and the necessary corresponding rejection of human culture's claim to loyalty. In addition to Jeremiah's injunction, we can also deduce significant biblical warrant for socio-political engagement and Pentecostal activism from the final judgement narrative of Matthew 25.31–46. Here we see an eschatological foreshadowing and disclosure of the seed of compassion sown in socio-political concern and transformation reaping a rich eternal harvest in the world to come – in the 'world without end'. From Jeremiah and Matthew we see how our motivation for socio-political and economic engagement can be both pragmatic and/or rooted firmly in compassion and concern for the other based upon our shared Imago Dei and love for God rather than love for the world.

Political Engagement and Spiritual 'Principalities and Powers'

Earlier I intimated that notions of the Imago Dei are replete with social and political implications; it speaks to a vision of our common life together and the sorts of political institutions we create and the political values we espouse. In a sense it is about the political culture we engender and the political climate we struggle for which best approximates to our understanding of the Christian ideal and vision of the common good. Political culture is best understood as the attitudes, beliefs and values which underpin and inform the operation of a particular political system (McLean and McMillan, p. 409). Dennis Kavanagh uses the term 'political culture' as a shorthand expression to denote the emotional and attitudinal environment within which the political system operates, or our orientation and predispositions to political action. These qualities are informed and influenced by factors such as traditions, historical memories and symbols (Kavanagh, pp. 11–12). Recent voting patterns in the US and the UK reveal the fragmentary, diverse and conflicting nature of our body politic as themes of race, migration and inequality take on toxic dimensions. We will have to be more attentive to what now looms large on the political horizon.

Understanding the formation and transformation of our political culture is important. And Pentecostals have to come to terms with the range of political and spiritual structures of power and how these are negotiated locally and globally. The apostle Paul gives us a number of clues and insights as to what we are up against when he says: 'For our struggle is not against enemies of blood and flesh, but against the rulers, against the authorities, against the cosmic powers of this present darkness, against the spiritual forces of evil in the heavenly places' (Eph. 6.12).

The implications of this insight/revelation for our political economy and communal well-being are conveyed in Amos Yong's work on Pentecostalism and political theology (Yong 2010). And here his logic is persuasive, inexorable: if the work of Satan is still to steal and kill and destroy (John 10.10) and his fall has produced chaos in the world's social and economic structures, then the key to the struggles of daily injustices, poverty and disenfranchisement resides in churches properly engaging in spiritual warfare prayer (Yong, p. 126). Pentecostals are attentive to this dialectic and dynamic relationship between prayer and politics and bringing spirits and powers under subjection to the lordship of Christ. A significant aspect of Pentecostal spirituality is the practice of taking authority and spiritual warfare (2 Cor. 10.3–6), recognizing, as Nigel Wright argues, that there is an extensive matrix of real but unseen forces that shape human life (Wright, p. 20).

Pentecostals are interested in social transformation and political engagement. The numerous Pentecostal-initiated projects and initiatives locally, nationally and globally testifies to this, especially in Latin America and Africa. Of course, from its early pioneering days there was an eschatological urgency for world evangelism to usher in the Parousia. There was also, as William Kay points out, the fear of liberal theology of the nineteenth century and its association with the social gospel of the early twentieth century (Kay, p. 302). In addition to this evangelism impulse, there was also a tendency toward what can be seen as an ideology of withdrawal from the world (Calley 1965). And given that many of the early Pentecostals were drawn from a lower socio-economic stratum of society, what Robert Mapes Anderson (1969) refers to as the 'disinherited', it is not surprising that evangelism and conversion were their major concerns as opposed to socio-political engagement and societal transformation.

Over the last 40 years or so we have witnessed changes in the stance and attitude of Pentecostal churches and leaders to politics and Christian activism. In the US one only has to look at how Pentecostal leaders have influenced the politics of the Right and the role of the Moral Majority, as well as a host of Pentecostals like Eugene Rivers and the Azusa Christian Community and the popular T. D. Jakes, et al. In Africa, Latin America and elsewhere Pentecostals are providing a range of social and welfare services in their communities; often they are filling the welfare gap left by the state. Pentecostal churches are also encouraging their members to be active citizens and agents of social transformation, including seeking public office. This is clearly seen in the global Pentecostal organization I have chosen to reference.

Encouraging Active Citizenship and Political Engagement in the Church of God

In its governing documents, the Church of God Cleveland, Tennessee, USA with offshoots in the UK, enshrines the importance of active citizenship and gives credence to the need for social and political engagement by its members through a number of its resolutions. Indeed, many of the resolutions are highly political. They demonstrate an acute awareness of some of the major social, economic, cultural and political challenges facing society and a willingness to speak out and guide its members to advocacy and action. There is an implicit and explicit espousal and commitment to neo-liberal political values in a number of the resolutions, especially the identification of these values with religious freedom and the flourishing of Christianity.

This is not at all surprising, given the cultural and political soil in which the Church of God took root. The creed of so-called 'rugged individualism' is constitutive of the liberal political values we identify with capitalism. Although its roots and progeny are varied its fruits culminate in the sort of political culture and institutional framework we readily associate with liberal democracy and what is triumphantly celebrated in Francis Fukuyama's *The End of History and the Last Man* (1992). In this modern classic Fukuyama informs us that in the wake of the post-Cold War era and the fall of the Berlin Wall in 1989, we witnessed a profound change: on the one hand there is the imaginative foreclosure of any socialist future and the ideological coherence once given by Marxism-Leninism to socialism and authoritarianism; on the other hand, we see 'one competitor standing in the ring as an ideology of potentially universality: liberal democracy, the doctrine of individual freedom and popular sovereignty' (p. 42).

The apotheosis of the triumph of liberal democracy – capitalism, in short – is summarized thus: 'Two hundred years after they first animated the French and American Revolutions, the principles of liberty and equality have proven not just durable but resurgent' (Fukuyama, p. 42). But Fukuyama's book was written before the recent financial crisis and its aftermath. Capitalism and liberal democracy are in crisis and in need of reimagining and rehabilitation (Williams and Elliot 2010); and inequality, as Thomas Piketty (2014) has shown, threatens to stir more discontent and further undermine liberal values. Although we hear echoes of Milton Friedman's (1963) political economy and Hayek's (2006) individualism and anti-collectivist sentiments in the association of freedom and rights with the democratic process, we also feel the tension of the cultural wars that characterizes modern America in the resolution on The Moral Responsibility of Those Who Control and Use the Media (1984), where the General Assembly of the Church of God calls upon those who control the media to respect the rights of all Americans and to desist from ignoring or ridiculing the Judeo-Christian moral and ethical values held by a majority of Americans.

While the implications for socio-political engagement are far-reaching in many of these resolutions, I want to focus on two of them, namely, the one dealing with voting and the other on political engagement, passed in 1984 and 1992 respectively. It's appropriate to quote both of the resolutions in full to get a feel for some of the subtext and socio-political assumptions inherent in them. Concerning voting, the resolution states:

Whereas it is constitutionally and Biblically right for Christians to become involved in government; and

Whereas the exercise of the right to vote is one of the most basic ways Christians can influence the issues and policies facing our society; and

Whereas Christianity has flourished in those areas where freedom and rights are guaranteed and safeguarded through the democratic process; and

Whereas Scripture promises that when the Righteous are in authority, the people rejoice;

Be it therefore Resolved That the Church of God urges its members, and especially its ministers, to consider carefully the guiding principles of scripture in deciding social, civil, political and religious issues. (60th A., 1984, p. 57)

Before we briefly consider some of the challenges of the resolutions we will quote the second one on political involvement which reads:

Whereas the Church of God as a member of the National Association of evangelicals has endorsed and agreed to support 'Christian Citizenship Campaign' (CCC); and

Whereas the two main objectives of the NAE resolution are to encourage Christians to pray for their leaders and to exercise their liberties to register and vote as part of the democratic process; and

Whereas the Church of God is an international organization which has historically encouraged Christians to seek godly means to improve standards of their respective societies;

Therefore Be It Resolved that in cooperation with the National Associations of Evangelicals, the Church of God encourages all constituents to avail themselves of every opportunity to peacefully and orderly register, vote and otherwise seek to improve the health, safety, and general welfare of all mankind (1 Peter 2.12); and

Be It Further Resolved that all political efforts should be effected with prayerful deliberation, knowing that we will give account to God for every deed done (Romans 2.12), or not done, in accordance with His divine and eternal plan for man. (64th A., 1992, p. 79)

A number of key points (implicit and explicit) can be deduced from the two resolutions. I will focus briefly on three of them. First, there is the assumption that civic participation and political engagement is a biblical imperative. Christians have a moral responsibility to be co-agents in social and political change and transformation. There is, therefore, a moral and theological legitimization of Christian involvement in all spheres of government. The dual foundation for this legitimization, that is, 'constitutionally and biblically right' raises questions about the nation's political culture and its historical treatment of minorities. For example, the disenfranchisement of African Americans from the political process even when they were constitutionally granted certain rights calls into question – and certainly engenders hermeneutical tension – any easy identification of a political regime with the Bible.

Second, there is concern for religious freedoms; and it's assumed that these are best protected under a liberal democracy. Of course, there are some of the assumptions I alluded to earlier about the relationship, freedom and democracy and its triumph in Fukuyama and others. The resolution identifies Christianity with American democracy. As pointed out by Philip Wogaman (p. 105), although Christians will always maintain the transcendence of God in Christ above all political systems, including democracy, they are nevertheless persuaded that 'the case for the superiority of democracy among possible political systems is irrefutable'.

Third, both resolutions contain elements on the importance of reflection on what is termed 'guiding principles of scripture' and 'prayerful deliberation' on political involvement. Because there are no serious or systematic attempts to tease out precisely what these 'guiding principles' are for the Church of God, it leaves open the possibility for a range of political responses to active citizenship. In the process of 'political education' it is not unlikely that members of the Church of God in the US and the UK, and beyond geographically and denominationally, may use these resolutions for political resistance against racial injustice and inequality in ways that fracture the assumed liberal consensus implicit in them knowing that we shall give account to God for every deed done or not done, in accordance with his divine and eternal plan for man (Rom. 14.12).

Political Mobilization and the New Activism of African and Caribbean Pentecostals

In this final section I want to turn to the manifesto produced by African and Caribbean Christian leaders under the auspices of the National Church Leaders Forum (NCLF), in anticipation of the 2015 General Election. NCLF began a major consultation with four sections of the black church constituency: social and political activists, church leaders, academics and young people.

Too often African and Caribbean Pentecostal churches in Britain are depicted as 'apolitical' and radically pietistic. Political engagement from this constituency is poor. In 1987 Marian FitzGerald published her *Black People and Party Politics in Britain* which showed that post-war generations of black migrants were 'very constrained in their political activity and development by various factors', including their obvious 'newness and unfamiliarity with the political system'. Crucially, apart from the 'struggle to establish a material foothold in this country' there was what FitzGerald calls 'a cherished fantasy (often referred to as "the myth of return") that their stay in Britain was only temporary' (FitzGerald, p. 9).

One inevitable consequence of this, according to FitzGerald, was that their political frame of reference remained their country of origin. Of course, as Mark Shelton Saint recognizes, there have been many attempts to engage in the political process, albeit with limited success, over the last two decades or so (Saint 2010). Included among the many socio-political activities and initiatives listed by Shelton Saint are Bishop Eric Brown's involvement in Citizens UK, Pastor Nims Obunge's development of the Peace Alliance and the formation of the Black Church Civic Forum (BCCF) in 1999. In respect of the BCCF, Shelton Saint argues that this was an attempt at a prophetic political connection – 'a valiant effort to bring together the disparate elements of the Black Church leadership to establish a powerful voice for justice' to 'increase the political involvement and social action of Black Christians nationally'. This prophetic political connection failed, according to Shelton Saint because it was ultimately stifled by the lack of cohesion and discord of the occidental orientation. Similar issues and themes concerning the need for Pentecostals to be much more intentionally active in the socio-political and economic spheres of public life are raised by authors such as Babatunde Adedibu (2012), Joe Aldred (2005), Robert Beckford (1998), R. David Muir (2010), Mark Sturge (2007) and Israel Olofinjana (2015).

What is clear from the authors cited above is that there is something of a paradigm shift, a conscious recognition that the separation of religion and politics, piety and socio-political participation, is neither desirable nor intelligible to a church seeking to be relevant in local communities or providing solutions to the creation of peaceful, prosperous and cohesive communities. Selwyn Arnold of the New Testament Church of God signalled this shift in articulating the implications of 'the social imperatives enshrined in the gospel of Christ and his kingdom' that legitimates socio-political engagement 'without compromising one's faith' (Arnold, p. 11). This shift in emphasis was continued under Bishop Eric Brown whose Big Move philosophy incorporated the notion of developing members of the church as social activists and political leaders in the community.

These are all signs of the changing trajectory from the 'apolitical' label often attached to Pentecostals, especially with the publication of a black church manifesto. Amos Yong in the 2009 Cadbury Lectures critiques this 'apolitical' characterization of Pentecostalism by reference to what he calls 'prophetic politics', that is, ways in which this Pentecostal apolitical rhetoric 'actually serves as a prophetic critique of the existing political order', and how its ecclesial practices function 'performatively to engage the domain of the political' (Yong, p. 11).

Ahead of the party conferences and the 2015 General Election, the NCLF produced its own manifesto for action (https://nclf.eu/down load-black-church-political-mobilisation-a-manifesto-for-action/). This marked a radical departure for the black church. The document is entitled 'Black Church Political Mobilisation – A Manifesto for Action' and it focuses on a number of key social and political issues. But what is the purpose of the manifesto? Why was it produced and what does it hope it will achieve?

The first thing to say about this manifesto is that it represents a 'first' for the black church in the UK. This is the first time that African and Caribbean church leaders have produced a document like this to politically mobilize its constituency. For some it demonstrates that the black church has 'come of age', signalling its willingness and commitment to fully engage in the wider social and political issues of the day. In the history of the black church in the diaspora, especially in America, there is a rich tradition of the church taking the lead in the fight for justice and equality. We think of radical and prophetic people like David Walker, Sam Sharpe, Sojourner Truth and Martin Luther King, Jr, to mention a few. We also call to memory a time when, according to the African American scholar Eric Lincoln, the church was the 'organizing principle around which life was structured' as it became the 'school', the 'forum' and the 'political arena' for individuals (Lincoln 1970).

Because the black church in the UK is often perceived as being silent – failing to speak out on social and political issues and challenging major injustices faced by the black community – it is sometimes referred to as 'a sleeping giant'. The manifesto challenges this view in two ways. First, by highlighting the range of social and community projects leaders of the African and Caribbean churches have established and led; it demonstrates what the churches have done and continues to do. Second, it advocates and recommends specific ways the church constituency should tackle some of the major problems facing the community.

Looking at the content of the manifesto it is clear that important issues are raised, but the document does not pretend to be comprehensive. It is anticipated that the manifesto will be a 'live document' with other issues added to it beyond the 2015 election. Questions will be raised in regard to its operationalization, communication and resourcing. We know that political communication is seldom budget neutral. In nine sections it deals with topics including church and community, policing and criminal justice, mental health and marriage, youth and education. Each section is divided into three parts, providing what it calls 'the current picture', 'the biblical picture' and concluding with 'where do we go from here?' There are some challenging and controversial statements about international aid and foreign policy, as well as on the disproportionate number of young black men incarcerated. It calls attention to the work of Michelle Alexander on what she terms the 'New Jim Crow', and what is referred to by cultural critic Cornel West as the 'prison industrial complex'(Alexander 2010). It is obvious that the disproportionate incarceration of black people in the UK and the US is both a moral and political issue that churches have to engage with. In the recommendations on the former the manifesto calls upon government to examine the conditions it attaches when giving aid to poorer countries if it wants to avoid charges of 'residual imperialism and cultural hegemony'; on the latter, the manifesto wants the government to work with black majority churches and other key agencies 'to facilitate a national dialogue on the disproportionate representation of black people in prison and work to reduce it'.

As a 'manifesto for action' and 'political mobilization', it recognizes, as with the two Church of God resolutions discussed above, the importance of voting and political engagement. It sees no dichotomy between the Christian faith and political engagement. Indeed, it argues that political engagement is 'a part of our civic duty and Christian responsibility'. This is certainly meant to be a challenge to those, both inside and outside the Church, who say that Christians should 'keep out of politics'.

Indeed, the manifesto argues that being 'salt and light' (Matt. 5.13–16) and taking seriously the welfare, peace and prosperity of 'the city where I have sent you' (Jer. 29.7), demands radical and prophetic Christian engagement in the political process. To this end, it calls upon Pentecostals and other church leaders to do more to promote and teach 'the importance of active civic and political engagement for the common good', as well as to host hustings, vote and support the National Voter Registration campaign.

We all know that political parties often forget about the electorate until elections looms large on their agenda. The manifesto challenges them not to play games with the BME constituencies, but rather to engage with Pentecostals and BME communities in the political process on an ongoing basis 'and not just during the election season'. And given the fact that Operation Black Vote had identified around 168 marginal seats in which the BME vote was a critical deciding factor in the 2015 election results, it is important that politicians take this message seriously.

The black church manifesto was produced in anticipation of the 2015 General Election, but was more than the usual exercise in the production of manifestos for political window-dressing. It was a declaration of a paradigm shift in political consciousness; it was African and Caribbean churches (largely Pentecostals) saying that they were making a step-change in how they think about some of the critical issues facing faith and nation, the Church and state; it was Pentecostals saying that their constituencies had 'entered a new era in their development in the UK'.

Ultimately, Pentecostals were saying that leaders in their community are ready to encourage, engage and resource a new form of Christian activism for the common good. I'm reminded of the wisdom and insight distilled by Bernard Crick when he said: 'Politics and love are the only forms of constraints possible between free people' (p. 11). In respect of the former, I have tried to provide a brief overview; the latter might prove more difficult.

References

Adedibu, Babatunde, 2012, *Coat of Many Colours: The Origin, Growth, Distinctiveness and Contributions of Black Majority Churches to British Christianity*. Gloucester: Choir Press.

Aldred, Joe, 2005, *Respect: Understanding Caribbean British Christianity*. Peterborough: Epworth.

Alexander, Michelle, 2010, *The New Jim Crow: Mass Incarceration in the Age of Colorblindness*. New York: New Press.

Anderson, Robert Mapes, 1969, *Vision of the Disinherited: The Making of American Pentecostalism*. New York: Oxford University Press.

Arnold, S. E., 1992, *From Scepticism to Hope: One Black-Led Church's Response to Social Responsibility*. Nottingham: Grove Books.

Augustine, 2003, *City of God*, translated by Henry Bettenson. London: Penguin Books.

Barr, James, 1980, 'The Bible as a Political Document', in *The Scope and Authority of the Bible*. London: SCM Press.

Barth, Karl, 2012, *Dogmatics in Outline*. London: SCM Press.

Bauckham, Richard, 1989, *The Bible in Politics: How to Read the Bible Politically*. London: SPCK.

Bebbington, D. W., 1989, *Evangelicalism in Modern Britain: A History From the 1730s to the 1980s*. London: Unwin Hyman.

Beckford, Robert, 1998, *Jesus is Dread: Black Theology and Black Culture in Britain*. London: Darton, Longman & Todd.

Brueggemann, Walter, 1997, *Theology of the Old Testament: Testimony, Disputes, Advocacy*. Minneapolis, MN: Fortress Press.

Bryant, Christopher (ed.), 1993, *Reclaiming the Ground: Christianity and Socialism*. Sevenoaks: Spire.

Calley, Malcolm, 1965, *God's People: West Indian Pentecostal Sects in England*. Oxford: Oxford University Press.

Crick, Bernard, 1962, *In Defence of Politics*. Harmondsworth: Pelican Books.

FitzGerald, Marian, 1987, *Black People and Party Politics in Britain*. London: Runnymede Trust.

Friedman, Milton, 1963, *Capitalism & Freedom*. Chicago and London: Phoenix Books.

Fukuyama, Francis, 1992, *The End of History and the Last Man*. London: Penguin Books.

Hayek, F. A., 2006, *The Constitution of Liberty*. Oxford: Routledge.

Hobbes, Thomas, 1985, *Leviathan*. London: Penguin Books.

Kavanagh, Dennis, 1972, *Political Culture*. London: Macmillan.

Kay, William, 2009, *Pentecostalism*. SCM Core Text. London: SCM Press.

Lincoln, Eric, 1970, Foreword, in Cone, James, *A Black Theology of Liberation*. Philadelphia and New York: J. B. Lippincott Company.

McLean, Iain and Alistair McMillan (eds), 2009, *The Concise Oxford Dictionary of Politics*, 3rd edn. Oxford: Oxford University Press.

Muir, R. David, 2010, 'Theology and the Black Church', in Aldred, Joe and Keno Ogbo (eds), *The Black Church in the Twenty-first Century*. London: Darton, Longman & Todd.

New Statesman, 11–17 November 2016, The Trump apocalypse: How his populist revolt threatens the world order, www.newstatesman.com/2016-11-10

Niebuhr, H. Richard, 2001, *Christ and Culture*. New York: HarperCollins.

Olofinjana, Israel Oluwole, 2015, *Partnership in Mission: A Black Majority Church Perspective on Mission and Church Unity*. Watford: Instant Apostle.

Piketty, Thomas, 2014, *Capital in the Twenty-First Century*. London: The Belknap Press of Harvard University Press.

Popper, Karl, 1966, *The Open Society and its Enemies*, 5th edn. London: Routledge & Kegan Paul.

Saint, Mark Richard Shelton, 2010, 'Politics and the Black Church', in Aldred, Joe and Keno Ogbo (eds), *The Black Church in the Twenty-first Century*, pp. 93–103. London: Darton, Longman & Todd.

Sophocles, 1974, *The Theban Plays*, translated by E. F. Watling. London: Penguin Books.

Stott, John, 2006, *Issues Facing Christians Today*, 4th edn. Grand Rapids, MI: Zondervan.

Sturge, Mark, 2007, *Look What the Lord Has Done! An Exploration of Black Christian Faith in Britain*. Bletchley: Scripture Union.

Walzer, Michael, 2012, *In God's Shadow: Politics in the Hebrew Bible*. New Haven, CT, and London: Yale University Press.

Williams, Rowan and Larry Elliot (eds), 2010, *Crisis and Recovery: Ethics, Economics and Justice*. Basingstoke: Palgrave Macmillan.

Wogaman, J. Philip, 2000, *Christian Perspectives on Politics*. Louisville, KY: Westminster John Knox Press.

Wright, Nigel, 2009, 'Government as an Ambiguous Power', in Spenser, Nick and Jonathan Chaplin (eds), *God and Government*. London: SPCK.

Yong, Amos, 2010, *In the Days of Caesar: Pentecostalism and Political Theology*. Grand Rapids, MI: Eerdmans.

Index of Names and Subjects